OKLAHOMA's MOST NOTORIOUS CASES Volume #2

Valentine's Day Murder

Clara Hamon, a Woman Scorned

Roger Wheeler's Bad Investment

The Geronimo Bank Case

The Death of Bill Tilghman

The Case of the Talking Pharmacist

Death, Oklahoma Style

KENT FRATES

THE ROADRUNNER PRESS
OKLAHOMA CITY, OKLAHOMA

Copyright © 2017 by Kent Frates
Cover copyright © 2017 by RoadRunner Press
Cover Photo by ColorBird / Shutterstock.com
Cover Design: Jeanne Devlin

All rights reserved.

In accordance with the U.S. Copyright Act of 1976, scanning, uploading, or electronic sharing of any part of this book, audio, written, or e-published, is strictly prohibited and unlawful. No part of this book may be reproduced in any form or by any means, including photocopying, electronic, mechanical, recording, or by any information storage and retrieval system without permission in writing by the copyright owner.

The RoadRunner Press
Oklahoma City, Oklahoma
www.TheRoadRunnerPress.com
Bulk copies or group sales of this book available by contacting orders@theroadrunnerpress.com

First Edition printed November 2017

Printed in the USA
by Maple Press, York, Pennsylvania

Library of Congress Control Number: 2017950782

Publisher's Cataloging-In-Publication Data
(Prepared by The Donohue Group, Inc.)
Names: Frates, Kent F.
Title: Oklahoma's most notorious cases. Volume #2 / Kent Frates.
Description: First edition. | Oklahoma City, Oklahoma : The RoadRunner Press, [2017] |
Series: Oklahoma's most notorious cases series | Includes bibliographical references.
Identifiers: ISBN 978-1-937054-52-6
Subjects: LCSH: Trials--Oklahoma--Case studies. | Murder--Oklahoma--Case studies. | Law--Oklahoma--Cases. | Hamon, Clara--Trials, litigation, etc. | Tilghman, William Matthew, 1854-1924--Trials, litigation, etc. | Wheeler, Roger, 1926-1981--Trials, litigation, etc.
Classification: LCC HV6793.O5 F732 2017 | DDC 364.109766--dc23

10 9 8 7 6 5 4 3 2 1

To my mother Mex L. Frates,
who taught me the value of reading and writing

Oklahoma's Most Notorious Cases Volume #2

Contents

Introduction 1

Valentine's Day Murder

Chapter 1   *Case #1: Valentine's Day Murder* 7
Chapter 2   *February 14, 2001* 9
Chapter 3   *The Scene of the Crime* 13
Chapter 4   *The Investigation* 17
Chapter 5   *Under Arrest* 23
Chapter 6   *Abusive Husband?* 27
Chapter 7   *Who Can Prove What?* 31
Chapter 8   *The Trial Begins* 35
Chapter 9   *The Case Against Dr. Hamilton* 39
Chapter 10 *The Defense* 45
Chapter 11 *The Verdict* 53
Chapter 12 *The Appeal* 57

Clara Hamon, a Woman Scorned

Chapter 13 *Case #2: Clara Hamon, a Woman Scorned* 65
Chapter 14 *Jake the Snake* 67
Chapter 15 *Clara and Success* 71
Chapter 16 *The 1920 Republican Convention* 75
Chapter 17 *Paying the Price* 79
Chapter 18 *The Lost Is Found* 83
Chapter 19 *Clara's Story* 85
Chapter 20 *The Rest of the Story* 89
Chapter 21 *The Surrender* 91
Chapter 22 *Trial Preparation* 93
Chapter 23 *The Trial Begins* 95

Chapter 24	*The Defense*	103
Chapter 25	*The Verdict*	107
Chapter 26	*What Next?*	111

Roger Wheeler's Bad Investment

Chapter 27	*Case #3: Roger Wheeler's Bad Investment*	119
Chapter 28	*The Crime*	121
Chapter 29	*Roger Wheeler*	125
Chapter 30	*The Telex Roller Coaster*	127
Chapter 31	*World Jai Alai*	131
Chapter 32	*The Investigation Begins*	135
Chapter 33	*The Winter Hill Gang*	137
Chapter 34	*Bulger Takes Control*	141
Chapter 35	*The Investigation Continues*	145
Chapter 36	*Breakthrough*	147
Chapter 37	*The Wheeler Case*	149
Chapter 38	*Cleaning Up the Witnesses*	153
Chapter 39	*The End of the Gang*	157
Chapter 40	*On the Run*	161
Chapter 41	*Bulger Goes Down*	165
Chapter 42	*Aftermath*	169

The Geronimo Bank Case

Chapter 43	*Case #4: The Geronimo Bank Case*	177
Chapter 44	*The Crime*	179
Chapter 45	*The Man for the Job*	183
Chapter 46	*The Timeline*	189
Chapter 47	*Bank-robbery Charges*	193
Chapter 48	*The Killers*	197
Chapter 49	*Preliminary Hearing*	201
Chapter 50	*The Trial*	205

Chapter 51	*The First Appeal and Related Foolishness*	209
Chapter 52	*Neill's Trial*	213
Chapter 53	*Johnson's Trial*	217
Chapter 54	*Further Appeals*	223

The Death of Bill Tilghman

Chapter 55	*Case #5: The Death of Bill Tilghman*	231
Chapter 56	*Frontier Days*	233
Chapter 57	*The Three Guardsmen*	237
Chapter 58	*The Wild Bunch*	241
Chapter 59	*Sheriff and Police Chief*	245
Chapter 60	*The Three Guardsmen Go Hollywood*	249
Chapter 61	*Cromwell*	251
Chapter 62	*Bloody Death*	255
Chapter 63	*Legal Maneuvering*	261
Chapter 64	*The Trial of Wiley Lynn*	265
Chapter 65	*Shoot-out in Madill*	269

The Case of the Talking Pharmacist

Chapter 66	*Case #6: The Case of the Talking Pharmacist*	275
Chapter 67	*The Talking Pharmacist*	277
Chapter 68	*The Surveillance Videos*	281
Chapter 69	*The Robbers*	283
Chapter 70	*The Charge*	285
Chapter 71	*Bail*	287
Chapter 72	*Still Talking*	291
Chapter 73	*The Preliminary Hearing*	295
Chapter 74	*There Goes the Judge*	299
Chapter 75	*Two Robbers Go to Court*	303
Chapter 76	*The Trial*	305

Chapter 77	*After the Verdict*	315
Epilogue		319

Death, Oklahoma Style

Chapter 78	*Case #7: Death, Oklahoma Style*	327
Chapter 79	*An Oklahoma Tradition*	329
Chapter 80	*The Lockett Case*	333
Chapter 81	*Lockett's Legal Mess*	335
Chapter 82	*You Can't Make This Stuff Up*	339
Chapter 83	*The Warner Case*	343
Chapter 84	*State v. Glossip*	347
Chapter 85	*Glossip v. Gross*	351
Chapter 86	*Don't Kill Glossip*	355
Chapter 87	*The Grand Jury's Report*	361
Chapter 88	*Recent Developments*	365

Acknowledgments	369
Bibliography	370
About the Author	378

Notorious: *well-known or famous especially for something bad: generally known and talked of; especially: widely and unfavorably known: from the Latin* noscere *to come to know*

Introduction

In its 110 years as a state, Oklahoma has had many notorious cases. In 2014, I wrote about six of them in the first volume of this series, including the bombing of Oklahoma City's Alfred P. Murrah Federal Building, unfortunately, Oklahoma's most notorious case. Seven more cases headline this second book. And rest assured, plenty more notorious cases still remain.

My goal in connection with each case included here is to accurately report the facts. To the greatest extent possible, I have relied on original sources such as trial transcripts and interviews with the lawyers, judges, and law enforcement professionals directly involved in the case. In some cases, I have also interviewed or corresponded with the criminal defendant who was convicted. The stories included here would not be as complete or as accurate without the information collected from these actual participants.

Much has been written about some of the cases, whereas for others, almost nothing at all has found its way into print.

In some instances, such as the killing of lawman Bill Tilghman, the "history" was sometimes false or exaggerated. In others, such as the case of Whitey Bulger and other members of the Winter Hill Gang, the record is voluminous and detailed because many people involved have sold their stories to writers who produced firsthand accounts of their crimes, including the murder of the Tulsa businessman Roger Wheeler.

The oldest cases, such as the Clara Hamon and Bill Tilghman cases, rely greatly on newspaper accounts. This source is more fertile than you might

Introduction

expect because in the 1920s, newspapers were the main source of news, and much space was devoted to detailed accounts of sensational trials. Newspaper articles involving those trials often contained verbatim quotations from testimony as well as lengthy accounts of trial proceedings.

If asked to rank the cases here by notoriety, I would have to say the most controversial cases in the book are the three most recent.

Did Oklahoma City physician John Hamilton, in the brief span of a few minutes, have time to beat and strangle his wife, clean up, dispose of the murder weapon, and return to Mercy Hospital, where he then calmly performed an operation with no indication that anything in particular had occurred? The jury thought so, but Dr. Hamilton still maintains his innocence. You will have to draw your own conclusion.

Should Oklahoma City pharmacist Jerome Ersland have been convicted of first-degree murder for having defended himself against armed robbers who threatened his life and the lives of two of his coworkers? Many gun owners and gun-rights advocates still say no, even though Ersland was convicted.

Does Richard Glossip, who still sits on death row, deserve to die? His case polarizes advocates for the death penalty and those who oppose it.

The other cases in this book have their own unique attraction. Jake Hamon led a life of political corruption and his widely publicized death occurred in 1920, but it is a tale that could happen today.

The facts surrounding Bill Tilghman's death are unclear and controversial. The bloody, savage murders at the Geronimo Bank rocked southwestern Oklahoma in 1984 and still give people pause.

Roger Wheeler's death remained a mystery for a long time, but the connection of the crime to the Irish-American mobster Whitey Bulger made it a national incident. It is again in the news because of Bulger's capture and conviction in the past several years and the Hollywood film staring Johnny Depp, *Black Mass*.

All these cases comprise part of the history of Oklahoma and ask to be memorialized. More important, I hope readers find them as interesting as I did.

Kent F. Frates
July 2017

Valentine's Day Murder

"Time is of the essence."

—A legal contractual term

CHAPTER ONE

Case #1: Valentine's Day Murder

IN LIFE, TIMING IS THE most important thing. For Dr. John and Susan Hamilton, that also proved to be true in death. In what came to be known as the Valentine's Day Murder, the key to Hamilton's innocence or guilt in the bloody death of his wife turned on timing. Was the doctor's schedule an alibi or a smoke screen designed to cover up the savage beating that left Susan Hamilton dead in her home on Valentine's Day?

The Hamiltons were an upscale, socially prominent couple in Oklahoma City, Oklahoma. Hamilton was a successful physician specializing in obstetrics and gynecology. Mrs. Hamilton was her husband's business manager, and like her husband, she was popular with friends in and outside the medical profession and at Oklahoma City's Quail Creek Country Club, where they were members.

From the outside, the Hamiltons seemed to be a happy couple, and the romance seemed to still be alive in their relationship. After the murder, some people would step up to describe Hamilton as "smothering" and "possessive," but others would say it was Susan who was controlling and obsessive about their relationship. By all appearances, the Hamiltons were devoted to each other. Married thirteen years, John and Susan Hamilton still lunched together on Tuesdays and spent Fridays and weekends together. They took frequent vacations, often jetting away for weekend jaunts that they liked to refer to as "quick-fix" trips. When home, Susan worked two days a week at the abortion clinic her husband operated along with his obstetrics and gynecology practice.

The murder came as a shock to friends and acquaintances, especially when Hamilton was almost immediately charged with Susan's death. The press feasted on the inherent interest of readers in the lives of the rich and prominent and the irony of a husband killing his wife on Valentine's Day.

The case, however, would come down to a matter of timing.

CHAPTER TWO

February 14, 2001

MUCH OF DR. HAMILTON'S TIME between 6:45 a.m. and 11:05 a.m. on February 14, 2001, is well documented. It is a matter of just minutes within those hours that remain in question and the key to who killed Susan Hamilton.

What is known is that between 6:45 a.m. and 7:00 a.m., Hamilton arrived at the Surgicare Center across the street from Mercy Hospital in northwestern Oklahoma City and performed a successful operation on a patient that finished by about 7:45 that morning. At about eight o'clock, he called Sally Sanzone, the Mercy scheduling coordinator for surgeries, and asked her to move up another operation, scheduled to start at 9:00 a.m. Sanzone informed him that the operation preceding his had started late, but she thought his could probably begin at 8:45 a.m.

Hamilton asked her to contact the doctor who would assist him, Donald Rahhal, and advise him of the change in schedule. Hamilton also requested that he be paged when the patient was ready to be taken to the operating room and sedated for surgery. Sanzone asked Sarah Cox, the circulating operating-room nurse, to do the paging. Hamilton then proceeded to Mercy Hospital, where he visited with the patient he was to operate on at 8:45 a.m. He also visited another patient, Kimberly Piper, in her hospital room to see if she was ready to be discharged. While visiting Piper, Hamilton was accompanied by nurse Karel Kraybill, who assisted him with Piper's discharge paperwork.

At 8:30 a.m., Hamilton left Piper's room. His former partner, Dr. Karen S. Reisig, saw him dictating notes in the doctors' lounge shortly thereafter.

At 8:50 a.m., the preoperative assessment nurse in the Mercy operating room paged Hamilton to tell him his patient was being sedated and taken to the operating room. Dr. Gregory Johnston, an anesthesiologist, thinking the operation was about to start, had given the patient a sedative and was preparing to fully anesthetize the patient. Dr. Rahhal had also arrived and was ready to proceed.

At 9:00 a.m., Hamilton called in response to the page and told the pre-op nurse he was on his way and not to put the patient to sleep until he arrived. This was conveyed to Johnston, who became upset, because it is not good practice to keep a patient under sedation and anesthetic any longer than necessary.

At about 9:15 a.m., Hamilton returned to Mercy. He had a brief conversation with Dr. Jack Metcalf in the doctors' dressing room. As he changed from street clothes to scrubs, Hamilton mentioned he had been buying his wife a "Valentine's present" and was in a hurry to get to an operation.

In the hall outside the operating room, Dr. Hamilton also had a very brief conversation with Dr. Rahhal, lasting about twenty seconds. He apologized for being late to surgery and explained again that he had been delayed while getting his wife a Valentine's gift. Hamilton also mentioned having had coffee with his wife.

At 9:25 a.m., Hamilton stuck his head into the operating room to let Dr. Johnson know he was there and then scrubbed up in preparation to operate. The operation finally began at 9:40 a.m. and lasted about twenty-five to thirty-five minutes.

During the operation, Hamilton removed a large ovarian cyst from the patient. At the conclusion of the operation, he volunteered to sew up the patient so Dr. Rahhal, who would have normally done that task, could return to his office for scheduled appointments.

The removed ovarian cyst was large enough and unique enough that Hamilton took time to show it to a nursing student who was observing the

Valentine's Day Murder

operation. The patient was taken to the recovery room at 10:22 a.m., and Johnston saw Hamilton dictating an operational note at about 10:30 a.m.

At about half past ten, Hamilton called Becky Davis, an employee at his clinic, and told her he was going to run by his house to pick up his "appointment book." The Hamiltons lived at 3056 Brush Creek Road in the Quail Creek neighborhood near Quail Creek Country Club and only six or seven minutes from Mercy Hospital.

At 11:05 a.m., a distraught Hamilton called 911 and informed the operator he thought his wife was dead. He identified himself as a doctor and said he was performing cardiopulmonary resuscitation and had to end the call to continue CPR.

The Oklahoma City Fire Department was notified of the 911 call at 11:06 a.m. and dispatched help from the station at Northwest 122nd Street and North May Avenue, only a few blocks from the Hamilton residence. The firemen arrived first and found Hamilton in the master bathroom holding the bloody, naked body of his wife.

All the known facts regarding Hamilton's activities during that time were largely uncontested. What became crucial to establishing his guilt or innocence in the murder were his activities during the forty-five minutes between 8:30 and 9:15 a.m. and the thirty-five minutes between 10:30 and 11:05 am.

What could he have done—and not done—in those short blocks of time? Therein lies the crux of the Valentine's Day murder.

CHAPTER THREE

The Scene of the Crime

THREE FIREMEN LED BY Lieutenant David Bradbury responded to Hamilton's 911 call. They had been advised that the emergency involved a "full arrest," which meant someone's heart had stopped beating.

They found the house with Hamilton's Jaguar parked in the front driveway and the front door closed but unlocked. Inside, they discovered Susan Hamilton naked on the floor of a first-floor bathroom, her head surrounded by a large amount of blood. Hamilton was next to her on the floor. The firemen had not seen any blood trail or signs of any disturbance between the front door and the bathroom.

Bradbury noticed that Hamilton's hands were not properly positioned to perform CPR. Meanwhile, it was obvious that his wife, who had an open wound on the left side of her head and a laceration over her right eyebrow, was either badly injured or dead. There was also severe bruising to her face and around her neck. A necktie was seen underneath her body and another near her on the floor.

As for Hamilton, his hands and shirt were covered with blood. He was not wearing shoes and his socks were bloody. A pair of men's shoes was found on a bathroom rug, and a woman's orange bath wrap, on the floor. Hamilton kept pleading with the firemen to help his wife. According to protocol, Bradbury removed Hamilton from the scene and escorted him into the kitchen. Hamilton was still shoeless, and his socks left a bloody trail of footprints between the bathroom and the kitchen. He remained frantic and made several attempts to return to the bathroom to help his wife.

With Hamilton out of the room, another fireman, Paul Michael Pierce, examined Susan. Pierce confirmed that she was not breathing and had no pulse. Although Pierce believed Susan was dead, he nonetheless began resuscitation efforts, which he continued until advised to cease by EMSA personnel on their arrival a short time later.

The police had arrived after the firemen. Christopher W. Spillman, an officer who had been patrolling in the area, was one of the first on the scene. He found an agitated Hamilton in the kitchen. "I don't know what happened to her," Hamilton kept saying. After a few minutes, Spillman escorted Hamilton to a patrol car.

With Hamilton in the patrol car, Spillman began to tape off and secure the house as a crime scene. He found no sign of forced entry but did find a back door unlocked and ajar. It had been raining that morning, and the back door opened to the back lawn. There was no evidence of any grass or mud having been tracked into the house.

In the patrol car, Sergeant Larry Sanders was speaking with Hamilton. At the time, Hamilton was in the backseat and not under arrest. When Sanders asked the doctor what had transpired, Hamilton said he had performed an operation at seven that morning at the hospital and had returned home to exchange valentines with his wife at about half past eight. At about nine o'clock, he received a page to return to Mercy Hospital for surgery, and he did so.

After the surgery, Hamilton realized he had left his address book at home and had returned to retrieve it. When he put his key in the lock of the front door, he found it unlocked. Inside, he noticed the kitchen light on and called out for his wife, who did not respond. He found her on the floor of the bathroom in a pool of blood. In administering CPR, he noticed something wrapped around her neck. He removed what proved to be a tie, called 911, and continued CPR until the firefighters arrived.

Valentine's Day Murder

Sanders asked Hamilton if anybody else was supposed to be at the home that day. Hamilton recalled an appointment with an appliance repairman and that someone was coming in the afternoon to repair the electric gate.

During their conversation, Sanders said Hamilton appeared to be upset but coherent. Repeatedly, Hamilton told him, "I'm a doctor. I can help her," expressing a desire to return to his wife. Before Hamilton was taken in for questioning, he was examined by EMSA paramedic Jerry Walker, who also found the doctor upset but not in shock. Walker did not observe any scratches or marks on Hamilton.

Sanders transported Hamilton to Oklahoma City police headquarters. During the ride, Sanders observed the doctor acting oddly, repeatedly rubbing the backs of his hands and knuckles against the protective screen that separated the back of the car from the front. Hamilton also kept tapping his head against the screen.

At the station, Sanders helped Hamilton out of the car, but Hamilton's legs "turned to jelly." The doctor slumped to the pavement in a puddle of water between the car and the curb. Two other policemen who happened to be nearby helped Sanders assist Hamilton into the station, where he was placed in an interview room.

In the interview room, Hamilton changed out of his bloody clothes and into a jail jumpsuit. In the process, Detective Jimmy Hatfield observed that Hamilton had several injuries. They included an elongated bruise or raised contusion to the center of his forehead, a scratch on the outer side of his right forearm, abrasions on his knuckles, a mark on his right little finger, a blood blister or bruise on his right middle finger, a bruise on the inside of his left knee, a finger-sized bruise on the inside of his left bicep, an abrasion on his left triceps, and finger-sized scratch marks on his right shoulder and right triceps. All the injuries appeared to Hatfield to be recent.

Detective Michael Burke noticed Hamilton checking his own injuries, including removing the jumpsuit to examine his right shoulder.

By five o'clock that evening, Hamilton was arrested as a suspect in the killing of his wife. After his arrest, he exercised his Fifth Amendment rights and did not give the police any further statements or information.

CHAPTER FOUR

The Investigation

IT WAS NOT DIFFICULT to declare Hamilton a suspect. No sign of forced entry or evidence of the presence of a third party in the house had been found. Couple that with the high percentage of murders, especially brutal murders, that are committed by a spouse or other family member, and it was logical for the police to see Hamilton as their prime suspect.

What was not so obvious was what Hamilton's motive could be for murdering someone with whom he was so seemingly in love. Detectives, however, would quickly learn that behind the Hamiltons' cloying displays of public affection, trouble had been brewing.

The detectives were first alerted to marital problems the day of the murder. While parked in front of the Hamilton residence, Detective Scott was approached by Susan Johnston, the Hamiltons' next-door neighbor, wanting to know what had happened.

"Is this a murder and suicide?" she asked.

In questioning Johnston, Scott began to learn what had been going on at the Hamilton house in the previous few months. That led to further interviews with the Hamiltons' family, friends, and employees. As the facts filled in, a disconcerting picture began to emerge.

The Hamiltons' marriage was not the first for either of them, and each had two children from previous marriages. At about Christmastime the year before, Hamilton had paid for some repairs on his son's car after agreeing with his wife not to do so. When Susan found out, she considered the matter a breach of trust and became upset.

The couple had largely reconciled that issue by February 2001 only to have Mrs. Hamilton discover that her husband had placed more than sixty calls to one of his female patients, Alliena Aguirre, over a two-month period. Aguirre made her living as a topless dancer, and Susan was convinced that Hamilton was having an affair with the woman—behavior he had been guilty of during his previous marriage. Hamilton denied an affair, claiming instead that he was only trying to help Aguirre overcome her struggles with depression. Susan found it difficult to accept his explanation, and it caused a marital rift that both had discussed with their friends.

That a rift of some kind remained between the two was evidenced by a Valentine's Day card discovered in the trunk of Hamilton's Jaguar after the murder. The card was from Susan to her husband and contained a mushy printed message in keeping with the holiday, but she had added a note of her own: "I bought my cards two weeks ago, so I guess maybe they don't seem appropriate now. But I do love you. Have a good day. Susan."

That cool, matter-of-fact valentine note stood in contrast to her husband's behavior when it came to his wife. Detectives soon realized Hamilton was possessive of his wife to the point of obsession. He spent nearly all of his nonworking hours with Susan, and when they were apart, he called her constantly. From all reports, Susan had appeared to love the attention. But she had her own obsessions, and when it came to Hamilton, they appeared to be fixated on the promise of his absolute loyalty and truthfulness. It might have seemed a minor thing to help a son fix his car, but that deception roiled Susan. It did Hamilton no good when the calls to the topless dancer surfaced.

But was any of this pertinent to Susan's death?

While the details surrounding the state of the Hamilton marriage began to fall into place, the police had been examining and analyzing the scene and the physical evidence to be found there.

Along with the two neckties, investigators found a rag soaked in blood, which indicated an apparent attempt by someone to clean up the blood pool.

Valentine's Day Murder

The bathroom floor was covered with Dixie cups and a hairbrush, evidence of a real or staged struggle. There were also the orange cover-up on the floor and Hamilton's bloody loafers on a bathroom rug near the body. Two mops and a cleaning bucket had been left out in the utility room rather than in their normal place. Police took many photographs of all that, and all the physical evidence was carefully preserved and documented.

The police had already secured Hamilton's Jaguar and transported the car to a police impound lot where it was examined for evidence. Blood was found on the steering wheel, and blood and tissue were recovered from the inside door panel on the driver's side. There was also a strand of bloody hair inside the car. Tests proved that the blood, hair, and tissue were Susan Hamilton's.

The detectives were also working to establish a timeline that would put Hamilton at the house at the time of his wife's murder. Hamilton claimed he had been home between 8:30 and 9:00 a.m. to exchange valentines with his wife. The police verified his comings and goings at the Surgicare Center and Mercy Hospital from their records and the statements of various medical professionals. What investigators couldn't find was any documentation for the doctor's time between 8:30 and 9:20 a.m. and between 10:30 and 11:05 a.m.

The murder was consistent with a crime of passion, and given the physical evidence, the police developed a theory of the case. Hamilton had come home shortly after 8:30 a.m. and found Susan preparing to dress in the bathroom. They argued, and she perhaps told him she wanted a divorce. Hamilton snapped, grabbed a tie or ties, and started to choke her from behind, smashing her face on the floor in the process. He then smashed an object on her head with enough force to break her skull. Then he returned to Mercy Hospital and performed his second operation of the day.

Somewhere, either before or after the second operation, Dr. Hamilto had disposed of the murder weapon and possibly his own bloody clothes. When he returned home the second time, he tried to stage the scene to look as if an intruder had been there by unlocking and opening the back door. He then called 911 and pretended to perform CPR.

To sew up this theory, the police needed to find the murder weapon. An all-out search was launched. The police scoured all the possible routes between Mercy Hospital and the Hamilton residence and even went through the trash at the hospital looking for the weapon. It was never found.

The police's scenario did have some flaws. For one, Hamilton had no history of violence, and more than one witness thought him incapable of physically overpowering Susan. For another, in spite of their recent difficulties, the couple had had a loving relationship for thirteen years. Most of the people who knew the couple could not imagine Hamilton killing his wife. Moreover, Hamilton had returned to Mercy and, by all accounts, calmly and competently performed a surgical procedure. Could someone who had just murdered his wife in the heat of passion pull that off?

And then there was the matter of time—or the lack of it.

The window of time in which Hamilton was by himself was so small that even the police questioned whether he could have killed Susan, changed clothes, disposed of the weapon and bloody garments, and still returned to the hospital and donned scrubs by 9:25 a.m.

The facts were the facts, but the accused did not seem to fit the crime. That would have required a Dr. Jekyll/Mr. Hyde transformation in Dr. Hamilton. The loving husband, devoted father and stepfather, and accomplished professional—with no history of violence—would have had to turn into a brutal murderer so violent that he could beat his wife to death and so coldhearted that he could perform a delicate operation only a few minutes later.

Hamilton's personality and reputation—combined with the couple's long history together—certainly put the detectives' theory in doubt. In those first few days, that doubt was reinforced from an unexpected source: Susan's first husband and Susan's children. In spite of what the family was hearing from Oklahoma City detectives, neither Dick Horton, the father of Susan's two daughters, nor his family could accept the idea that Hamilton was a murderer, much less Susan's killer. Angela Horton, one of Susan's daughters, even went and visited Hamilton in the Oklahoma County Jail in the days immediately after losing her mother.

Although the Hortons could think of no one else who would have had reason to kill Susan, and even in light of the speculation that her death might stem from Hamilton's possible affair with the topless dancer, they could not see Hamilton as the perpetrator—at least not in those first days after the murder.

Dick Horton remembers vividly when the family's attitude changed. Three days after the murder, Horton sent one of Susan's best friends to the

Valentine's Day Murder

Hamilton house to pick out some jewelry to go with the outfit Susan would be buried in. At first, the friend could not find the jewelry, but after some searching, she located it in Susan's underwear drawer. That was not where Susan ever kept her jewelry, and knowing Susan's impeccable habit of keeping everything in its place, Horton and his children immediately knew something was wrong.

To them, it now appeared that Hamilton had hidden the jewelry to fake a robbery. From this moment forward, the detectives' theory of the case began to ring true to them.

CHAPTER FIVE

Under Arrest

REGARDLESS OF HIS guilt or innocence, Hamilton was incarcerated in the county jail and in need of counsel. He immediately hired Mack Martin. One of Oklahoma's premier criminal defense lawyers, Martin was experienced in defending cases of all kinds, including murder charges. Martin chose attorney J. David Ogle to assist him in the defense of the case.

Martin realized the importance of examining the physical evidence and the need for employing a forensic expert. He quickly obtained the services of Tom Bevel to act as a consultant to the defense. This was seen as a coup for the defense, Bevel being the preeminent expert in crime-scene reconstruction not only in Oklahoma but also nationally. Bevel was particularly expert in the analysis of blood spatter.

A twenty-seven-year veteran of the Oklahoma City Police Department, Bevel had retired from the force in 1996. He taught courses in crime-scene reconstruction all over the country and, along with with Ross Gardner, had written the definitive book on blood-spatter analysis. The Oklahoma County district attorney's office had used Bevel as an expert in other cases, and it probably would have liked to have employed Bevel in the Hamilton case if Martin had not gotten to him first. The police and district attorney suspected that the defense had hired Bevel not only for his expertise but also to keep him from testifying for the state.

Bevel went to the Hamilton residence two days after the murder and examined the scene. He later studied the police reports, photographs, autopsy report, and exhibits, including Hamilton's blood-spattered clothes. He shared his findings with the defense lawyers and helped them prepare for trial. Initially, Bevel was employed as a consultant and not as an expert witness. This is an important legal distinction because as a consultant, his findings would be privileged and confidential to the defense only. If he was identified as a witness, then his opinions would become subject to discovery by the prosecution. Obviously, the defense wanted to know what Bevel's conclusions were prior to determining whether he would be used as a witness in the case.

* * * * *

February 21, 2001, turned out to be a bad day in John Hamilton's life. The doctor was charged with the murder of his wife, and his wife was buried at Rose Hill Burial Park in Oklahoma City.

Hamilton's lawyers obtained an order that allowed him to attend Susan's funeral. According to the *Oklahoman*, he arrived "clad in a black suit, white shirt, and manacles," accompanied by two sheriff's deputies. It had to have been a humiliating experience for Hamilton, who by all accounts had loved his wife.

At the time the charges were filed against Hamilton, longtime Oklahoma County District Attorney Bob Macy was still in office. Macy assigned the case to Assistant District Attorney Wes Lane. Lane had been with the district attorney's office since 1981 except for a short break in private practice and business. He was an experienced prosecutor. Shortly after the case was filed, Macy resigned for health reasons. Governor Frank Keating appointed Lane to the empty post in July 2001. Lane, who continued as the lead prosecutor on the Hamilton case, would be elected district attorney in 2002.

District Judge Ray Elliott was assigned to the case. A former prosecutor who had taken the bench in 1999, Elliott had a reputation as a strict no-nonsense judge, although some defense lawyers felt that his past experience as a prosecutor made him more prosecution oriented.

Valentine's Day Murder

After the charges were filed, Martin made an attempt to have Hamilton released on bail. A hearing on the bail request was held on March 16. The request included an offer by Hamilton to live under strict monitoring and armed guards. Martin called ten witnesses on the doctor's behalf, including three medical doctors who offered to make daily checks on their peer. The defense also offered numerous letters from patients, colleagues, and friends attesting to Dr. Hamilton's good character.

In spite of the proposed restrictions on his release, Hamilton's request for bail was denied by Judge Elliott. An appeal was filed with the Oklahoma Court of Criminal Appeals, where bail was once again denied in a four-to-one vote on May 8.

Dr. Hamilton would remain in the county jail until his trial, a far cry from the luxury accommodations of his accustomed lifestyle.

CHAPTER SIX

Abusive Husband?

HAMILTON'S PRELIMINARY HEARING was set for May 25, 2009, before Special Judge Don Deason. That morning, spectators—many of them affluent friends of the Hamiltons—lined up in advance. The courtroom was so full at one point that someone remarked it was probably a good day to get a tee time at Quail Creek Country Club given that all the members were obviously at the courthouse.

The hearing took off on an unexpected tangent almost immediately. Lane had bought into a theory advanced by a little-known volunteer witness named Melissa Marshall. After the murder, Marshall had telephoned Lane with unsolicited information, and she became the prosecution's first witness. Claiming to be an intimate friend of Susan Hamilton's, Marshall was in reality unknown to any of Susan's friends or family, and she told a tale that was patently unbelievable to anyone who knew the Hamiltons.

According to Marshall, she had met Susan in 1995 at a service at Church of the Servant, a local church Susan did not normally attend. Marshall testified that their chance meeting had blossomed into a close friendship, and they met periodically for lunch and shared confidences about their abusive husbands. Marshall, who had subsequently divorced, testified that Susan had told her about mental and physical abuse by Hamilton. Marshall described Susan as fearful and insecure, when all who knew Susan regarded her as a strong and confident woman.

Marshall claimed that she and Susan became involved in a support group for abused wives, a group so secret that participants addressed each other only by first names and did not even exchange telephone numbers. None of the events Marshall testified to were documented, and her statements seemed to be couched in a way that made them difficult to verify or refute. The reliability of Marshall's testimony was tested on cross-examination. She stated to have last seen Susan in early December 2000, even though she had testified about the Hamiltons' marital difficulties, which had not occurred until January and February 2001. Caught in an obvious falsehood, the drama queen did not back down but kept spinning her incredible tale.

Continuing this line of questioning, Lane called Martha Serna, a Hispanic cleaning woman who had previously worked for the Hamiltons for about six years, cleaning their house weekly. Although she seemed to understand some English, Serna testified through an interpreter, saying that several times, she had heard an enraged Hamilton hurl insults at Susan and on two occasions, she had seen bruises on Susan, including a black eye. In one instance, Susan told Serna that her injuries had been caused by a bug bite or a virus and on the other occasion by a fall in the shower. Serna testified that she did not believe either explanation.

The other reason Lane had called Serna to the stand soon became clear. The housekeeper described, and then drew a picture of, a small marble statue she had seen in the Hamiltons' master bathroom. The police had not found the statue anywhere in the house after the crime, and the implication was that it could be the missing murder weapon used to bludgeon Susan.

One can only speculate as to Hamilton's state of mind as he heard the testimony of the two women. Marshall and Serna's testimony was later debunked by that of Susan's best friend, Shary Coffey, who knew the Hamiltons intimately, had never seen or heard of any abusive behavior by Hamilton and believed he was incapable of any physical violence against his wife.

Oddly, Lane remained so enamored of his theory that Hamilton was an abusive husband that after the hearing, he publicly asked for any other battered women who knew about Hamilton's abuse of Susan to come forward.

Valentine's Day Murder

Because the alleged acts almost certainly never happened, it surprised no one when no credible witnesses stepped forward to support the testimony of Marshall or Serna.

In preparing his defense, Martin took no chances, employing an investigator named John Floyd who worked many hours to discredit Marshall's tall tales. Martin prepared for trial believing that the state would pursue the theory that Hamilton was an abusive husband.

Because of the state's theory that Susan Hamilton was an abused wife, Connie Pope, another assistant district attorney, joined the prosecution. Pope was the head of the domestic-abuse division of the district attorney's office. Now Connie Smothermon, she is an assistant professor at the University of Oklahoma College of Law. Pope became deeply involved in the preparation and trial of the Hamilton case.

In Oklahoma, the state does not have to prove guilt at a preliminary hearing. The state needs to prove only that a crime has been committed and that probable cause exists to believe that the defendant committed the crime. The question of guilt or innocence is left to a jury trial.

To meet this burden of proof, the preliminary hearing was devoted to establishing the opportunity Hamilton had had to kill his wife and his possible motivation because of their known marital problems.

There was certainly no question that a crime had been committed on Valentine's Day, and at the end of the hearing, Judge Deason ruled that the state had presented sufficient evidence to link Hamilton to the crime.

Dr. Hamilton would stand trial for first-degree murder.

CHAPTER SEVEN

Who Can Prove What?

THE HAMILTON CASE SOON consumed Mack Martin's practice. He not only had to organize the doctor's defense but he also had to sort through hundreds of photographs, reports, and other exhibits, many technical in nature.

Fortunately, he had a client who could afford an investigator and pay a decent fee. In most criminal cases, the state has the inherent advantage of being armed with the full spectrum of the investigative and scientific resources of the police department. In this case, the defendant at least had an investigator and an expert witness in Tom Bevel, although Bevel's role in the case would ultimately prove to be a curse rather than a blessing.

Preparing for trial, Mack Martin and David Ogle worked closely with Bevel. What they were unaware of was the contact Bevel was also having with the police and Ross Gardner, the prosecution's expert witness. Gardner and Bevel were friends and colleagues. In fact, Bevel was Gardner's mentor. The two had written a book together, and Bevel had recommended Gardner to the district attorney's office as a possible expert in the Hamilton case. Indeed, Bevel and Gardner were so close that they later formed a business together, Bevel, Gardner & Associates, a forensic analysis firm.

Eventually, Gardner prepared a written report for the D. A.'s office. The report had to be furnished to the defense, and Bevel disagreed with some of Gardner's findings. He called his friend and got Gardner to partially change the report. According to telephone records, the two men talked numerous times between the time Bevel was employed by the defense and the trial. It should be said that the frequent phone conversations between Bevel and Gardner were not unusual, and on occasion they concerned matters other than the Hamilton case, but they also sometimes touched on the Hamilton case.

Because of his years on the force and his continued service for the district attorney's office as an expert witness, Bevel was acquainted with Teresa Sterling and Randy Scott, the lead detectives on the case, as well as with Detective Craig Gravell, one of the police department's leading experts on blood spatter. All of those officers were anxious to know Bevel's conclusions about the case, and on five or six instances, they directly asked him about his findings. In each case, he refused to give out any information, but still they persisted.

At one point, Bevel was in the district attorney's office working on another case. He ran into Richard Whinery, an assistant district attorney with whom he had worked several times before. Whinery brought up the Hamilton case, and when Bevel declined to give him any information, Whinery mentioned that he could always subpoena Bevel. Bevel reported this encounter to Ogle.

Martin had yet to decide if he would call Bevel as a witness. That would be a decision he would make at trial, but for Bevel to testify, he had to be listed as a witness to the court and a summary of his testimony provided to the district attorney. Martin listed Bevel as a witness, and Bevel prepared a vague and generic report that indicated disagreements with Gardner but gave few specifics as to why. That further raised the curiosity of detectives and prosecutors.

Meantime, while interviewing countless people in preparation for trial, John Floyd was finding that the testimony about Hamilton's supposed spousal abuse had no basis in fact. It was contradicted by everything he could learn from credible witnesses who knew the Hamiltons. None of the Hamiltons' friends, family, or employees had ever seen any evidence of abuse by Hamilton. Most of them described Susan as a strong-willed woman who would never have put up with any such abuse. Those people insisted she would have

Valentine's Day Murder

left Hamilton if he had done anything to her such as described by Melissa Marshall. Floyd also dug up information that could be used to discredit Marshall's truthfulness and credibility.

This was all important and necessary prep work, but it failed to answer the question as to who might have committed the murder if Hamilton had not. A new theory emerged, one based on the doctor's work at his abortion clinic. Could the murderer have been an enraged antiabortionist? The idea was not without precedent. Other doctors who performed abortions had been killed or their property had been vandalized.

Hamilton had received anonymous threatening telephone calls, and antiabortion groups had picketed both his clinic and his home. In one instance, antiabortionists had printed a "Wanted" poster accusing Hamilton of murder and marched around with it.

Martin wanted to raise the possibility to the jury that Mrs. Hamilton had been the victim of an antiabortion zealot, but he never got the chance. The state filed a motion to exclude any such evidence from the trial. In a pretrial hearing, Judge Elliott sustained the motion, ruling that without a specific suspect, such evidence was too vague and irrelevant.

That, however, did leave the possibility Susan had been killed by an unknown intruder.

CHAPTER EIGHT

The Trial Begins

THE TRIAL STARTED ON December 3, 2001. After almost ten months in jail, John Hamilton would finally get his day in court. Picking an impartial jury, however, presented a problem, particularly for the defense. Hamilton was an abortionist in a strong pro-life state. The defense had to be sure that all the jurors could give the defendant a fair trial, regardless of how they felt about abortion. The prosecution, on the other hand, wanted jurors who would focus on rendering a verdict on the facts of the crime and not be inclined to acquit Hamilton because of his previously spotless record, professional status, or apparent love for his wife.

Both sides extensively questioned the jury on those and other issues over the course of three days. Finally, a jury was sworn in, composed of five men and seven women. One man and one woman were also sworn in as alternate jurors. Meanwhile, during voir dire, Judge Elliott set the tone for the trial by having a juror arrested who failed to show up as ordered, based on a flimsy excuse.

The prosecution had wisely decided not to pursue the theory that Susan Hamilton was the subject of spousal abuse prior to her murder. No credible evidence existed to support the theory. Martin only learned of this change in strategy during voir dire, so Judge Elliott granted him a short delay to revise his opening remarks to the jury.

Wes Lane established the prosecution's theme for the trial with the first sentence of his opening statement: "Ladies and gentlemen, John Hamilton loved his wife to death."

That assertion foreshadowed the prosecution's theory that the good doctor had killed his wife in a fit of rage occasioned by his fear that she intended to divorce him. Lane said the state would prove that sometime during that short window of time between 8:30 a.m. and 9:25 a.m., Hamilton had killed Susan, changed his clothes, attempted a crude cover-up, and returned to Mercy Hospital for his second operation of the day. Then, after completing the operation, he returned to the crime scene on the false pretense of picking up his appointment book. His actual objective was to fake finding his wife's body, cover up his crime, and make that crucial call to 911. Somewhere during all this, he also disposed of the murder weapon and his bloody clothes.

In his opening statement, Martin countered Lane's narrative by pointing out that the state's case was circumstantial and based largely on speculation and supposition. He emphasized that Hamilton had been quickly targeted as the only suspect, placed in a patrol car, and taken to the police station for questioning within sixteen minutes of the detectives arriving at the scene. Martin suggested that the police first determined Hamilton was guilty and then built their case on that theory alone, never investigating any possible alternative or any other suspect.

As the evidence developed over the next ten days of trial, the prosecution would try to convict Hamilton by eliminating the possibility that anyone else could have committed the crime. If there were no one else with motive or opportunity, the state would argue that the killer had to be Hamilton.

Given Martin's opening statement, the prosecutors could not be sure if the defense intended to call Bevel as a witness or not. Martin's comments seemed to indicate that Bevel would not testify. Based on that assumption and their review of Bevel's report, the prosecutors felt confident that Bevel substantially agreed with Gardner, so they served Bevel with a subpoena, setting the stage for him to be called as a witness on behalf of the state.

Valentine's Day Murder

Subpoenaing the other party's expert witness is highly unusual, especially when the prosecution is unsure what the witness will say. The defense reacted to that move by filing a motion to quash the subpoena on the grounds that Bevel was acting only as a consultant until such time as the defense called him as a witness. Given his status as a consultant, he was privy to information and defense strategy that was privileged and confidential.

The defense's efforts to block the state from calling Bevel made the prosecutors even more curious about his testimony, assuming that they did not already know exactly what it would be. What knowledge the prosecutors did or did not have would soon become the subject of intense controversy. In any event, Judge Elliott overruled the defense's motion to quash, ruling that once Bevel was listed as a witness, he was subject to being called by either side.

CHAPTER NINE

The Case against Dr. Hamilton

THE PROSECUTORS BEGAN their case by first trying to prove Hamilton's motive. Susan Hamilton's longtime best friend, Shary Coffey, was called as the first witness. Coffey painted a picture of a loving couple whose marriage had hit a snag over Hamilton's perceived relationship with the topless dancer because it fueled Susan's belief that her husband could no longer be trusted.

Susan and John Hamilton had both confided in Coffey about their marital problems, and Coffey said that in spite of their efforts to reconcile, Susan remained upset.

On cross-examination, Coffey described Hamilton "as a gentle, caring man." She also said that she did not believe he could ever hurt Susan and that she did not believe he had committed the murder.

The state called a procession of Hamilton's employees to establish that his behavior toward Susan was "smothering," "possessive," "obsessive," and "controlling." One witness, Teresa Henderson, an employee at Hamilton's clinic, said the couple was "possessive of each other." Those same witnesses also painted a picture of the couple as inseparable and of Susan as a wife who basked in the attention her husband bestowed on her.

To establish the couple's marital rift, Alliena Aguirre was presented as a witness. The dancer denied any sexual involvement with Hamilton but did testify that he had phoned her so frequently, she stopped answering his calls. On two occasions, he had come to see her perform, and he had also supplied her with prescription drugs she needed but could not afford.

Cell phone bills showing that Hamilton had made more than sixty calls to the dancer over the course of about three months were then introduced into evidence, supporting Aguirre's testimony. The bills had come from the Hamilton residence and bore notes in Susan's handwriting, indicating that she had reviewed them.

The prosecution also wanted to establish that Susan was extremely security conscious and would never have left the back and front doors unlocked as they were found on the day of her murder, particularly while she was in the house alone. In fact, Susan's daughter, Angela Horton, testified that her mother was so security conscious, she made Angela lock the doors even when Angela went out for a short run in the neighborhood. The Hamiltons' current part-time housekeeper, Cathy Brainard, confirmed this.

Having established the background for the crime, the state presented evidence to support its theory about when the crime occurred that morning. At 9:19 a.m., Susan's mother, Louise Shibley, called her daughter. Susan did not answer. Unknown to Shibley, her daughter was already dead. Other testimony pertained to a meeting of the Oklahoma County Medical Society Alliance, hosted by one of Susan's friends on the morning of the murder. Susan was expected at the meeting, which started with a social at 9:30 a.m. followed by the program at 10:00 a.m. Janie Axton, the hostess, testified to being both surprised and disappointed when Susan failed to show. The prosecutor used this evidence to try to prove that Susan was killed between 8:30 a.m. and 9:15 a.m. while John was unaccounted for at the hospital.

A parade of nurses and doctors from the Surgicare Center and Mercy Hospital established Dr. Hamilton's known whereabouts on February 14. Because of the maintenance of medical records, including the meticulous timekeeping necessary in the operating room, much of the time was documented down to the minute. Although Hamilton's unaccounted-for time did give him the opportunity to commit the crime, it would have had to take place in a very narrow window.

Valentine's Day Murder

Martin was able to elicit on cross-examination of the medical professionals that Hamilton's behavior at the hospital was professional, competent, and, other than being late for surgery, normal in all respects. It raised the question of whether anyone could maintain such calm and cool control just after having bludgeoned his spouse and left her in a pool of her own blood.

Although the judge had excluded any defense evidence of abortion protests or anonymous threats against Hamilton, in a few cases, the prosecution asked questions that allowed Martin to draw some of this evidence out of witnesses. Although not allowed as a defense, a juror could have been influenced by hearing about antiabortion protests at Dr. Hamilton's clinic.

The prosecution pursued the idea that Hamilton had changed his clothes after he murdered Susan and before he returned to Mercy. The evidence for this turned out to be not only conflicting and inconclusive but also proved that most people have no reason to care or remember what someone else is wearing. Various witnesses put Hamilton in khaki pants, a blue blazer, and white shirt with a pattern; a light blue shirt; a tweed blazer; a dark suit coat; and something akin to an overcoat and a white sweater.

Although the clothes Hamilton was wearing at the scene and the blood on those clothes played a prominent role in the trial, the testimony as to what if any clothes he might have changed into between surgeries was in serious doubt.

After framing the time during which Dr. Hamilton had been at home, by his own statement to police, the prosecution moved on to describe the crime scene. The firemen, police, and EMSA personnel who responded that morning testified to what they had found and described Hamilton's behavior. Although they remembered him as being agitated and frantic, no one recalled seeing any tears. His odd scratching of his arms and hands in the patrol car was also pointed out.

Detective Jimmy Hatfield, who had seen Hamilton examining the injuries to his own body, testified that Hamilton's injuries appeared to be recent and consistent with injuries inflicted by a victim fighting for her life. That was particularly true of a contusion to Hamilton's forehead that swelled in size while he was at the police station, as well as what appeared to be fingernail scratches on his arm and back. All of Hamilton's injuries had been photographed. The photographs were placed in evidence, along with hundreds of other exhibits by the prosecution, including horrific photographs of Susan's bloody and beaten body and the clothes Hamilton was wearing that morning.

Another succession of witnesses, all Oklahoma City police officers, testified about the details of the crime scene, including the location of the physical evidence and the subsequent results of several scientific tests. Some of the most damning evidence came from Hamilton's Jaguar, which was found parked in front of the house. Tests confirmed the presence of Susan's blood on the steering wheel and elsewhere in the car, along with her hair and body tissue. An innocent explanation of that evidence would be hard to come by.

Dr. Jeffery J. Gofton, a forensic pathologist at the Oklahoma office of the chief medical examiner's office, performed the autopsy on Susan Hamilton. He had also observed her body at the residence before it was removed. He ruled the cause of death to be "blunt force head trauma." He had found "ligature abrasions to the neck, defensive abrasions to the anterior neck, facial contusions and lacerations, and underlying facial fractures."

In his opinion, Susan was first strangled and then her face was pounded on the floor; she was finally killed by blunt-force trauma to the head.

In view of what he had observed at the scene, Gofton's said his opinion was that Susan had been strangled with the neckties found at the scene, and the wounds and scratches on her neck were made by her own fingernails as she tried to pry the ties loose. Gofton said the wounds Susan suffered were slow to bleed, and the amount of blood found in the bathroom would have taken some time to accumulate. The autopsy pictures introduced during Gofton's testimony were so gruesome that they left three female jurors in tears.

As well as building a case against Hamilton, the prosecution witnesses offered testimony that helped to eliminate the possibility of an unknown assailant committing the crime. It was stressed that there had been no sign of forced entry, nor was there motive for anyone else to kill Susan. There were no tracks in or out the back door of the Hamilton residence and no blood trail leading from the bathroom to the front or back door. There was also no sign of robbery and no proof of sexual assault. Believing that the killer was an enraged antiabortion fanatic required also believing that such an intruder was able to time his attack to the rare occasion when the doors to the Hamilton house were unlocked and professional enough to leave no trace of entry or exit.

Valentine's Day Murder

The prosecutors had baked their cake, but they decided to ice it by calling Ross Gardner. Gardner was presented as "an independent consultant in bloodstain pattern analysis, crime scene investigation," but he had also been called in anticipation that the defense might call Tom Bevel to the stand. The chief of police of Lake City, Georgia, Gardner had written a book with Tom Bevel on the subject and had testified as an expert witness on numerous occasions. He was certainly qualified in the field of bloodstain analysis.

Whether such analysis was a reliable scientific tool at the time is another matter. Wes Lane has since called bloodstain analysis "a powerful tool," and he believes wholeheartedly in its scientific reliability. Recent studies have questioned whether such analysis is valid, much less scientific. Nevertheless, it is an area in which expert testimony is allowed in court, and given the idea, fueled by television and films, that every crime can be solved by forensic analysis, opinions about bloodstains remain persuasive to juries.

Gardner started at a disadvantage. He had not been employed in time to examine the crime scene or the body. His opinion was based on photographs, exhibits, and the testimony of the state's witnesses. He had paid particular attention to the blood-soaked and blood-spattered clothes worn by Hamilton and had reached two opinions about them that were especially damaging to the defense.

Gardner had determined that Hamilton's left shoe showed a blood-spatter pattern that could have been created only by a forceful act. He ruled out the source of the spatter being created by the doctor's supposed CPR efforts on his wife or stepping in the blood pool. In Gardner's opinion, the shoes were present when Susan was attacked, leading to the inevitable conclusion that Hamilton committed the crime. Gardner said he had no conclusive opinion as to whether the shirt, pants, and coat were or were not present when the crime was committed.

Gardner's second damaging opinion related to the blood pattern on Hamilton's shirt. By studying and measuring the wound to Susan's head, Gardner concluded that the bloody weapon used to bludgeon her had made an imprint on the shirt. Since the weapon was unknown and had never been found, that conclusion was a stretch. Gardner also opined that the killer would have had to pass behind Susan to get to the ties in the closet and that there was no blood trail leading away from the bathroom.

Mack Martin effectively cross-examined Gardner. He established that Gardner's opinion on the imprint of the weapon in blood on the doctor's shirt was highly suspect and that many other things could have caused that imprint. Martin also pointed out that the blood spatter on the doctor's shoe could have been caused after the fact by his activities in and around the blood pool. Under questioning by Martin, Gardner also admitted that an attacker could have entered the closet when Susan was not in the bathroom, concealed himself, and then surprised her from behind. Importantly, Martin also led Gardner to admit that he could not testify that the shirt had even been worn at the time of the murder. Gardner said the minor spatter on the outside of the cuff and sleeve was inconclusive and that 99 percent of the blood on the shirt came from the blood pool.

After Gardner, the state briefly called one more witness to establish the identity and location of the shoes and then rested its case.

CHAPTER TEN

The Defense

D R. JOHN HAMILTON HAD ALWAYS adamantly insisted that he was innocent of his wife's murder, and it was time for him to tell his story. He was the first witness called by the defense.

Hamilton began by describing his background as a doctor and his lengthy history with Susan. They had met in 1985 at a birthday party, and after dating for more than two years, had married in 1987. They were constantly together during their marriage. Hamilton had altered his schedule at work to give him more time to spend with his new wife. He bought her gifts and took her on vacations; nonetheless, she was jealous of any time he spent away from her. He described a close and loving relationship.

During his testimony, Hamilton frequently spoke in a very soft voice. At one point, one of the jurors asked that he please speak up so his testimony could be heard, and the court reporter prompted him several times as well.

Hamilton described the rift with his wife about paying for his son's car repairs and the issues caused later by his contacts with the dancer, Alliena Aguirre. He denied any affair with Aguirre. In his opinion, the relationship with his wife had improved greatly by Valentine's Day, with Susan beginning to overcome her doubts about him.

After describing their life before February 14, Hamilton then began his explanation of what had happened leading up to his wife's death. Two days before the murder, he claimed to have been working on the landscaping around the house and having been scratched in the process—hence the scratches found on him by the police.

His recount of what occurred the day of the murder began with what he was wearing when he left the house that morning for his first surgery. He identified those as the same clothes he was wearing when he was found at the scene of the crime, the same ones that had been placed in evidence.

According to Hamilton, after his first surgery and his visit to Mercy Hospital, he returned home between 8:30 and 8:45 a.m. He drove directly home. He found Susan dressing in the master bathroom. The two exchanged Valentine's Day cards and "hugged and kissed and got a little romantic." When he received a pager call at 9:00 a.m., he left immediately for the hospital. He tossed Susan's valentine on the kitchen counter and placed the one she had given him in the trunk of his Jaguar, because it was his habit to put all his papers or belongings there.

After his second surgery, Hamilton said he left Mercy Hospital at about 10:40 or 10:45 a.m. to return home and pick up his PalmPilot, a Christmas gift from his office employees in 2000. He was also carrying his appointment book because he had yet to transfer all of its contents to the PalmPilot. He was headed to the florist to pick up a plant he had bought for Susan for Valentine's Day, but about a mile from his house at 122nd Street and May Avenue, he changed his mind and returned home, parking his Jaguar in the circular driveway in front of the house.

He had not expected to find Susan home and was surprised when he found the front door unlocked. He looked in the kitchen where the light and the coffeepot were still on. He also saw a light on in the utility room and glanced in there.

As he went into the master bedroom, he heard a space heater running in the bathroom. When he entered the bathroom, Susan was lying on her right side with a pool of blood above her head. He took her by the left shoulder and rolled her onto her back. Her head lolled into the blood pool. He jumped over her, and his shoes came off. Although he found no pulse, he gave Susan two quick blows to the sternum and then attempted chest compressions and

Valentine's Day Murder

mouth-to-mouth recitation. He felt something around her neck, picked up her head to remove it, and felt her head fall back into the blood pool. That created a spatter event that Bevel would later say could have accounted for the spatter on the doctor's shoe.

Hamilton then called 911. Despite his repeated efforts to put on his shoes, they kept slipping off. There was standing water in the sink, and he washed his hands in it. Worried that his car would block the EMSA vehicles, he decided to move it. He stated that he was "not coherent" at the time. When he reached the car, he opened the driver's door, put his right leg into the car, and attempted to put his key in the ignition. He was so upset that his hand was shaking, and he dropped his keys. Unable to get the key in the ignition, he relocked the car and returned to the bathroom, where he was found by the firemen, the first responders to arrive at the scene.

In the police car, Hamilton said he was frantic to return to Susan, which was why he kept beating his head and dragging his hands on the metal screen. When he finally exited the car, he fell and hit his head on the curb, which explained the subsequent knot on his head. He specifically denied killing Susan.

During cross-examination, Wes Lane stressed the couple's marital discord. He also extracted an admission from Hamilton that it was uniquely unusual for him to be late to any surgery, and in fact, he had never before had a patient ready to be anesthetized when he was not available. Hamilton blamed this situation on the hospital not calling him as he had requested.

Lane then led Hamilton through a series of questions that caused him to admit that an intruder could not have passed behind Susan to hide in the closet, obtain the ties, and then attack her without being detected because she was sitting in front of a mirror and the intruder would have had to pass right behind her in the bathroom.

In response to that, Hamilton pointed out that that was not the way he thought the murder had happened. He theorized that the initial attack could have occurred after Susan put on the orange wrap, which was later found on the floor of the bathroom, and had gone to sweep leaves off the front porch, as she had done in the past on several occasions. That, Hamilton noted, could have been when the attacker slipped into the closet.

As far as the open back door, Hamilton felt responsible for that, saying he might have left the door open while watering the plants two days before the murder. Lane implied that Hamilton had actually opened the door after the murder to create the idea that a thief had entered the home. As far as the scratches on his body, Hamilton said he did not know how he had gotten them. He was sure the abrasion on his forehead, however, was the result of him falling while exiting the police car and hitting the curb.

Lane also extracted from Hamilton that as he was running through the closet to move his car so EMSA could access the house more easily, he had found Susan's jewelry on the counter and had stopped to place it in her underwear drawer. Hamilton said he had been concerned about having the jewelry out with so many people in the house. Lane, however, suggested that Hamilton had hidden the jewelry so he could come back later, remove it, and claim that a robbery had taken place, an assertion Hamilton denied.

All in all, Lane shone a spotlight on the parts of Hamilton's testimony that did not make sense, including those that might have been contrived to cover up the weaknesses in his story.

Whether Hamilton had managed to talk his way to freedom remained in question.

In the opinion of some of the participants, Hamilton's testimony might have done him more harm than good. Detective Sterling described it as "cold-hearted and cold-blooded." Assistant District Attorney Connie Pope said Hamilton seemed to have too many explanations for everything he did. And Lane remembered feeling as though he wanted to keep Hamilton on the stand for as long as he could because "the longer he talked the more he hurt himself."

As for Hamilton's own lawyer, Mack Martin had worked patiently to prepare the doctor for trial and thought he would make a good witness. Martin was sorely disappointed. He particularly recalled the response to his final question asking Hamilton to face the jury and tell them whether he had killed his wife or not. Rather than turning and looking the jurors in the eye, Hamilton hung his head and mumbled that he was not guilty and had not killed Susan. Martin recalled feeling the doctor looked "defeated" in that moment, not innocent.

The defense then called on Dr. Jack Metcalf, Dr. Karen Reisig, and Dr. Gregory Johnston to testify that Hamilton's appearance, demeanor, and actions at Mercy Hospital on the day of the murder were perfectly normal.

Valentine's Day Murder

Reisig, Hamilton's former business partner, had seen Hamilton between 8:30 and 8:45 a.m. before Hamilton left Mercy Hospital for the first time. Metcalf had observed Hamilton upon his return to the hospital at about 9:15 a.m. And Johnston, the anesthesiologist who had participated in Hamilton's second operation of the day, testified that Hamilton had performed professionally in surgery. Johnston recalled no hint of any unusual behavior.

Perhaps the highlight of Johnston's testimony, however, came when Pope asked him, "How many individuals have you've spoken to that have killed their wives?"

Johnston calmly replied, "At least two."

When Pope asked if either of those people had acted markedly different, Johnson, relying on his emergency-room experience, replied, "They did—they had been either shot or stabbed."

The defense put Barbara Westerman, Evelyn Handke, and Kyle Cates on the stand to establish that everything seemed normal between the Hamiltons just the day before the murder. Westerman and Handke worked at Hamilton's clinic, and Cates was a friend and the manager of Tommy's Restaurant, where the couple had eaten lunch on February 13.

To underscore the fact that the police never really considered any other suspect, Detective Teresa Sterling was called to testify. She went on record as having arrived at the crime scene at 12:01 p.m. and seen Hamilton placed in a patrol car and transported to the police station at 12:17 p.m.

The defense had had its own autopsy of Susan Hamilton's body done by Dr. Adam Merchant. He was called to provide an opinion calculated to undermine some of Gardner's testimony. Merchant said that in his opinion, the tearing and abrasions on Susan's head made it impossible to determine either the shape or size of the weapon with any specificity. He also contended that using the wound to measure the weapon with the precision Gardner had testified to was not possible.

The question as to whether the defense would call Tom Bevel was answered when he was placed on the stand as the last defense witness. His opinions, given on direct examination, were important in refuting Gardner's testimony in two respects. First, in Bevel's opinion, the blood-spatter pattern on Hamilton's left shoe could have been caused by Hamilton giving CPR to Susan and moving in and around the blood pool after he found her body.

Second, Bevel contended that without knowing what the murder weapon was, it was sheer speculation to say the blood spatter on Hamilton's shirt was caused by some unknown weapon. Bevel scored some important points for the defense.

Lane's cross-examination was initially uneventful and did little or nothing to change or discredit Bevel's opinions. However, as Lane neared the end of his cross-examination, everything changed dramatically when he asked Bevel: "In your view, is there anything that the police or that Mr. Gardner missed in the examination of these items that has not been presented to the court?"

Posing such an open-ended question to a hostile expert is unusual and dangerous. It opens the door for the witness to expound on matters that might be unknown to the questioner and, in most cases, helpful to the party that had sponsored the witness.

In Bevel's case, however, the opposite proved to be true.

"Yes sir, there are a couple," Bevel responded.

Lane asked him to explain. Bevel mentioned the blood spatter found on both sides of the bathroom door. Lane declined to pursue the significance of that particular revelation and instead pushed Bevel for another example.

In doing so, he struck gold for the prosecution.

Bevel noted that no one had focused on the blood spatter on the inside of the right sleeve of Hamilton's shirt. Lane showed Bevel the shirt, and Bevel identified what he referred to as "directional" blood spatter on the inside of the right sleeve. He later referred to it also as "back spatter."

Under further questioning by Lane, Bevel testified that the spatter was not consistent with someone who had been administering CPR but rather with someone smashing a person's face on the floor or hitting the face with his fist. When Lane asked if such spatter was consistent with "John Hamilton holding a blunt instrument in his hand and beating her skull in," Bevel's response was short and to the point. "It would be consistent with such an occurrence, yes, sir," he answered.

Bevel then testified a blunt instrument applied to the victim's head was "the most probable" source of the spatter on the inside of Hamilton's sleeve.

Martin and his associate David Ogle were shocked. They had discussed that very same issue with Bevel in detail to different effect. Martin recalled with great certainty that Bevel had previously told him the blood spatter on

Valentine's Day Murder

the inside of Hamilton's cuff could have come from three sources: giving CPR, contact with the blood pool, or a blow to Susan's head such as Lane suggested. In their private conversations, Bevel had told them he could not say which of the three sources was the more likely. He certainly had not said that a blow with a blunt instrument was "most probable."

Hamilton also vividly and "absolutely" remembered Bevel saying in one meeting that there was no way "anyone" could be sure of the way the few drops of blood came to be on the inside of Hamilton's cuff.

On redirect, Martin regained some ground. He got Bevel to state that the spatter on the inside of the shirtsleeve could have come from Hamilton's administering CPR on Susan if a sufficient volume of blood was present on her chest during the process. Bevel also said the spatter could have come from Hamilton's striking the blood pool with his fist. Because Hamilton had testified that he gave Susan two hard blows to the sternum in an effort to start her heart, this seemed a possible alternative.

Next, Martin pursued Bevel's comments about blood being found on both sides of the bathroom door. Bevel said he believed this indicated that the door was closed during at least some of the events that morning.

Martin had done what he could on redirect, but the damage had already been done. The defendant's own expert had given an opinion that linked him to the commission of the crime. Bevel's testimony was particularly damaging because he was the last witness to testify before the case went to the jury.

Did Lane know how Bevel would answer his open-ended question? Both Bevel and Lane would subsequently deny that under oath. But why would Lane ask such a question in the first place—without knowing the answer? And why would Bevel answer the way he had?

Lane later explained his open-ended question to Bevel by saying his cross-examination was going nowhere and he had felt like "he was drowning." He felt Bevel knew something more and was "an absolutely honorable man" who would not lie on the witness stand. That sentiment was reiterated by both Detective Teresa Sterling and Assistant District Attorney Connie Pope.

Lane also noted that prior to Bevel's taking the stand, his office had been trying to work out a deal with Martin that would have kept both sides from calling Bevel as a witness. As Lane would later say, "If I had known there was a silver bullet, why wouldn't I have called him?"

He claimed Bevel's testimony "took my breath away." It definitely elicited an "audible gasp from the defense table."

Detective Sterling has said that Scott pestered Lane to ask Bevel for more information based on Scott's study of Bevel's report. Scott supposedly picked up on differences in the report between areas that were specific and areas that were vague, particularly as it came to Hamilton's clothes. Scott surmised that this was an area of testimony that would help the prosecution that had been left out of the report and encouraged Lane to follow it up with Bevel.

Lane has said he resented the subsequent attempts to try to suggest that Bevel had furnished confidential information to the prosecution. In Lane's opinion, such efforts were "an attempt to destroy the messenger" and were motivated by "frustration over an overplayed hand."

As for Bevel, he said only that he was obligated to tell the truth—an honorable and professional response, but it was not a fact he had testified to. It was an opinion, and experts frequently dodge or finesse questions relating to opinions because there is no true absolute in these arenas.

In any event, the defense was saddled with Bevel's testimony.

CHAPTER ELEVEN

The Verdict

IN A CRIMINAL CASE, the prosecution presents the first closing argument. That is followed by the defense's closing statement and then a final argument by the prosecution.

Assistant District Attorney Connie Pope made the first closing statement for the prosecution, recounting the evidence against Hamilton and stressing the violence of the murder. She noted that it revealed an intense rage in the killer. She also pointed out that Hamilton had the opportunity and the motive to commit the murder.

Pope then talked about the importance of "the presence of blood and the absence of blood" as it pertained to the doctor's guilt.

She reminded the jury about the presence of blood on Hamilton's shirt, pants, shoes, and coat and, most important, in his car—as well as the absence of blood on his mouth, which one would have expected to find if he had been doing mouth-to-mouth resuscitation and CPR on his wife.

She recalled that no blood had been found on Susan's chest, and no bloody trail led to the front door to confirm Hamilton's story of having abandoned his attempts to save his wife's life to move his car. There was also no bloody trail to the open back door.

Pope argued that this evidence—coupled with all the other evidence against Dr. Hamilton—proved his guilt.

Martin's argument for the defense focused on how the police and prosecution had both prejudged Hamilton as guilty and, as a result, had slanted every fact against him. Martin pointed out that no one had seen blood on Hamilton when he returned to Mercy Hospital for the second operation and that his behavior there had been perfectly normal.

As far as the scratches on Hamilton's back, Martin argued that if the state's theory was to be believed, Susan would have had to scratch Hamilton while being attacked and controlled from behind—and the scratches would have to have been made through her husband's coat and shirt. Martin reminded the jury that according to the state's own witnesses, no flesh or DNA was found under the victim's fingernails—from her husband or anyone else.

As far as the damaging testimony by Bevel with regard to the blood spatter on the inside of Hamilton's shirt cuff, Martin reminded the jury that Bevel had also said it could have been caused by giving CPR or coming in contact with the blood pool.

Finally, Martin made perhaps the most telling argument in favor of Hamilton's innocence. The doctor simply had not had time to do the crime.

Dr. Hamilton left Mercy the first time between 8:42 and 8:45 a.m. and arrived home at about 8:48 that morning. He returned to the hospital about 9:15 a.m. Given the distance to his house, Hamilton would need to have committed the murder—and done all the things the state accused him of—between 8:48 to 9:08 a.m. or 9:10 a.m. After committing the crime, he would have to have returned to Mercy Hospital and professionally performed in a normal manner.

This just did not seem possible, beyond a reasonable doubt.

Lane made the closing argument for the prosecution.

He noted Hamilton's activities were unaccounted for from 8:30 to 9:25 a.m.—or fifty-five minutes, a greater window of time than the defense referenced. He bore down hard on the blood-spatter evidence, emphasizing Bevel's testimony and noting that "whoever is in that shirt and whoever is in those shoes was there."

Whatever spin the lawyers might have put on the evidence, in the end, the jury, as always, had the final say. In this particular case, it took the jury

Valentine's Day Murder

just two hours to find Hamilton guilty and to recommend a sentence of life without parole for the good doctor.

Hamilton was formally sentenced to life without parole on January 8, 2002. At the sentencing, Judge Ray Elliott said his communications with jurors indicated that they were very disappointed that they did not have the option of giving Hamilton the death penalty.

"You should consider yourself very lucky," he told Hamilton.

To add insult to injury, Elliott ordered Hamilton to reimburse the state for the cost of his time in jail pending trial, $11,104.

CHAPTER TWELVE

The Appeal

MACK MARTIN IMMEDIATELY filed a notice of appeal with the Oklahoma Court of Criminal Appeals. After the appeal was filed, Hamilton employed two new attorneys, Clark Brewster and Rob Nigh, both of Tulsa. Brewster was a high-profile lawyer who had been involved in many controversial cases; Nigh, later a Tulsa County public defender, was one of the lawyers who had represented Timothy McVeigh in the Oklahoma City bombing case.

Meanwhile, Susan Hamilton's estate, her children, and her mother filed a civil action for wrongful death, seeking monetary damages from Hamilton. That case was later settled under a confidential agreement, but while it was pending, Brewster and Nigh used the civil suit as vehicle to try to collect evidence to overturn Hamilton's murder conviction. As his lawyers in the wrongful-death action, they took the depositions of Tom Bevel, Wes Lane, and Connie Pope.

Brewster and Nigh tried to establish Bevel had indulged in unlawful and unethical contact with the police and the district attorney's office prior to trial and that he had disclosed both confidential defense information and strategy.

Brewster aggressively and accusatorily questioned Bevel. Yet Bevel steadfastly denied that he had given any information regarding his opinions to the police detectives or the D.A.'s office, even though they had repeatedly asked him about the case. He claimed that he had told Martin about his conclusion prior to trial regarding the blood spatter on the inside of the shirt cuff and that Martin had been "in shock" when originally told about Bevel's opinion.

Based on information they accumulated during discovery in the civil case, Brewster and Nigh filed an application for an evidentiary hearing with the Court of Criminal Appeals. Besides raising Bevel's supposed breach of confidentiality, they alleged that Martin's representation of Hamilton had been rendered ineffective because he had been misled by Bevel and failed to seek other expert testimony, which was available and which would have refuted Ross Gardner's theories. In support of this argument, the report of another expert was submitted which disagreed with both Gardner and Bevel.

One of the principal arguments on appeal was that Judge Elliott had erroneously excluded the evidence and magnitude of threats by antiabortionists to the life and safety of the Hamiltons.

If allowed, the defense would have offered evidence that the abortion clinic and the Hamilton home had both been picketed by antiabortion protesters in the past and that an antiabortion group had obtained a permit to demonstrate in front of the Hamilton home in February 2001. The defense would have introduced an undated "Wanted" flyer, purportedly distributed by an antiabortion group called the Army of God, accusing Dr. Hamilton of murdering unborn children.

The defense team would also have offered evidence that Susan had received anonymous "hang-up" telephone calls a few days before her death and that an unidentified person or persons had been seen in the Hamiltons' neighborhood on the day of the murder.

On September 2, 2003, the Court of Criminal Appeals issued its opinion refuting all the defense arguments and affirming the verdict and sentence.

Hamilton's lawyers then filed a habeas corpus proceeding in the U.S. District Court for the Western District of Oklahoma. Brewster and Nigh again argued that the verdict should be set aside because of Bevel's surprise testimony and his failure to disclose to Hamilton and his lawyers what he would say on the stand.

Valentine's Day Murder

A hearing was conducted before U.S. Magistrate Judge Doyle Argo. Wes Lane, Mack Martin, and David Ogle were called as witnesses, and Tom Bevel's deposition testimony was offered to the court. After receiving a report from Judge Argo recommending denial of the writ, U.S. District Judge Ralph Thompson denied the request.

His decision was appealed to the Tenth Circuit Court of Appeals, which affirmed the denial, thus upholding John Hamilton's conviction.

Dr. Hamilton, who continues to adamantly assert his innocence, remains in prison.

It all came down to a matter of minutes.

Clara Hamon,
a Woman Scorned

"Heaven has no rage like love to hatred turned.
Nor hell a fury like a woman scorned."

—**William Congreve,**
The Mourning Bride (1697)

CHAPTER THIRTEEN

Case #2: Clara Hamon, a Woman Scorned

JAKE HAMON NEEDED killing—at least, a Carter County jury thought so in 1921. Twelve stalwart citizens reached this conclusion, even without knowing that Hamon was knee-deep in one of the most sensational scandals in the history of American politics at the time.

The honors came at the hands of his young mistress, Clara Smith Hamon, in the Oklahoma town of Ardmore in November 1920.

Their shared last name was the result of a marriage—just not their own. Jake Hamon had paid his nephew to marry Clara so the young woman could live and travel with him under the auspices of their being man and wife, despite Jake being still married to, albeit separated from, his own wife.

Needless to say, Clara and Jake's story and the circumstances of his death at the hand of his paramour captivated the country. It was a story made for Hollywood, which is where it was ultimately told. Yet before reaching the silver screen, the couple generated headlines across the nation, focused attention on the Oklahoma town of Ardmore, and later became part of the backstory behind the infamous Teapot Dome Scandal that rocked the Republican administration of President Warren G. Harding.

CHAPTER FOURTEEN

Jake the Snake

BORN JUNE 5, 1873, in Grenola, Elk County, Kansas, Jake Hamon grew up in a series of small southern Kansas towns, including Sedan, where his father was the town marshal. As a boy, he once ran away with the circus but quickly returned home. In 1898, he graduated from the University of Kansas School of Law in Lawrence. His law degree would prove to be a license to steal.

This son of a small-town law enforcement officer started out respectable enough, marrying Georgia Perkins and briefly operating a country store in Cherryvale, Kansas, before moving to Newkirk in what was then Oklahoma Territory. By then, the couple had two children.

In 1901, the Hamons relocated to Lawton in southwestern Oklahoma, and Jake took up politics. Elected as Lawton's first city attorney, Hamon found himself two years later accused of using his office to extort protection money from gamblers. When it came to light that he had also been spending his off-hours boozing, gambling, and womanizing, he was defeated for reelection. Respectability was a thin veneer for many people in Oklahoma's early days, and memories had a convenient way of fading. In spite of his tarnished reputation, Hamon was later elected mayor of Lawton.

Hamon was not only active in local politics but also started worming his way into Republican Party politics. In short order, he was elected to the territorial committee of the Grand Old Party. He maintained his private law practice in Lawton, but his real intent was making as much money as he could as fast as he could, legally or not.

He began to cultivate relationships with Oklahoma politicians on a state and national level, including Oklahoma's first governor, Charles Haskell, and U.S. Senator Thomas P. Gore. Gore, who was blind, was a Lawton resident. He and Hamon became friends and in some cases business associates, and Hamon supported Gore even though Gore was a Democrat.

In 1909, when Governor Haskell was indicted by a federal grand jury for fraud involving the sale of city lands in Muskogee, Oklahoma, Hamon went to Washington to lobby Congress to intervene on the governor's behalf.

Back home, McAlester lawyer J. M. McMurray had signed contracts with the Choctaw and Chickasaw tribes that included an unprecedented twist: a 10 percent attorney's fee on proceeds from a land/mineral sale. Many people in Congress, including Hamon's old friend Senator Gore, opposed the attorney fees in the contracts and sought to block the sale.

But Gore and company failed to appreciate the magnitude of what was at stake. The tribes were selling four hundred thousand acres of coal and asphalt rights valued at $30 million to $140 million in 1910 dollars ($383 million to $1.7 billion in 2017 dollars) to a New York consortium of investors. The mere 10 percent attorney's fee would be worth millions, and it would open the door to the promise of lucrative attorney fees on future big-money contracts. And that proved irresistible to Hamon. As usual, his approach was simple: bribe the McMurray opponents.

That is how Gore came to announce on the floor of the U.S. Senate in 1910 that he had been offered a bribe of twenty-five thousand dollars to fifty thousand dollars to support the McMurray contracts, including the attorney's fee. He declined to name names but revealed that the individual who offered the bribe had said an offer had been made to a congressman and that the names of high officials had been brought up as people "interested" in the approval of the McMurray contracts.

Gore's remarks made the front page of newspapers across the country and led the House of Representatives to appoint a committee to investigate

Clara Hamon, a Woman Scorned

the charges. The committee convened in Muskogee and also held hearings in McAlester.

Gore was the committee's first witness, and he named Jake Hamon as the person who had offered him the bribe. Hamon also dropped the names of Vice President James Sherman, a sitting senator, and two former senators as people interested in the contracts. Gore testified that the congressman involved, according to Hamon, was C. E. Creager of Oklahoma's Third District. Creager testified that Hamon had indeed approached him and suggested Creager could have an interest in the contracts if he supported their approval.

Hamon flatly denied all charges. He did testify that he and Senator Gore were friends and that on one occasion he had raised five thousand dollars and given it to Gore to help the senator pay off a debt. Hamon also brazenly admitted that he, the senator, and others had conspired to bid on Indian lands sold at government auction as a way to keep the price down and buy the lands cheaply. Hamon denied knowing about a federal statute prohibiting such a conspiracy, and when asked if he thought such behavior was "honorable toward the Indians," he replied, "We did not look at it that way. In fact, we don't do things out west just the same way you do in the east."

Perhaps the most revealing testimony at the hearings came from Senator Gore's stenographer, who said Hamon had once told him, "I want to make a lot of money and I don't care much how I make it."

After some delay, the committee came up with a report and a recommendation denying approval of the McMurray contracts. In the end, committee members believed Gore and not Hamon. However, they also found no evidence that Hamon had acted on behalf of McMurray—a remarkable finding given that the two men had shared a suite at a Washington, D.C., hotel during the proceedings.

Vice President Sherman and the senators Hamon had attempted to implicate were all exonerated, and although Hamon was publicly discredited, he managed to skate by without any real legal trouble or fines. He was only thirty-eight years old when he headed back to Oklahoma. He had suffered his first major political setback, and his personal life was about to take a turn that would sign his ultimate fate.

CHAPTER FIFTEEN

Clara and Success

HAMON MET CLARA Smith in a Lawton store. Given his history of womanizing, it probably surprised no one when Hamon began an affair with the nubile teenager. What was surprising was the impact the pretty shopgirl would have on the rest of his life.

From the start, the relationship with Clara was different than Hamon's other dalliances. In short order, he hired her as his personal assistant and then paid his nephew ten thousand dollars to marry her so she could become Clara Hamon. This allowed Hamon to travel the country with the young beauty under the guise that they were husband and wife. Hamon also anted up the money to send Clara to business school in Lexington, Kansas, near Kansas City.

His wife Georgia might have turned a blind eye, as she had on so many of her husband's previous antics and affairs, if Hamon had not been so blatant about this one. How could she ignore the money and attention he publicly lavished on Clara? Eventually, Georgia had had enough. She left Hamon and moved to Chicago with their two children.

After Georgia left, Hamon moved Clara to Ardmore and took up residence with her in two adjoining rooms in the Randol Hotel. Over time,

Clara became Hamon's confidant and adviser, which he needed more than she knew. Although he'd maintained an appearance of wealth when they met, he was struggling financially. Intelligent and with a head for business, Clara played a role in turning around Hamon's financial interests. He rewarded her with furs, more than ten thousand dollars in jewelry, and the perks of what soon became a lavish lifestyle by any standards, then or now.

Hamon was still practicing law in Ardmore as the women in his life played musical chairs, but increasingly, he was looking for the next fast buck. Soon he had a new scheme. He wanted to build a railroad from Ardmore to Lawton.

There was only one problem. He lacked the capital to fund the venture. Ever the hustler, Hamon headed to the 1912 Republican National Convention in New York City seeking investors. While in New York, he wrangled a meeting with John Ringling, the famous circus owner, and convinced Ringling that the railroad was a sound venture. Backed by Ringling's investment, the Oklahoma, New Mexico, and Pacific Railway Company was chartered in January 1913. The ONMP was reported to be the only privately owned railroad in the United States not financed by debt or the sale of bonds.

Financing secured, Hamon began to buy up right-of-way for the railroad route. Using hardball tactics, he forced towns along the route to cough up money if they wanted to be a stop on the line. In some cases, unsatisfied with the town's proposed payment, he moved the line, and in one case, he even started a new town.

Envisioned by Hamon as a steady income-producing investment that would pay out over many years, the ONMP railroad shocked even him when it became an instant financial bonanza. Construction of the line began in August 1913. Just six days later, the first well in the Healdton oil field, twenty-eight miles west of Ardmore, was completed, and a local oil boom began.

Hamon rushed to complete the line.

Soon, oil-field equipment was moving into the Healdton field via the ONMP and barrels of oil were riding it back to Ardmore, where the line connected with a main line of the Santa Fe Railway. Not one to let dollars just sit, Hamon began to use his profits to buy up leases in the

Clara Hamon, a Woman Scorned

Healdton field. The money rolled in. Hamon had finally created the wealth he had always coveted. He continued to do oil deals and once again met with success, this time in the Hog Creek field in north Texas. He decided to build another railroad there, stretching 110 miles south from Wichita Falls, Texas. Never one to think small, he even founded a Texas town that he modestly named Jakehamon.

It had been not even ten years since Hamon's Washington disgrace over the tribal land deals, and he was now reportedly the richest man in Oklahoma. Some men would have rested on their laurels and enjoyed a young mistress and wealth, but not Hamon. He was already setting the stage for his next and even more ambitious scheme. First, however, he needed to get himself elected as a Republican National Committee member from Oklahoma.

Hamon financed his own campaign and won the post despite a heated election in which his opponent understandably questioned his honesty and morality. Then he was off to Chicago as a delegate to the 1920 Republican National Convention.

Being a GOP delegate was all well and good, but it was only a stepping-stone to Hamon. What he was after was nothing less than the right to choose the next U.S. secretary of the interior to gain influence over the vast government oil reserves at Teapot Dome in Wyoming and Elk Hills in California, both of which were under the control of the U.S. Department of the Interior.

Hamon enlisted two oil tycoons, Harry Sinclair of Kansas and Edward Doheny of California, to help. He promised that once he controlled the secretary of the interior, he would see that the oilmen obtained leases on the government reserves on the cheap. The three men would then split the profit from any oil production that followed.

Former Carter County District Judge Thomas Walker, who has studied Carter County history, says that according to local stories, Hamon's plot was hatched at a meeting with the oilmen at a notorious bootlegger's establishment in Ardmore frequented by Hamon.

What transpired among the three there became a scandal that one historian declared the "greatest and most sensational scandal in the history of America politics," prior to Watergate. It would see Albert B. Fall, who served as President Warren G. Harding's secretary of the interior, become the first member of a presidential cabinet to go to prison.

It became known as the Teapot Dome Scandal.

CHAPTER SIXTEEN

The 1920 Republican Convention

HAMON'S SCHEME REQUIRED HIM to control a significant bloc of votes at the GOP convention. His plan was simple: He would buy delegates' votes. With this in mind, he borrowed one million dollars from the National City Bank of New York. Now all he lacked was a candidate who not only could get the nomination but would play ball.

Two months before the convention, Hamon visited Washington, D.C., and met with Harry M. Daugherty, a shrewd and ruthless political operative who was the campaign manager for U.S. Senator Warren G. Harding of Ohio. Daugherty and his friends were the power behind Harding, and Daugherty would later become U.S. attorney general in the Harding administration.

Like Hamon, Daugherty had a reputation for bribery and shakedowns. As for Harding, he was a long-shot candidate with no real interest in being president of the United States. In fact, he had been talked into heading the ticket by Daugherty and other political cronies anxious to capitalize on the office of the presidency. Hamon had previously met Harding, but now he learned that his estranged wife, Georgia, was a cousin of Harding's wife. This does not appear to have caused him any immediate concern.

Hamon told Daugherty he could control Oklahoma's eighteen-member delegation and another thirty votes. Hamon had already committed his votes to Illinois Governor Frank Lowden, one of the convention favorites, along with General Leonard Wood, but he struck a deal with Daugherty to shift his support to Harding if it appeared that Lowden could not win the nomination.

The Republican Convention convened in Chicago on June 8, 1920. It was soon evident that the delegates were deeply divided among Wood, Lowden, and Governor Hiram Johnson of California. Harding was a distinct dark horse with seemingly little chance of success. It was also apparent that the convention was going to be decided by a few powerful cliques of insiders and big-money backers. The struggle for votes would take place largely in hallways and hotel rooms, not on the convention floor, and money would change hands in return for votes.

Four ballots were cast on the first day of voting. The fourth ballot results were Wood 314.5, Lowden 289, Johnson 140.5, Pennsylvania Governor Cameron Sproul 79.5, and Harding 61.5, with the rest of the votes scattered among numerous lesser candidates. Wood was in the lead but still 119 votes short of the necessary majority. In spite of his front-runner status, Wood did not stand a chance. He was just too damned honest.

After the convention recessed for the night, the real politicking began. A group of political leaders, including the chairman of the convention, U.S. Senator Henry Cabot Lodge, gathered in a room at the Blackstone Hotel. According to legend, the convention's outcome was decided in this "smoke-filled room," giving rise to a political term that would define American politics for years to come. In reality, the final outcome of the voting was probably far more influenced by Hamon, Daughtery, and their cohorts.

Hamon, who had all the loyalty of a cur dog, first called on General Wood. According to Wood's son, who was present at the meeting, Hamon offered to trade the general his bloc of votes in return for being able to name the secretary of the interior and the ambassador to Mexico. The old general blasted Hamon, shouting, "I am an American soldier! I'll be damned if I'll betray my country. Get the hell out of here."

Unfazed and undeterred by this rejection, Hamon and Daughtery went next after the Pennsylvania delegation controlled by U.S. Senator Boies Penrose. They offered him the opportunity to name three cabinet members

Clara Hamon, a Woman Scorned

and sweetened the deal with $250,000. Penrose agreed to deliver his delegates to Harding once General Wood was defeated.

Early the next morning, Hamon ran into an acquaintance, Oklahoma journalist E. J. Costello. Costello pressed Hamon for information, and Hamon told the newspaperman, "Warren Harding will be the nominee. I'll be in the cabinet." Costello was the first to predict Harding's victory.

During the second day of voting, six more ballots were taken. Harding finally took the lead, garnering 374.5 votes to Wood's 249 and Lowden's 121.5; the handwriting was on the wall. Hamon delivered his bloc of votes to Harding, and sixty of Pennsylvania's seventy-six delegates followed suit. Those delegates put Harding over the top. Calvin Coolidge was named vice president; Hamon and his pals got ready to ride the gravy train.

There was just one small detail left to attend to: Harding had to win the general election. This was something of a problem, because he was almost as bad a campaigner as he was a public servant. Harding declared he would run a "front porch" campaign, with the intention of not leaving his home state of Ohio during the election. This strategy did not suit Hamon who, after all, had future riches at stake. Hamon, along with some of Harding's other backers, strongly counseled Harding to get off his porch and into the fray. They finally goaded him into making a campaign tour throughout several eastern states and then into the Midwest. At Hamon's urging, Harding also went to Oklahoma City for a banquet and torchlight parade, while Hamon basked in his own notoriety and proximity to national political power.

Fortunately for Hamon and friends, the Democrats chose a lackluster candidate as well, James M. Cox, a newspaperman also from Ohio. Cox's running mate was Franklin D. Roosevelt. In the end, who was on the ticket didn't matter much because the country was tired of Democratic leadership after eight years of the Woodrow Wilson administration.

Meanwhile, Harding's campaign was well funded; he outspent Cox four to one. The Republican nominee also had the advantage of looking more presidential, with his stately visage and head of silver hair. So in spite of his general disinterest in politics, Harding won a landslide victory. He carried thirty-seven states and received more than 60 percent of the popular vote.

Harding also became the first Republican presidential candidate to carry Oklahoma, which had gone Democratic since statehood in 1907. The big

Harding win was unusual enough that the *Daily Ardmoreite* ran a banner headline stating, "We had some roosters to show you but the Republican Pole Cat broke into our poultry house last night." Hamon's hometown paper also gave him credit for Harding's victory, declaring he would be "the biggest Republican in the Nation except the man who will occupy the White House."

Hamon wasted no time testing the truth of that. Huddled with Daughtery and other insiders in Ohio, Hamon began to divide up the spoils, while the president-elect was seemingly more concerned with whether he would be able to smuggle his mistress into the White House and continue his weekly poker game.

CHAPTER SEVENTEEN

Paying the Price

IT WAS SOON CLEAR THAT Hamon would play an important role in the new administration, possibly even as secretary of the interior. Before he could cash in on Harding's victory, however, Hamon had to take care of a personal matter. Given the mores of the time and the fact that his estranged wife was the soon-to-be first lady's cousin, there was no way he could continue his relationship with Clara. He had to break up with his young mistress and return to his wife.

As usual, Hamon thought he could fix things with money. He promised Clara an unknown sum of cash with the understanding that she could also keep all her expensive gifts from him.

At first, Clara appeared to take the breakup remarkably well, signing a release of all claims against Hamon and agreeing to move out of town before the return of his wife and children. In retrospect, Clara must have been seething, because during that time she made a shopping trip to Oklahoma City and purchased a .25 caliber pistol.

On Sunday November 21, with her bags packed, Clara wrote in her diary that she was ready to leave Hamon and head to California. Hamon spent most of the day at his office conferring with Oklahoma City insurance man

Kellie M. Roach and retired Oklahoma City police chief W. B. Nichols. The three men were preparing for a trip to Texas later that week, and they discussed business and politics until six o'clock, when Hamon finally excused himself, saying he needed to meet an acquaintance. The three men agreed to meet for dinner later that evening.

Hamon never made it. At 8:30 p.m., he staggered down the stairs of the Randol Hotel bleeding from a gunshot wound to the stomach. He made it two blocks to the Hardy Sanitarium, owned by Dr. Walter Hardy. Hardy's examination revealed that a bullet had entered Hamon's abdomen, penetrated the right lobe of his liver, and lodged an inch from his spine. The doctor sedated Hamon, removed the bullet, and confined him to the hospital. Hardy reportedly then notified Roach and Nichols that Hamon was resting and that the wound would not be fatal.

According to Roach, Hamon had carried the gun with which he was shot, a .25-caliber pistol, with him to the sanitarium. Roach said Hamon showed the gun to Dr. Hardy and to his surprise told him the shooting was self-inflicted: "There's the damned old thing I did it with. Isn't it a pretty looking little old damn thing to have caused all this trouble?"

Through his business manager Frank Ketch, Hamon later let it officially be known that the shooting was an accident. Ketch quoted Hamon as saying, "I shot myself, but I know nobody will believe me when I say that."

One person who definitely did not believe Hamon was the county attorney for Carter County, Russell Brown. Within a day, Brown charged Clara with assault with intent to kill. He also filed charges against both Hamon and Clara for the crime of immorality. Exactly what motivated Brown to file charges is hard to say, but the filing of the shooting charge against Clara must have been based on the thinnest kind of hearsay evidence. As far as the immorality charge, the couple's long-term relationship was an open secret, and Brown probably added that charge simply for how it would play in the headlines.

Because of Hamon's condition, Brown did not attempt to serve a warrant on him, and Clara could not be found. Brown, believing she had taken the northbound Santa Fe train from Ardmore to Kansas City headed for California, alerted authorities at Guthrie and Ponca City. Clara was not located, but her baggage did arrive in Kansas City the next day.

Clara Hamon, a Woman Scorned

It was soon clear that even without a suspect in hand, Brown had more than a local case of interest. The charges combined with the backstory of the relationship between Hamon and Clara, generated a nationwide explosion of publicity. The cocktail of attempted murder with money, sex, and national politics was welcome fodder for newspapers all over the country, many of which quickly sent reporters to Ardmore to dig into the details.

For three days, Hamon's condition seemed to improve. During that time, Dr. Hardy received a phone call from a member of the president-elect's transition staff inquiring about Hamon's condition. Harding, who was traveling in Panama, also sent an encouraging letter and allegedly a telegram confirming that the job of secretary of the interior was Hamon's if the Oklahoman wanted it. Letters and wires from Republican big shots all across the country, including Daughtery, poured in, wishing Hamon a speeding recovery. Georgia Hamon arrived from Chicago and went to her husband's side.

On November 25, Hamon's condition changed. He began to fail instead of improve, and on November 26, he succumbed to his injury and died. According to Dr. Hardy and several other local doctors, the cause of death was acute dilation of the stomach, which had caused acute dilation of the heart.

Jake Hamon was buried in Ardmore on November 29, 1920, after a funeral attended by local and national business and political leaders and including a host of prominent pallbearers and honorary pallbearers.

Brown quickly amended the charge against Clara to murder, although her whereabouts remained unknown. Unconfirmed rumors about the shooting were rampant. One story had Hamon drunk and on his beds when Clara entered his room and approached him. She began to stroke his hair with one hand while she shot him where he lay with the other. Hamon supposedly then disarmed Clara and walked himself to the hospital, where he first told Hardy he had shot himself, but later, realizing he might die, told friends what actually had happened.

CHAPTER EIGHTEEN

The Lost Is Found

IT IS UNCLEAR WHAT EFFORTS U.S. law enforcement made to find Clara after Hamon's death; what is known is that she continued to hide until December 19. That day, she was found not by any law enforcement officer but by Sam Blair, an enterprising reporter for the *Chicago Herald-Examiner*. Blair had already established his cleverness by retrieving Clara's diary from her luggage in Kansas City and publishing its contents. His articles, circulated nationwide by Universal Services, painted Clara as a naïve, romantic, and sympathetic young woman led astray by a corrupt older man.

Blair, probably sensing that he had stumbled onto the story of his life, followed what in retrospect seemed an obvious lead. Clara's parents and her nineteen-year-old brother, James, lived in El Paso, Texas. Suspecting that her parents knew Clara's whereabouts, he traveled to El Paso to interview them. After meeting with them, Blair was convinced that the couple did not know exactly where their daughter was. They had, however, indicated that she might have fled to Mexico.

Based on a tip, Blair and Clara's brother crossed the Mexican border and traveled south to Chihuahua City. After making inquiries for several days, James was approached by an anonymous Mexican who said he was aware of

Clara's whereabouts and asked for a photograph of James. The photograph was provided, and a day later, James received a note intended for Blair. The note was from Clara, and it said she wanted Blair to tell her story to the world, but she was not yet ready to return to Ardmore and face trial. Blair responded with a note asking Clara to meet him.

A telephone call set up the night meeting with Clara at the Central Plaza in Chihuahua City. Clara appeared as scheduled, accompanied by two distinguished-looking Mexican gentlemen whom Blair described as two of the most prominent men in Mexico. Clara and James shared a brief reunion, and then she agreed to tell her story to the reporter.

Clara and Blair walked into the park, leaving the others behind, and settled on a park bench. Clara began to recount the tale that would be the basis for her defense to the Oklahoma murder charge. She also told Blair that contrary to her first note, she was ready to return to Ardmore and face trial, reportedly declaring at one point: "I am going back gladly. I have nothing to fear. Where is there a jury that would find me guilty after the story I … told you?"

She had had several weeks to plan and practice her story, so maybe it should not have come as a surprise that her tale was a compelling one that rang true to the reporter.

But then again, maybe it was compelling because it was true.

Whether true or not, Clara's strategy was clear.

Rather than remain silent, she would tell her story to the public as though she had nothing to hide and would conduct her defense in the press. She would play the poor, innocent shopgirl, seduced by a rich and sleazy older man who dominated and ultimately abused her.

Before their meeting in the park was over, it was also clear that Clara's story had swayed at least one person, Blair, the scribe who would launch her version of the circumstances of Hamon's death to the world. To Clara's credit, whether through guile or innocence, she would stick with her story through the trial and to the very end.

CHAPTER NINETEEN

Clara's Story

CLARA CHOSE TO BEGIN her story at the end rather than the beginning, describing in detail what happened on the day Hamon was shot. November 21 was supposed to be the last day the couple was to be together. From Clara's standpoint, the separation was a mutual decision. Mrs. Hamon was returning, and Hamon needed to regain his respectability. Clara, who both loved and hated Hamon, was also ready to move on with her life.

She and Hamon had planned to spend the day together, but he had political people in town, so he ended up shuffling back and forth between the hotel and his office across the street. Each time he returned to the hotel, he appeared more intoxicated. This in itself was not unusual. Hamon often drank but generally was able to hold his whiskey.

At about six in the evening, Hamon met Clara on the veranda of the hotel, and an ugly scene ensued. He yelled at her and at one point threw her into a chair. She begged him not to make a scene. His reponse was to once again return to his office.

Upset over his foul mood and violent behavior, Clara left the hotel and went for a long drive in her car. On her return, she decided to stay in her own room until Hamon sobered up. Clara was in Room 28 and Hamon in Room 29, with a connecting door between. She locked the connecting door and the hallway door to her room. She heard Hamon ranting and raving for her next door for her but refused to let him in. Clara ordered dinner in, and when the hotel porter brought her meal, Hamon forced his way inside. Seeing an ugly scene coming, she asked the porter to leave.

By then in a drunken stupor, Hamon threw himself onto the bed. While he lay sprawled there, Clara took the precaution of retrieving a small pocketknife he kept on a chain, hiding the knife under a newspaper on the nightstand. When Hamon subsequently sat up and demanded to know who had gone driving with Clara that evening, she insisted she had gone out alone. He refused to believe her and began to work himself into a blind rage. Clara described his demeanor like this to Blair: "Crazy is the word. The way his eyes were glowing—his lips twitching—his fingers clenching."

She said he then attacked her, grabbing her first by the throat and choking her. He began to torture her, bending her fingers back and twisting her wrists until the skin on her forearms was torn and bloody. At this point in her story, Clara stopped to show Blair the lingering bruises on her neck and the marks on her arms from what she said was Hamon's attack. She told Blair that at one point, Hamon lit a cigar and said, "I would as easily slit your throat as draw on this cigar" and then reached for his knife, only to find it gone.

"His face set in a way that's horrible to remember. He started to lunge toward me across the floor. His arms outstretched and his fingers clutching the air grotesquely," she told Blair. "Instinctively," she grabbed the gun, which she claimed Hamon had bought for her, from a handbag on the windowsill.

Clara turned the gun on Hamon and motioned him toward the door. At first, he backed up as if he was going to leave, but as he reached the door, he turned off the lights and grabbed a chair. He swung the chair over his head and then down on Clara. The gun went off, even though Clara claimed she did not pull the trigger, and Hamon was shot in the abdomen.

"It's true I held it in my hand and had it pointed at him, but I swear to God I didn't pull the trigger." In a later conversation with Blair, Clara supposedly asked: "A blow like that naturally would make it fire, wouldn't it?"

Clara said Hamon responded to the shot by shouting, "Clara you hit me; you've hit me."

Clara Hamon, a Woman Scorned

She screamed in return: "Oh, I didn't, you know I didn't, you know I never could have done it. I didn't do it; I didn't do it."

At this point in telling her story, Clara began to shriek so loudly she drew the attention of passersby as well as her two Mexican friends and her brother, who had quietly been watching Blair and Clara. James stepped forward to comfort Clara, and she collapsed from emotion.

If Clara had made up her story, she had done it well.

Blair penned it the way she told it and added a melodramatic flavor referring to Hamon as a "pudgy masher" and describing how Clara had sobbed and wept at all the appropriate times. Blair had his scoop, and the story hit the wire the next day under his byline. The story circulated nationally and crashed the front pages of the *Daily Oklahoman*. Clara had rolled the dice. This was her story and she would stick to it.

Clara said she offered to call a doctor for Hamon that night, but he insisted on walking to the hospital. Neither Hamon nor Clara thought the wound would be fatal. She spent a sleepless night suffering from her injuries and worrying about Hamon. The next day, she went to the hospital. At first, the doctor refused to let her see Hamon, but he wanted to talk to Clara, and so the doctor relented.

Clara's story took another turn then. Rather than minimizing his injuries, Hamon then said, "Clara, I am going to die. There isn't a chance in the world of my getting over this. You did right, Clara. You should have done it before. You did right. And remember this, I'm going to tell the world that I did it myself, accidentally."

Hamon then told Clara she should leave town and that he had arranged for Frank Ketch to give her five thousand dollars to help. She offered to stay by his side, but Hamon told her to leave. When her escape began, she did not initially feel that she was in any trouble, but by the time she reached El Paso, she realized she was being "hunted" and thus went on to Mexico.

Thus far, hers had been a story of love and self-defense, so Blair must have been shaken when she suddenly said, "The bullet which killed him should have been fired ten years ago."

That's when she confided that "several of the biggest men in Oklahoma" had advised her much earlier to kill Hamon, but she hadn't.

"I loved him. I still do love him."

CHAPTER TWENTY

The Rest of the Story

CLARA'S CONVERSATION WITH Blair lasted several hours, and the two met again the next day to discuss what would happen next. Clara asked Blair if the *Herald-Examiner* could arrange for her surrender and her return to Oklahoma. She did not want to surrender to some unknown lawman who might parade her before the press to capitalize on her notoriety or, worse, hold her in Mexico or Texas.

Blair agreed to help, and legal arrangements were set in motion so Clara could return to Ardmore. She was placed in the custody of the United States consulate, which arranged with the Mexican government for Clara to cross the border at Juárez.

In the meantime, a group of forty Ardmore businessmen employed the law firm of Coakley and Mathers to represent Clara. On December 22, Mathers announced that his partner Charles Coakley and Carter County Sheriff Buck Garrett were on their way to pick up Clara. Mathers had spoken to the county attorney, who had agreed he would not oppose a bond of ten thousand to fifteen thousand dollars. The Ardmore businessmen would cover the bond.

The wheels were turning for Clara's return to Oklahoma, but she was not through talking. Over the twelve-hour train ride from Chihuahua City to Juárez, she told Blair her life story—from the time she first met Hamon to why she was willing to take her chances with a jury.

She frequently referred to Hamon as "a masterful man" who always got his way. He had pursued her forcefully from their very first meeting, offering to buy her "all the furs" in the store where she worked. He pressed her more than once on his visits to the store to come to his office. She finally did, and he further impressed her by taking her for a ride in his car, which in 1910 was one of the few in Lawton.

Clara described a man who could be sweet and loving one minute and cruel and hateful the next—but always domineering. She seemed to want to make clear her importance to Hamon as well as to his success. "He depended on me. He loved me too. He would seek out other women but he always came back to me," she told Blair. She also insisted that "every dollar he had—every political influence he developed I helped him achieve."

Clara recalled sleeping in Hamon's car while visiting various oil prospects when he was working his way up in the oil business. She recounted how she had helped Hamon entertain influential people in New York and Washington and how, as he grew rich, his ego grew as well. Near the end of his life, she told Blair, he took to calling himself the "biggest man" in the country, "bigger than Wilson," referring to President Woodrow Wilson.

By 1920, Hamon had convinced himself that he would be president in eight years and was taking all the credit for Harding's victory. Clara believed that Hamon would reach his ambition because, in her eyes, "Jake Hamon won—he always won. But won regardless of the means." According to Clara, when it came to politics, Hamon "played a dirty, money-peddling game." Certainly, she knew him well.

Clara also disclosed to Blair another reason she was willing to return and face trial: Hamon's will left her one-fourth of his estate, which some people had estimated at more than fourteen million dollars.

If found not guilty, Clara stood, at least in her mind, to become a very rich woman.

CHAPTER TWENTY-ONE

The Surrender

AFTER SURRENDERING IN Juárez, Clara returned by train to Ardmore, accompanied by Sheriff Garrett and her lawyer, Charles Coakley. They reached Ardmore at noon on Christmas Day and were met by a crowd of curious citizens and an army of reporters.

The wheels of justice had already been greased, so Clara was taken directly to the courthouse by her lawyers. In an unusual Christmas Day court session, she went through a speedy arraignment, entered a plea of not guilty, waived a preliminary hearing, and posted a bond of twelve thousand dollars. District Judge T. W. Champion, who would preside over Clara's trial, signed the bond and released her, promising her a speedy and fair trial.

The Jake Hamon murder case would become the most publicized case in the history of the young state of Oklahoma and surely the biggest event that had ever occurred in Ardmore. Clara was treated more as a celebrity than an accused murderess. Even seasoned lawmen were susceptible to her charm, as indicated by a photo of her flanked by Sheriff Garrett and Judge Champion, taken at the request of a news photographer. Gifted at making the most of every opportunity, Clara reportedly exclaimed at the time how flattered she was to be photographed between "two big men."

After Clara's release on bond, the sheriff drove her the twenty-two miles to the town of Wilson so she could stay at her sister's house. The whole event transpired more like a coming-home celebration than a criminal proceeding.

Even before Clara's return to Oklahoma, the *Daily Oklahoman* had recognized the public's overwhelming interest in the case and tellingly sent its society editor, Edith C. Johnson, to cover the story. Johnson arrived in town on December 24. She interviewed the women of Ardmore and with only one exception found them sympathetic to Clara. In Johnson's words, the women believed that Clara "was caught in a black spider's web, that she was more sinned against than sinning, and that not a few women said very frankly that she should have shot Jake Hamon many years ago."

Clara and Johnson took a liking to each other, and Clara granted the society editor access and a series of exclusive interviews. A flowery, polite, and formal writer, Johnson penned a series of stories hugely sympathetic to Clara. Her articles humanized Clara, portraying her as a misunderstood damsel in distress. The substance of the articles was largely trivial, covering such topics as Clara's choice of a church, but the tone was entirely sympathetic.

Whatever else Clara was, she was a natural at handling the press.

CHAPTER TWENTY-TWO

Trial Preparation

CLARA'S CASE WOULD EVENTUALLY go to trial on March 10, 1921, but before that, the representation of both the defendant and the state had to be sorted out.

The county attorney who had filed the charges, Russell Brown, had been defeated in the November 1920 election. More problematic, the victor was James Mathers, one of the lawyers who had already agreed to represent Clara. Mathers was set to take office in January 1921. Prosecuting Clara would present a direct conflict of interest. Yet Mathers, sensing a winning high-profile case and unwilling to miss out on a good fee, professed his determination to represent Clara at trial. He said he was even willing to delay taking office, if need be, so he could represent her.

The matter was resolved when Governor J. B. A. Robertson replaced Mathers as prosecutor with Attorney General S. P. Freeling. Mathers continued on Clara's defense team, which included noted criminal defense lawyer William P. "Wild Bill" McLean of Fort Worth, Texas, and Joe Champion, Judge Champion's twin brother.

In one interesting twist, it looked for a while as if the case would be handled by Kathryn Van Leuven, one of the rare women lawyers in the 1920s and an assistant attorney general for Freeling. In the end, however, Freeling decided to conduct the trial himself, saying, "It wouldn't do to have one woman prosecute another." It is doubtful that his decision had to do with any worry about where Mrs. Van Leuven's sympathies lay. She was on record as calling Clara a "modern vampire."

Freeling did take care, however, to involve the local Ardmore bar, hiring associate attorney H. H. Brown to help him prosecute the case. Brown was the brother of Russell Brown, the former country attorney who had filed the original charges against Clara.

As preparations for trial began, Freeling also disclosed that he was seeking to locate a missing witness. It had come to his attention that a traveling salesman from New York had occupied the hotel room next to Clara's, leaving the possibility that the man might have overheard what transpired between Hamon and Clara on November 21. Mysteriously, the page from the reception book for that night had disappeared, and so the witness could not be easily identified. The salesman, if he ever existed, was never found.

The attorney general arrived in Ardmore a few days before the trial accompanied by Georgia Hamon and her children. Their party also included attorney James C. O'Brien of Chicago, whom Georgia had employed to represent her interests. O'Brien had, as an assistant state's attorney of Cook County, Illinois, gained a national reputation for his dogged prosecution of murder cases—hence his nicknames: "Ropes" and "Red Necktie." The first was a reference to all the men O'Brien had convicted who had been hanged and the second to the signature red necktie he always wore to court. Although it was originally thought O'Brien would participate in the prosecution, he ended up only consulting with Mrs. Hamon and Freeling.

If Clara was nervous about the upcoming trial, she was not alone. Hamon's political cronies and Mrs. Hamon were also nervous. The politicians worried the investigation or questioning might stray into areas they wanted to keep secret, and Mrs. Hamon was concerned with both protecting the family name and her children from the tawdry details of Hamon and Clara's affair.

In the end, both the prosecution and the defense announced they had no intention of offering evidence outside the facts of the case. The politicians breathed a sigh of relief. Unfortunately for Georgia, Hamon and Clara's relationship was integral to what had transpired that fateful night.

CHAPTER TWENTY-THREE

The Trial Begins

FOR DAYS BEFORE THE trial began, Ardmore had been packed with reporters. The trial was covered not only nationally but also internationally by reporters from as far afield as France and England. There was hardly a local resident who did not want to view the trial or at the least get a look at Clara.

So on Thursday, March 10, 1921, the first day of the trial, no one was surprised to find the courtroom filled beyond capacity with reporters and spectators. Clara and her lawyers were seated at the defense table, and in a show of support, Clara's mother, sister, and two brothers were present. The petite Clara was conservatively dressed and wearing a wide-brimmed hat.

Just before the proceedings began, Freeling, H. H. Brown, O'Brien, and Georgia Hamon—the latter still dressed in mourning black—entered the gallery. Accompanying Mrs. Hamon were her eleven-year-old daughter, Olive Belle; her eighteen-year-old son, Jake Jr.; and her aged father. Mrs. Hamon's animosity toward Clara manifested itself in a perpetual glare in the direction of her late husband's mistress.

Freeling, conceding that it would be virtually impossible to find jurors who had not heard about the case, said he would not object to any juror on those grounds, as long as the juror had no preconceived opinion of guilt or innocence. Given Clara's relentless public relations campaign on her own behalf, the defense had a similar attitude. Freeling also declared that the state would not seek the death penalty, which further expedited jury selection.

The picking of a jury in a murder case is often a tedious task, but this one moved ahead with unusual speed. By the end of the first day, a jury of twelve white men had been seated (women not being legally authorized to serve as jurors in Oklahoma until 1951).

One juror was unmarried, one juror had no children, and ten jurors were family men with one to ten children each. Their ages ranged from thirty-three to seventy-three. Six were dairymen or farmers; the rest included three merchants, a barber, a banker, and the owner of a carriage works. Unusually, the *Daily Oklahoman* published the names and a short biography of each juror.

The standard rule barring witnesses from the courtroom except during their own testimony was initially invoked, but in a display of cooperation, the parties agreed that Mrs. Hamon, Clara's mother, Mrs. Smith, and the Chicago reporter Sam Blair would be exempted from the rule and allowed to remain in the courtroom. Blair had been subpoenaed by the state to testify regarding the statement Clara had given to him in Mexico.

In an opening statement described as "careful and concise," Freeling laid out the facts of the case that the state intended to prove and revealed some evidence that had not previously been made public. According to the state, Hamon had feared going to the hotel the night he was murdered, knowing that Clara had carried a gun for years. This held to the narrative that Hamon had returned to his room and taken to his bed, and Clara had shot him.

Freeling said Clara then left the room about half past ten, went downstairs, and calmly told a person at the hotel that Hamon had not been shot and nothing was wrong. In his account, Clara later admitted that she would have shot Hamon with an old gun if she had known it would have been more likely to cause death. The state's timeline also had Clara telling a taxi driver on her way out of town that the man she had shot was not dead yet, but she hoped he would die.

In one of the shocking new pieces of information that day, Freeling also declared Clara had tried to kill Hamon twice before the fatal shooting on November 21.

Clara Hamon, a Woman Scorned

A deputy sheriff had thwarted one of the attempts. When Freeling finished, the defense waived the right to make an opening statement.

Prior to the beginning of testimony, because of the perceived immoral nature of some of the evidence to be heard, the judge had barred anyone younger than sixteen from the courtroom. Olive Belle, the younger of Hamon's two children, was thus spared hearing about her father's affair with Clara and the gory details of his death.

The state called a series of witnesses to establish that Hamon and Clara had lived together in the Randol Hotel since 1913. Clara was known to carry a gun, and she had bought the murder weapon in November shortly before Hamon was shot. This, of course, contradicted what Clara had told Blair, that Hamon had bought the gun and given it to her for her own protection and to guard the jewelry he had given her.

The murder weapon was also introduced into evidence.

It quickly became apparent from the cross-examination of witnesses by Clara's lawyers that the defense would try to paint Hamon as a profligate drunk who was domineering, abusive, and possessed of a bad temper.

After the testimony of the preliminary witnesses was concluded, Freeling called Dr. Walter Hardy to the stand. Hardy was the state's key witness. It was through Hardy that Hamon's story as to how Clara murdered him would be introduced to the jury. Hardy's testimony as to what Hamon had said to him after the shooting was clearly hearsay. It would be admissible only under an exception to the hearsay rule, which Freeling received. In this case, it would be offered as a "dying declaration." The words someone speaks in contemplation of death are deemed in law to be reliable enough to avoid a hearsay objection. However, such statements are admissible only if the person making the statement believes he is dying.

Hardy, whether because of excellent coaching or in the spirit of complete truthfulness, took great care in describing Hamon's state of mind the night of the shooting. He said his friend walked into the clinic, embraced the doctor, kissed him on the forehead, and then said, "I am shot by Clara Smith. I am going to die. I am very weak and want to go to bed." Hardy said he then operated on Hamon and removed the bullet.

The next day, Hardy testified, Clara came to see Hamon but stayed only about four minutes.

After she left, Hamon told the doctor, "That's the woman that did the work. I was laying in the same position as I am now." At that time, Hamon was lying on his back with his head propped up about six inches off the bed.

Hardy went on to describe how the bullet had entered between Hamon's eighth and ninth ribs, damaged the liver, and lodged four inches lower near the spine. Under Freeling's questioning, Hardy confirmed that the trajectory of the bullet was consistent with Hamon's story. On several occasions, Hardy mentioned that Hamon had asked him to swear he would never tell how Hamon was shot for the sake of Hamon's family.

Freeling also had Hardy identify Hamon's bloody clothing, which included a set of long underwear. This elicited a volley of objections from the defense attorneys and provoked an outpouring of sobs from both Clara and Mrs. Hamon. Mrs. Hamon was so distraught she had to be excused from the courtroom.

Hardy's cross-examination by "Wild Bill" McLean led to more courtroom theatrics. After removing his coat and vest, McLean handed Hardy a pencil and then lay down on his back on the courtroom floor with his head supported by law books. McLean asked Hardy to step down from the witness chair and mark on the front of his shirt where the bullet had entered Hamon's body and on the back where the bullet had subsequently lodged. Hardy did as requested.

McLean then told Hardy to take the pistol and hold it in the position necessary to carry out the shooting as Hamon had described it to him. According to reporters, this led to a series of contortions by Hardy that made it difficult to believe the shot could have been delivered as Hamon had described.

McLean's demonstration was not over. Rising from the floor, he stood in front of Hardy. McLean then raised his hands above his head as though he were ready to crash a chair down on the witness. He asked Hardy to "shoot" him again with the gun.

To shoot McLean in the spot now marked on the front of his shirt for the bullet hole, Hardy pointed the gun in a relatively level position, one consistent with the story Clara had told Blair and was prepared to tell the jury.

Still, McLean wasn't through with Hardy. He next asked a series of questions designed to get Hardy to say Jake Hamon was drunk when he arrived at the clinic that night, but McLean's efforts proved unsuccessful, thwarted

Clara Hamon, a Woman Scorned

in part by a series of Freeling's loud objections. McLean persevered with a probe into Hamon's medical history—implying that Hardy had been treating Hamon for syphilis. This line of questioning was quickly halted by Hardy's claims of doctor-patient privilege. McLean did, however, get Hardy to state that Hamon's death had been hastened by his drinking earlier in the day and by cirrhosis of the liver. According to Hardy, Hamon's liver problems were so advanced, he would "not have lived over two years in any event." The doctor said that probably 70 percent of people suffering the same liver damage caused by the bullet would have survived such a shooting if they had had a healthy liver.

Another telling point made by the defense on cross-examination was that Hardy had not originally told County Attorney Russell Brown that Clara had shot Hamon. This was a line of questioning that Clara's lawyers would pursue with many of the state's witnesses. Hardy's explanation was to reiterate that Hamon had sworn Hardy to back his story that the shooting was accidental.

Before the day was over, the jury was taken to the Randol Hotel to view the scene of the crime, which the press had taken to calling "the death chambers." Neither the lawyers nor the judge made the trip; instead, Sheriff Garrett and Clara accompanied the jurors. With the aid of the sheriff, Clara was allowed to recreate the scene according to her version of how the events of the night had transpired.

It had been a busy first day of testimony. At its end, the defense attorneys looked visibly pleased with how their case was going.

Day two of the trial saw two more prosecution witnesses called, both of whom recalled deathbed statements that Hamon had made.

W. B. Nichols, former Oklahoma City police chief and a business associate of Hamon's, had spent most of the day of the shooting with Hamon in his friend's office. When he visited Hamon in the Hardy Sanitarium the day after the shooting, Nichols testified Hamon had told him, "Bill, I was lying on my bed in my room. She came and put her hand on my head. Then she shot me. I jumped down from the bed and knocked the pistol from her hand."

Nichols also testified that Hamon had gone on to tell him: "Clara suggested after she had done it, 'Let's say it was an accident.' And I said alright." In keeping with Dr. Hardy's testimony, Nichols also testified that Hamon thought he was dying, and he made Nichols promise not to reveal his dying statement for the sake of his wife and children. Nichols tried to cheer Hamon up by reminding him of an upcoming trip to Palm Beach, Florida, only to have him say, "Where I am going there are plenty of palms but no beach."

Nichols also testified to being in Hamon's office the day after the shooting and witnessing an exchange between Clara and Hamon's business manager, Frank Ketch, in which Ketch had advised Clara to leave town because Hamon's wife and children would be arriving shortly. Clara then demanded five thousand dollars from Ketch, and Ketch agreed. Clara denied shooting Hamon, saying it was an accident. Ketch told her that he did not want to talk about it, but he did give her the money she had requested.

On cross-examination, Nichols admitted that Hamon had been drinking the day he was shot. This particular question would be directed to all the witnesses who had been with Hamon throughout that day. Kellie Roach later testified that he had had two drinks and Hamon had had three the afternoon of the shooting.

A little moral drama was added to the day when the prosecution called Hamon's Presbyterian preacher, the Reverend T. J. Irwin of Lawton, to testify. According to Irwin, who also gave the eulogy at Hamon's funeral, the dying man admitted to having lived in sin with Clara for ten years and said she had indeed shot him: "Preacher, Clara came to my bedside yesterday and told me it was a frame-up and that she was sorry for what she done. She was gone out of my life forever. I have paid her off. It is the third time I have paid her."

On cross-examination, McLean grilled the reverend as to why in his funeral address, knowing Hamon had been shot by Clara, he had nonetheless preached, "Why God permitted the accident which resulted in his passing we do not know."

The state also called E. W. Sallis, the Dallas taxi driver who had driven Clara from Dallas to Cisco, Texas, where she had boarded a train to El Paso on her way to Mexico. Sallis testified that Clara had displayed two automatic pistols and had confided that she had shot a man and "hoped he would die." That was the exchange that had led to her inquiry as to whether it was better to shoot someone with an old or new gun. Sallis told her an old gun would make the wound worse because of rust, and he recalled her saying she wished she had used an old gun.

By all accounts, Sallis was a shaky witness at best, one who came across

Clara Hamon, a Woman Scorned

more as a slimy, cheap hood than a reliable source of information. On cross-examination, he denied having ever served time in the McAlester prison and a previous armed-robbery allegation, but he still managed to leave a lingering poor impression after he stepped down from the witness chair.

When court adjourned on Saturday, the jury was sequestered for the remainder of the weekend. The judge took the precaution because the case remained the center of attention locally and in the national press.

Meanwhile, Clara continued her relentless public-relations campaign, granting an interview to Universal Services staff correspondent Winifred Van Duzer. The defendant once again charmed the reporter, who filed a melodramatic story portraying Clara as a poor young girl seduced by an evil old man. She referred to Clara as a "poor little moth!"—and, in fact, the article included a photo of the couple with Hamon marked "Flame" and Clara identified as "Moth." The news service distributed the story nationally.

Sam Blair also continued to cover the Hamon case, publishing a story about a member of the Mexican Spiritualist community who had harbored Clara in Chihuahua City right after the shooting. According to this emissary, a medium associated with the Spiritualists had spoken with Hamon who, from the grave, reportedly forgave Clara and confirmed her innocence.

Interestingly, the press almost universally had started to refer to Clara as Hamon's "sweetheart," the word *mistress* being far too racy for the daily news or family newspapers.

The trial resumed Monday on a more earthly note with the prosecution calling Frank Ketch to the stand, but not before an assistant county attorney named John Hedge injected himself into the trial. Taking a uniquely odd position on behalf of the people of Carter County, Hedge, who represented the state, objected to Ketch testifying as a witness for the state given that Ketch was complicit in a homicide. No doubt a plant by the defense, Hedge's objection was overruled with great effect. Ketch would be deemed the most persuasive witness called by the prosecution. In his testimony, the understated businessman told the court that Hamon had admitted that Clara had shot him, but he wanted "people to believe I did it myself."

Just when it seemed the court drama had reached its peak, the trial took another emotional turn: Letters written by Clara to Hamon were introduced. The correspondence illustrated the confused thoughts of the young woman and reflected the mixed emotions of love, guilt, jealousy, and fear that the affair had generated in Clara. The letters also contained veiled threats as to what Clara might do if Hamon did not leave his wife. The letters were offered by the prosecution to show premeditation.

A legal release of all claims against Hamon was also introduced into evidence. The release, dated January 27, 1916, recited valuable consideration and reflected one of the times the parties had split and Hamon had paid off Clara. The release was offered to prove that Clara was a gold digger and not the naïve, wronged young woman she professed to be.

This same charge led the prosecution to put Georgia Hamon on the stand. Claiming that the prosecution was not offering a "tear appeal to the jury," Freeling nonetheless appeared to hope that her testimony would turn the tide of sentiment in favor of the wronged widow and thus against the other woman.

Under oath, Mrs. Hamon then testified that about three years after her husband took up with Clara, she confirmed his infidelity by going through Hamon and Clara's two adjoining rooms at the Randol Hotel. She found a gun and two expensive fur coats and, although denying any bitterness, pointed out that she herself had no fur coat. She took the gun with her. While Mrs. Hamon was still there, Clara came into the room, threw her hat on the bed, and bolted. At the conclusion of Mrs. Hamon's testimony, the state rested its case.

It was now time for the defense to fight back.

CHAPTER TWENTY-FOUR

The Defense

THE DEFENSE OPENED ITS CASE by calling Russell Brown, the county attorney who had filed the original charges against Clara. Brown was called principally to discredit the testimony of Frank Ketch, and he did just that, testifying that during Brown's investigation of the shooting, Ketch had misled him not only by saying that Hamon's bloody underwear, already placed in evidence, had been disposed of but also by failing to reveal Hamon's statement that Clara had been the one to shoot him.

Sheriff Buck Garrett was sworn in and testified that he had visited Hamon in the sanitorium, and Hamon had told him that he had shot himself. "Bud" Bellew, the sheriff's first deputy, who was present at that conversation, confirmed this testimony.

The defense called several witnesses to impeach the character of E. W. Sallis, the Dallas taxi driver who had testified for the prosecution. The witnesses were from McAlester, Oklahoma, Sallis's hometown, and they swore that Sallis had been in jail and had a reputation for not telling the truth.

The two nurses who had cared for Hamon in his dying days testified that they had never heard him tell anyone that Clara had been the one who shot him. When testimony ended for the day, Clara's attorneys announced that they had only three remaining witnesses: Clara; her mother, Mrs. J. L. Smith; and Clara's sister, Mrs. H. W. Walling.

During the trial thus far, the courtroom had been packed to overflowing each day. Seats were almost impossible to get, with spectators arriving at the courthouse as early as 6:00 a.m. to stand in line for a chance to crowd into the courtroom. With the anticipation of Clara's long-awaited appearance on the stand now imminent, the crowd swelled larger. By some estimates, as many as eight hundred people jammed into a courtroom designed to hold 250.

Those who got a seat would not be disappointed. The fireworks started even before Clara took the stand. Her sister, who lived in Wilson, testified that Clara had come to her house the day after the shooting. and she had observed bruises on Clara's throat, breast, and hand.

Mrs. Walling went on to tell how, several years before, her father, J. L. Smith, had learned of Clara's affair with Hamon and had gone from El Paso to Ardmore to kill Hamon. A deputy sheriff had disarmed Smith or he would have completed the job, Mrs. Walling swore.

At one point during Mrs. Walling's testimony, H. H. Brown, the special prosecutor, casually referred to Clara's mother as "the old woman," a comment that so offended McLean that he responded with a remark about Brown's own mother. The two men lunged at each other as if to fight, and the courtroom went wild, with spectators clapping, yelling, and cursing one another. One reporter described it as a "near riot," and another said he saw guns drawn. Judge Champion had the sheriff's deputies clear the courtroom and called for a one-hour recess to let tempers cool.

When court reconvened, Mrs. Walling's fourteen-year-old daughter confirmed seeing bruises on Clara during her visit, and Mrs. Smith testified that the bruises were still visible in El Paso four days after the shooting.

During cross-examination, the prosecutors repeatedly pointed out that Clara was now twenty-nine years old, something also confirmed by both Mrs. Smith and Mrs. Walling. Clara had often said she had met Jake when she was a mere seventeen years of age. Yet if she was twenty-nine at the time of trial, she would have been nineteen when she met Jake and, under the prosecution's theory, a more mature woman and not a child, one who knew just what she was doing entering into a relationship with an older man.

Clara's own testimony was pure theater. She took the witness stand

Clara Hamon, a Woman Scorned

dressed in a long dress, a fur collar, and another wide-brimmed hat. This was her moment, and she was clearly up to the task. In more than four hours of direct and cross-examination, Clara told much of her own life story as well as the details surrounding Hamon's shooting. Her testimony held almost word for word to the story she had told Sam Blair in Mexico, a story that had since circulated the world.

After court adjourned for the day, Freeling reportedly predicted, "There will be a verdict two minutes after the jury retires to deliberate." An experienced lawyer, Freeling was referring to a "not guilty" verdict, sensing that opinion had swung against the prosecution's case.

During Clara's testimony that day, she had described Hamon on the night of the shooting as "drunker, crazier than in all the years I had known him."

She reiterated how he had choked her, tortured her, thrown her to the floor, kicked her, and then attacked her again one last time—forcing her to pull the gun from her purse in self-defense. The courtroom held a collective breath as she described how she had backed Hamon toward the door. "I held the gun on him. When I unlocked the door I had to let him out of my sight. That instant he turned off the light and raised the chair to strike me. He did strike me with that chair and the gun went off. I didn't mean to shoot him."

At the close of Clara's testimony, the defense, having played its best card, rested.

CHAPTER TWENTY-FIVE

The Verdict

THE NEXT DAY, THE PROSECUTION called several rebuttal witnesses, including Sam Blair. The witnesses did little to discredit Clara's story. In fact, Blair, who was questioned about the statement Clara had given him in Mexico, presumably to point out changes in her story, recited an account of the facts almost identical to Clara's trial testimony.

After the rebuttal testimony, Judge Champion instructed the jury on the charge of murder and the lesser charges of first- and second-degree manslaughter. His instructions also reminded the jurors that killing someone was lawful if it occurred by accident, in self-defense, or when someone is the victim of a murder attempt or a felony.

It was time for closing statements.

H. H. Brown, one of the few people left in Ardmore on record as believing that Clara was guilty of anything other than a public service, spoke first. His speech recalled more a sermon than a closing argument. To quote Brown, Clara was "like a serpent, a slimy thing stealing into the nest, she went into their home—this woman. She who sings like a dove and sells her body for years to come and sells her children to be—she went into their home to take the husband away from the wife and the father away from the children."

Brown also found some way to relate the trial to the lives of Jesus Christ, John the Baptist, Davy Crockett, and George Armstrong Custer. His oration lasted almost two hours. At the end of Brown's closing argument, the defense was entitled to respond. Anxious to get the case to the jury and betting on the power of Clara's testimony, the defense attorneys, in a gutsy move, waived a closing argument. This was designed to keep Freeling from making the last argument to the jury in rebuttal to a defense argument. The move caught the judge and prosecution by surprise.

Freeling objected and argued that the state was entitled to a second argument, even if the defense did not make a closing statement. Because it was already evening, Judge Champion decided to adjourn court until the next morning so he could review the law on that question.

When court commenced the next day, the judge ruled in favor of Freeling. He would be allowed to address the jury. Why he wanted to speak was unclear. His final argument was surely one of the strangest ever given by a prosecuting attorney, amounting more to an apology than a plea to find the defendant guilty.

Freeling appeared to feel compelled to address the accusations made by the defense during the trial that Freeling intended to run for governor. Freeling denied that he would be a candidate, claiming any notion that he might have had of running for high political office had been dashed by the way the attorneys had torn down Hamon, a man of political standing, during the trial.

At one point, Freeling observed, "In this case innocence seems to need a louder voice than is usual. If there is doubt about her guilt I'd say let the innocent sister go." With those words, Clara's attorneys lost any need to respond because Freeling had just made the classic "reasonable doubt" argument common to the defense of all criminal trials.

As something of an afterthought, Freeling tied up his final statement with a plea for a "truthful" verdict and a request to the jurors not to "crucify a man in his grave." The attorney general then closed with yet another curious remark. "Nobody wants a great penalty for her," Freeling said. "We agree with anybody on Earth that she has been wronged."

Reaching a verdict took slightly longer than the predicted two minutes, but not much. After just thirty-nine minutes of deliberation, the jury returned a "not guilty" verdict.

Clara Hamon, a Woman Scorned

Clara and her mother embraced in tearful relief. In spite of Judge Champion's warnings to the gallery, the spectators went wild—clapping, yelling, and glad-handing each other. The jurors beamed like sports stars, posed for a collective photograph, and one by one proudly shook hands with Clara.

Mrs. Hamon was not present when the verdict was read, warned away by friends who had anticipated the outcome.

CHAPTER TWENTY-SIX

What Next?

CLARA WAS FREE AND THE hoopla was over, but what would she do now? She had sold her jewelry to pay for her legal "dream team," and now, cleared of murder, she had need of income.

She also needed to clean up her image.

In this regard, Clara chose to show up at a local Baptist church, admitting and repenting her sins, and then accepting her Savior—after which she was baptized in the water. She also made an appearance at a women's meeting at another Ardmore church, where she recited an inspirational poem. Publicly, she talked of making a speaking tour in which she would warn young girls against pursing a life of sin. Her national notoriety and compelling story also had Hollywood calling. The idea of a film about Clara's life, with Clara playing herself, met with varied responses.

Given the state of movie censorship at the time, it was not unexpected that the idea of such a film was rejected by several large movie distributors, all of whom worried about the immorality of her story and the idea of Clara profiting from the shooting. In explaining its decision, the Oklahoma Theater Managers and Owners Association said viewers would be attracted to such a film only through "sheer morbid curiosity," and then it went a step farther, declaring that its members would refuse to show any films in which Clara "was a featured player."

On the other hand, Hollywood, where the appeal of morbid curiosity was well regarded, did express interest, and Clara quickly signed a contract to star in a movie based on her life story. Like so many Oklahomans would in the coming decades, Clara made plans to depart for California. Before she left the state, however, the question of her claim on Hamon's estate needed to be resolved.

The very existence of the will remained in dispute. James Mathers had confirmed that the will existed. However, Frank Ketch, who was appointed administrator of Hamon's estate, denied that Hamon had left one behind. If what Ketch said was true, Hamon's estate would be divided among his lawful heirs—his wife and his two children—and Clara would get nothing. Georgia Hamon, incensed by what she believed was the fake claim of a woman she still believed to be a gold-digging murderess, had vowed to fight any claim by Clara to her husband's estate.

With the clock ticking, the wily Ketch wasted no time in taking care of the matter. He met with Clara, who was no longer represented by counsel, and reached a settlement without ever confirming whether a will existed or not. Purportedly, he authorized Clara to be paid a lump sum of ten thousand dollars in cash along with some oil royalties that she said Hamon had promised her.

Oklahoma's newest would-be movie star was free to head to Hollywood.

The movie the case wrought was titled *Fate*, and Clara would play herself in the film. Prior to her trial, Hamon's nephew had divorced Clara, and before her film was completed, Clara married her director, John Gorman, in August 1921. The movie was filmed on the Warner Brothers lot in Los Angeles and financed by a wealthy Texas oilman. It was also a financial failure. *Fate* was largely banned from theaters all over the country and certainly was never shown in Ardmore, having also been banned by the Oklahoma attorney general. In some cities, the film was even confiscated, and in San Francisco, the producer was charged with indecency. He was found not guilty, but regardless, the film would never secure any wide distribution.

Clara's marriage to Gorman didn't fare much better; the two divorced in 1924. In 1932, Clara married Charles Diggs, director of the Los Angeles

Clara Hamon, a Woman Scorned

County Regional Planning Commission. Diggs later became planning director for Orange County. Clara never appeared in another movie and henceforth stayed out of the press. The couple stayed together until Clara's death in San Diego in 1962.

President Harding died in office of natural causes in 1923. After his death, the Teapot Dome Scandal was uncovered, and both Harry Daugherty and Albert Fall, the man who had become secretary of the interior after Hamon's death, were implicated. Fall eventually went to prison, but the other crooks—Daugherty, Harry Sinclair, and Edward Doheny—avoided any criminal convictions.

The Teapot Dome Scandal—along with the revelation of Harding's own extramarital affair, carried on in the White House itself—discredited Harding and left him widely regarded as one of the worst presidents in American history.

Would these events have transpired differently if Hamon had not been shot? It's hard to say, but Jake Hamon was a slick enough crook that he might just have pulled off the crooked scheme that did not bear his name but most certainly reeked of the kind of conniving that drove him to wealth and political influence.

Roger Wheeler's Bad Investment

"If you lie down with dogs, you get up with fleas."

—Attributed to *Poor Richard's Almanack*
by Benjamin Franklin

CHAPTER TWENTY-SEVEN

Case #3: Roger Wheeler's Bad Investment

ROGER WHEELER WAS AN unlikely murder victim. The time, the place, and the way he was killed in 1981 shocked the community of Tulsa, Oklahoma.

The prominent fifty-five-year-old businessman was assassinated at four-thirty in the afternoon in the parking lot of Southern Hills Country Club in Tulsa. There was no obvious motive and no easily identifiable suspects. For years, it appeared to be one of those infamous crimes that might never be solved. Finally, however, the murderer and the reason for the crime were revealed in 1997—when it became known that the sixteen-year-old murder was one of many performed by one of America's most notorious criminal gangs, the Winter Hill Gang of Boston.

What made the Winter Hill Gang so dangerous was not only the ruthless leadership of James J. "Whitey" Bulger but also its criminal involvement with the Boston office of the FBI. The gang was, in effect, given a federal license to kill by a group of corrupt FBI agents who for years protected a rogues' gallery of savage Irish thugs. Bulger and his cohorts controlled loan-sharking, bookmaking, drug dealing, and extortion in Boston and enforced their power with violence and death.

Much credit for exposing the web of corruption that existed between the FBI and Boston's Irish mobsters deservedly goes to the Massachusetts and Connecticut State Police, but contributions by the Tulsa Police Department and its own Detective Michael Huff proved crucial. Perhaps even more critical to the case being closed was that Wheeler's son David Wheeler continued to press the authorities to solve it.

The pressure brought by the Tulsa police and David Wheeler, who refused to let his father's killer go unfound, helped not only in solving the Oklahoma crime but also in keeping alive the investigation of the Boston crime ring until the worst of the worst, Whitey Bulger, was finally brought to justice.

CHAPTER TWENTY-EIGHT

The Crime

NONE OF THAT BACKSTORY of the crime was known on Wednesday, May 27, 1981, when Wheeler met his death at the hands of a stone-cold killer in the parking lot of Southern Hills Country Club in south Tulsa.

Wheeler, chief executive officer and principal owner of Telex, an electronics company listed on the New York Stock Exchange, had finished his regular Wednesday golf game at about four o'clock. As usual, Wheeler, a club member, played with his three golfing pals: Evans Dunn, a drilling contractor; Robert Allen, the owner of a charter bus company; and Thomas Clark, chairman of the board of the Tulsa Beechcraft distributorship. In a hurry to make a meeting at Telex, Wheeler quickly showered and changed into his business clothes. On the way to his car, he stopped briefly in the pro shop to commiserate about his golf game with George Matson, a club employee.

It was a sunny late spring day, and the swimming pool near the lot where Wheeler's Cadillac was parked was busy with children swimming and playing. Groundskeepers were also working in the area.

Carrying his sports bag, Wheeler walked to his car and got in just as a man exited a nearby parked car and walked briskly toward him. Wheeler started to close the car door but the man held the door open, pulled a revolver, and shot Wheeler one time between the eyes. The assailant then jogged to a waiting car driven by another man, got in, and was driven away. No one saw which exit the car took to leave the club grounds. Wheeler was found shot, sitting in the driver's seat with his feet outside the car. He might have lived for a few minutes after the shooting, but he was dead when police arrived.

Several unfired .38-caliber shells were found on Wheeler's lap and another unfired shell next to the car. Wheeler had eight credit cards and $996 in his suit pocket.

Police were called, and three homicide detectives arrived at the scene just minutes after the crime was reported. One of the detectives was twenty-five-year-old Michael Huff, who had recently been assigned to the homicide division. Huff had no way of knowing it at the time, but the Wheeler case would come to define his long and illustrious career with the Tulsa Police Department.

The officers were quickly able to identify several eyewitnesses. The most useful of them proved to be an eleven-year-old girl who had been at the club swimming pool. Witnesses described the getaway car as a gray Ford or Pontiac and even provided a partial license number, but the car was never found. What proved more helpful were descriptions of the shooter and the driver of the getaway car.

One witness who had been standing within fifty feet of Wheeler's car described both men, giving a detailed description of a five-foot, ten-inch-tall gunman weighing about two hundred pounds with dark gray, coarse, collar-length hair. The witness said the man also had a gray mustache, large arms, and a thick neck.

As for the getaway driver, he was said to be light complected and in his early forties with wiry brownish gray hair, a receding hairline, and a salt-and-pepper mustache. Both men wore dark glasses. The descriptions were sufficient to allow Harvey Pratt, the renowned Oklahoma State Bureau of Investigation forensic artist, to create likenesses that were circulated nationwide to law enforcement.

Meanwhile, the Tulsa Police Department formed an eleven-member task force to investigate the case, and Telex hired its own private detectives to dig up clues. Police Detective Major Stanley Glanz said the police were looking

Roger Wheeler's Bad Investment

at three possible motives, including assassination, armed robbery, or kidnapping-extortion.

Tulsa was rocked by the killing. Wheeler was a prominent businessman who headed a company that was one of Tulsa's premier employers. Southern Hills was an exclusive club in an upper-class, safe neighborhood where crime just wasn't supposed to happen. If someone could be killed in broad daylight at Southern Hills, no one was safe anywhere.

For the good of the community, the perpetrators needed to be caught, a task that would prove to be far from easy.

CHAPTER TWENTY-NINE

Roger Wheeler

WHO WAS ROGER WHEELER? And why would anyone want to kill him? These two questions would prove central to solving the crime.

Born in 1926 in Boston, Roger Wheeler grew up in Reading, Massachusetts, a suburb of Boston. The son of a printer who worked for thirty years at the *Christian Science Monitor*, Wheeler had one sister and two brothers.

While still in school, Wheeler began to show the entrepreneurial drive that would spur him on to future business success. At fourteen, he started a neighborhood newspaper and a stamp-collecting service. Before he graduated from high school, he was the owner and operator of a company that hauled wood from Vermont to Massachusetts.

Wheeler joined the U.S. Navy during World War II and while serving, still managed to attend the University of Notre Dame in Indiana and meet Patricia Wilson, who would become his wife.

He finished his college education at Rice University in Houston, Texas, graduating in 1946 with an engineering degree. Roger and Pat Wheeler would go on to have five children, four sons and a daughter. After the war, Wheeler entered the oil business, working for Gulf Oil and Standard Oil.

One of his work assignments took him to Venezuela, where he observed how pipelines were kept free of rust and related leaks by attaching an anode of magnesium metal to them. The magnesium anode then rusts instead of the pipe.

A natural entrepreneur, Wheeler relocated to Tulsa in 1948 and went to work for Cathodic Protection, a manufacturer of magnesium anodes. Only a year later, he started his own company, manufacturing the same kind of anodes from scrap metal left over from World War II.

This was the kind of ambitious and innovative thinking that drove Wheeler's success in business. Fifteen years later, he sold his anode company to Kaiser Aluminum for $9.8 million.

Afterward, he worked briefly for Kaiser in Oakland, California, but he was just not meant to be anyone's employee.

CHAPTER THIRTY

The Telex Roller Coaster

IN 1965, WHEELER AND a group of investors purchased Telex and moved the company from Minnesota to Tulsa. Originally formed to develop an innovative type of hearing aid, Telex had moved into marketing audio electronics such as headsets. Under Wheeler's management, Telex also expanded into the quickly developing computer business and began to manufacture tape drives. This put the company in direct competition with computer giant IBM, which controlled the market at the time. Telex competed with IBM by pricing its tape drives cheaply and using aggressive sales methods all over the country. Under Wheeler, Telex also began a pattern of hiring engineers away from IBM so Wheeler could pick their brains.

Telex became a stock sensation.

Listed on the American Stock Exchange, Telex shares soared to 300 percent of their initial value. The company then moved its listing to the New York Stock Exchange, where its stock continued to be traded heavily as one of the new innovative electronic companies that emerged in the 1960s and 1970s.

Although Telex was his main business, Wheeler invested in many other businesses as well, including oil and gas projects. Most of his companies prospered, and he accumulated millions of dollars in assets.

Along the way, Wheeler earned a reputation as a tough, aggressive businessman always looking for another buck. Like many successful people, he made both friends and enemies. His lifestyle was that of a millionaire. He built a mansion on acreage in Tulsa and acquired a ranch in Wyoming and a house in Nantucket. For business and pleasure, he traveled in his own private jet.

There was no denying that Telex was doing well, but not everything was rosy at the company. IBM had initially more or less ignored minor competitors such as Telex, but as the smaller companies began to eat into IBM's market share, the computer giant launched a campaign to drive out its competitors by cutting prices, even if that meant selling below cost.

Wheeler came to believe that IBM was violating antitrust laws, and in 1972, Telex filed an antitrust case against IBM in the U.S. District Court for the Northern District of Oklahoma. Telex asked for actual damages of some $238 million, which could be tripled under the antitrust statutes. Telex also sought injunctive relief against IBM, with the objective of stopping IBM from any further predatory practices. The mighty giant responded by hiring a phalanx of defense lawyers with an obvious strategy: It would litigate Telex to death. IBM also filed a counterclaim against Telex for stealing IBM's trade secrets.

The fact that Telex would sue someone surprised no one.

Wheeler had a contentious personality and a litigious reputation. Former Tulsa County District Judge Robert G. Green remembered Wheeler appearing in his court on several occasions. He described Wheeler as someone "who loved the courtroom," observing that when Wheeler was in court, he always appeared to be "enjoying himself."

Telex appeared at first to be outgunned by IBM, but IBM's haughty big-firm lawyers soon learned that they had underestimated their opponent. Wheeler had the resources and combativeness to fight, and Telex's lead attorney was Floyd Walker, a salty Tulsa courtroom veteran who knew his way around a lawsuit. Walker's bread-and-butter was garden-variety tort cases, but he had also done legal work for Telex. When Wheeler approached him about suing IBM, Walker saw the makings of a winning case. It had that classic David-versus-Goliath narrative that is irresistible to plaintiffs' lawyers. Walker agreed to take the case on a contingent-fee

Roger Wheeler's Bad Investment

basis (a decision that would later lead to controversy with his client), and the slugfest began.

IBM's legal team was spearheaded by the venerable New York City firm of Cravath, Swaine & Moore. Interestingly, one of the attorneys representing IBM was David Boies, who would later gain national prominence by representing Al Gore in 2000's *Bush v. Gore* case over the presidential election controversy and championing gay marriage before the U.S. Supreme Court. IBM's Tulsa counsel was Rucker, Tabor, McBride and Hopkins.

The case was assigned to U.S. District Judge Sherman Christensen, Salt Lake City, Utah. Prior to trial, both sides waived a jury, and the case was tried to the court from April 16 through May 24, 1973. Walker was assisted during the trial by Jack Bailey, Telex general counsel, and Serge Novovich, who was an engineer as well as an attorney.

On September 17, 1973, Judge Christensen dropped a bombshell, ruling in favor of Telex and awarding damages of $353 million. He later amended the judgment to a mere $259.5 million plus costs and $1.2 million in attorney fees. He also enjoined IBM from continuing certain business practices. Wheeler was jubilant. He had bested Goliath and ensured Telex's future. What was almost lost in the euphoria of victory was the judgment awarded to IBM against Telex for stealing trade secrets, in the amount of $21.9 million.

IBM had to have been shocked by the judgment, and it quickly appealed the case to the Tenth U.S. Circuit Court of Appeals in Denver, Colorado. The lead counsel for IBM was Nicholas Katzenbach, a former U.S. attorney general. One can only imagine the mood around the Telex offices when in 1975—two years after its big court win—the appellate court reversed Telex's judgment against IBM and found for IBM, upholding IBM's judgment against Telex in the amount of $18.5 million plus interest, costs, and attorney fees.

Telex now faced a major problem. It could not pay the IBM judgment; the company had neither the cash nor the credit to do so. Wheeler had to contemplate the possibility of bankruptcy.

Telex filed a motion for rehearing, which was overruled by the Circuit Court, and then Telex threw a Hail Mary by asking the U.S. Supreme Court to review the case. While the request for review was pending, Telex negotiated what in legal parlance is known as a *dogfall*, meaning the two parties walk away and neither takes anything from the other. The settlement saved Telex, but the suit's cost and distraction had badly damaged the company, already overextended by several new projects. And there was other trouble brewing back home.

Floyd Walker, Wheeler's attorney in the IBM case, claimed he was owed an attorney's fee based on a percentage of the amount saved when IBM agreed to drop its counterclaim judgment. Walker's claim led to another fight. Telex not only denied owing Walker anything but also asserted that Walker was negligent in his representation of Telex and owed the company trial costs just shy of a million dollars.

The Walker case was tried, appealed to the Oklahoma Supreme Court, and then tried again before Walker finally dragged a fee out of Telex.

Although Telex had been beaten up by the IBM case and the subsequent court loss to Walker, Wheeler showed his usual resiliency and kept the company going. On the prowl for investments that might add to his still considerable wealth, he made an acquisition in 1978 that was literally a fatal mistake.

CHAPTER THIRTY-ONE

World Jai Alai

As early as 1976, Roger Wheeler had begun to consider investing in the gambling business. This was decades before the explosion of Native American casinos and at a time when gambling, outside of Nevada, was mostly at horse and dog tracks. Wheeler at one point looked at buying two horse tracks in West Virginia but never closed a deal.

Wheeler had a good relationship with the First National Bank of Boston. The bank had loaned Wheeler money for previous business investments, and Wheeler had been a solid customer. Wheeler's loan officer, David McKown, knew Wheeler had cash to invest and was looking into a possible gambling investment. McKown also knew John B. Callahan.

Callahan was a Boston accountant and president of World Jai Alai. Jai alai is a fast-paced wall game similar to racquetball but played with a hard ball thrown from a curved basket attached to the player's hand. The game, which originated in the Basque region of Spain, is fast and dangerous. At the time, it was one of the few sports it was legal to gamble on—at least, in some locations.

Callahan's World Jai Alai owned four such facilities, known as frontons, three in Connecticut and one in Florida.

There were a few downsides in the possible investment. For one, jai alai games had gained a reputation for being fixed, partly because of a 1977 game-rigging scandal in Connecticut. The sport was also known to have mob involvement—the huge amounts of cash involved made it ideal for skimming and money laundering, typical mob areas of interest.

Yet on the surface, Callahan appeared to be a legitimate businessman. In 1974, he was made president of WJA. Three years later, however, he was tossed out as president when he lost his Connecticut gaming license for associating with known criminals, some of whom were notorious members of Boston's Winter Hill Gang.

Callahan subsequently tried to buy WJA but was unsuccessful. Still, he retained friends and influence in the company. His successor as president was Richard B. Donovan, who had previously been Callahan's partner in a consulting firm. Callahan's hire for head of security at WJA, H. Paul Rico, also remained in his post. Rico was a retired FBI agent who lived in Florida and was best known for having started the FBI's witness-protection program.

Wheeler's loan officer not only touted WJA as a real moneymaker but eventually, First National Bank of Boston loaned Wheeler thirty-three million of the fifty million dollars that Wheeler's real-estate investment firm would use to buy the company in 1978.

Wheeler did not go into the deal blind.

The Tulsa businessman had been warned about the kind of people who were attracted to the jai alai business, but Wheeler bought WJA anyway, reassured by the presence of Rico, the enthusiasm of his banker, and the host of other former FBI agents who handled security for WJA.

Wheeler's romance with gambling was short-lived. WJA never performed up to its projections. The cash gambling handle went up, but the profits went down. In less than two years, Wheeler began to take measures to correct the downward spiral of WJA. He sold one of the Connecticut frontons and decided to investigate WJA's operations.

Convinced that someone was skimming at least one million dollars a year out of the operation, Wheeler sent two of his sons—Larry, an accountant, and David, a computer and business professional—to Florida to audit and investigate the operation. Wheeler's sons met with a cold reception, especially from Rico, who looked more gangster-like than ex-FBI and who had begun

Roger Wheeler's Bad Investment

to fancy himself a hard-ass. At that point, Wheeler still believed he was dealing with an investment gone south—not an ideal scenario, but nothing he hadn't dealt with before. His opinion of the extent of his problem would soon change.

Wheeler had traveled to Miami to question a cashier, Peggy Westcoat, about the handling of cash at the company. Shortly thereafter, Westcoat and her boyfriend were brutally murdered.

There was no direct evidence that Westcoat's murder, which has never been solved, was connected to WJA, but the crime shocked Wheeler. He began to look for a buyer for WJA and became determined to fire Donovan and several other employees. He even asked Rico to take a polygraph test, which Rico refused to do.

Wheeler also started to have concerns about his own safety. At least once, he made his pilot check his personal jet for a possible bomb, going so far as to have the pilot take the plane for a short test flight before Wheeler would board.

That trip ended peacefully.

Unfortunately, Wheeler's concerns were well founded.

CHAPTER THIRTY-TWO

The Investigation Begins

WHEN THE CALL OF A possible murder at Southern Hills came in that weekday afternoon in 1981, Michael Huff and two other detectives were killing time and discussing where to have dinner. Dinner would have to wait. The detectives took off for the country club, reaching the scene within minutes after the commission of the crime.

Huff's first thought was that it was probably a robbery gone bad. About two weeks before, there had been an armed robbery at Fifty-Eighth Street and Harvard Avenue, not far from Southern Hills, and the perpetrator had yet to be caught. It did not take the detectives long, however, to conclude the Wheeler shooting was no botched robbery but rather a professional hit.

The clues were all there: a killing done in broad daylight with a single shot to the head, the calm behavior of the killer as observed by witnesses, and the fact that the unfired shells had been wiped of fingerprints. There was nothing amateurish about this shooting. And if anyone had had any doubts, the fact that Wheeler's cash, watch, and Cadillac were all left behind should have quelled them.

Telex immediately offered a reward of one hundred thousand dollars, and the local detectives began to dig into the case.

Two of the first suspects were a pair of hoods out of Oklahoma City, Patrick Earley and Dennis Bates Fletcher. Both were connected to a group of criminals known as the Dixie Mafia that had terrorized Oklahoma during the 1950s, 1960s, and 1970s, with crimes that included killing grand-jury witnesses and bombing a Tulsa district judge.

The main members of the group—Rex Brinlee, Tom Lester Pugh, and Albert "Big Al" McDonald—were all in jail or dead, but Earley and Fletcher were also known to associate with the Dixie Mafia in the commission of crimes, including contract killings.

Earley had been previously convicted of arson for hire and was believed to have killed several people. Fletcher, a bail bondsman, had convictions for bank robbery and illegal possession of firearms. Detective Huff and his partner, Dick Bishop, wore out the road to Oklahoma City trying to find the piece of evidence that would connect Earley and Fletcher to Wheeler's murder, but nothing ever surfaced.

This came as no real surprise to the president of Telex, Steve Jatras, or to Wheeler's sons David and Larry. All three suspected almost immediately after the shooting that Wheeler's murder was connected to his ownership of World Jai Alai. With local leads exhausted or turning into dead ends, Tulsa police began to pursue the WJA theory. They had started down a long and winding road.

In June 1981, Detective Huff went to Boston to follow up on leads pointing to people involved in WJA. It was there, with the help of the Massachusetts State Police, that Huff's education in Boston crime, particularly as it pertained to the behavior of the Winter Hill Gang, began.

CHAPTER THIRTY-THREE

The Winter Hill Gang

TO UNDERSTAND THE Wheeler murder, it is necessary to understand the Winter Hill Gang. To understand the Winter Hill Gang, it helps to know that Irish mobs are the oldest organized crime group in the United States. Born in the Irish street gangs of the early 1800s, the Irish mobs trafficked in everything from petty theft and prostitution to bootlegging and murder for hire. They operated for almost a century before facing competition in the form of recently arrived Italian and Jewish gangs in the 1880s and 1890s.

A consolidation of several tough Irish gangs, the Winter Hill Gang derived its name from the Winter Hill section of Somerville, Massachusetts, north of Boston. It would terrorize Boston for more than half a century, and by 1981, its territory had grown to include the city's south side, known as Southie. The gang was ruled by James J. "Whitey" Bulger.

Bulger's basic leadership style was rule by terror. He ruthlessly enforced member discipline with beatings, torture, and murder. Central to the gang's success was the idea that nobody ever ratted out any other members of the gang. Rats were exterminated. What most of the gang didn't know was that Bulger was the biggest rat of all.

Born in 1929, James J. Bulger was one of six children. A towhead, he got the nickname "Whitey" early in life, but he preferred to be called Jim or Jimmy. His was a rough childhood. His father was disabled from a work accident, and the Bulger family lived in the projects in Southie, a poor neighborhood near the waterfront. The Bulgers were poor even by Southie standards, but at least one of Bulger's siblings managed to escape the neighborhood for a better life, even one of regional prominence.

That sibling was Billy Bulger, who became a lawyer and then president of the Massachusetts State Senate. As a state senator, Whitey Bulger's younger brother gained a reputation for being one of the most powerful political figures in the state. After retirement from politics, Billy Bulger was named president of the University of Massachusetts.

Whitey Bulger took another route. He was first arrested at age thirteen for larceny and shortly thereafter for assault and battery. In 1948, he joined the U.S. Air Force and served until 1952. He received an honorable discharge, but not without going AWOL, serving time in a military jail, and getting in off-base trouble on several occasions.

When Bulger left the military and returned to Boston, he quickly returned to his criminal activities, graduating from petty larceny to hijacking trucks and then robbing banks. He took part in several successful bank robberies, including one in Indiana, but that career did not last long, and in 1956, he was arrested by the FBI. Coincidentally, the man who put the cuffs on Bulger for that crime was H. Paul Rico, the same Rico who would become the head of security for WJA during Wheeler's ownership.

Bulger was sentenced to twenty years in federal prison. He did his time in Atlanta, where he reportedly volunteered as a guinea pig for LSD experiments, and in the federal prison on Alcatraz Island in California's San Francisco Bay. Released eleven years early, Bulger returned to Boston in 1965 just as mean and crooked as when he had left, but he must have learned something because it would be more than forty-five years before he served time again.

Before his first year of freedom was over, Bulger once again was involved with the Irish mob, this time with a gang known as the Killeen Gang, led by Irish mobster Donald Killeen. Bulger extorted money and acted as an enforcer for the Killeens.

Roger Wheeler's Bad Investment

By this time, several Irish gangs and the Mafia were active in Boston. A turf war exploded between two of the Irish gangs in 1971 when Kenny Killeen, Donald's brother, got in a brawl with Mickey Dwyer of the Mullen Gang, shooting Dwyer three times and biting off his nose. Dwyer survived, but the Mullen Gang quickly retaliated, and the war was on.

Revenge killing followed revenge killing until, after about a year, the Mullens killed Donald Killeen. Having chopped off the head of the snake, the Mullen Gang's victory led, of all things, to peace between the two gangs, and they merged into a new gang known as the Winter Hill Gang, led by Howie Winter.

CHAPTER THIRTY-FOUR

Bulger Takes Control

AS THE WINTER HILL GANG consolidated its territory, Whitey Bulger was moving up the ranks. And in 1979, when gang leader Howie Winter was indicted and convicted for extortion and fixing horse races, Bulger took control.

Interestingly, the federal indictment brought against Winter named a long list of Winter Hill members but significantly neither Bulger nor his pal Stephen "Stevie" Flemmi. Why the two were not charged with the others would not become clear until more than fifteen years later.

At that point, Flemmi was Bulger's closest and most trusted associate. Of Italian-Irish descent, Flemmi had been reared in Roxbury, Massachusetts. At age seventeen, he enlisted in the U.S. Army and served in the Korean War with the 187th Airborne Regimental Combat Team. He was awarded both the Silver Star and the Bronze Star but chose not to stay in the military. Instead, Flemmi returned to Boston, where he ingratiated himself with both the Italian Mafia and the Irish mob.

Flemmi earned the nickname "the Rifleman," not for his service record but for his weapon of choice when it came to killing gangland rivals. Involved in any number of murders and other crimes, Flemmi was never convicted and never served any time over the course of forty years of criminal thuggery. He was indicted at least once. He fled to Canada that time only to return to Boston when the charges were dropped. He was such a prolific killer that when Bulger once asked him about a specific hit, Flemmi had to say, " 'show me the list.' "

What Flemmi's associates didn't know was that much of his good fortune with the law stemmed from his being an informant for the FBI. As early as the 1960s, Flemmi was recruited as an informant by none other than FBI agent H. Paul Rico. Flemmi was considered such a valuable resource that he was all but untouchable, protected not only by Rico but also his successors at the FBI.

Over the years, dozens of other hoods were identified as part of the Winter Hill Gang, but only two of them would become involved in Wheeler's murder: Brian Halloran and Johnny Martorano.

Halloran, a small-time thug known as "Bubblehead," had a reputation for drinking too much. His value came in the number of crimes he committed on behalf of the gang, including murder.

Martorano was, quite simply, a killer. He would eventually admit to twenty murders and undoubtedly committed even more. Martorano, another Italian-Irish American, was born in Somerville, Massachusetts. A high school football star good enough to attract Division I scholarship offers, he nonetheless never made it to college because of poor grades, taking up crime instead. He served a valuable role for the Winter Hill Gang: If the gang had problems with someone, Martorano was the guy they called on to fix it. He was rewarded with money, but Martorano later testified that his motive to kill was based more on loyalty. If a rat talked to law enforcement or otherwise betrayed the Winter Hill Gang, such a rat needed killing, as far as Martorano was concerned.

In 1979, Martorano was indicted for having fixed horse races, along with Howie Winter and others, but Martorano got wind of the charges and fled to Florida, where he eluded capture for sixteen years, until 1995. He might have lived like a retiree in Florida, but the gang still fed him money and called on him to kill people as needed.

The Winter Hill Gang's connection to legitimate business was John B. Callahan. Callahan looked like a respectable, law-abiding citizen. He attended

Roger Wheeler's Bad Investment

Yale University and graduated from Bentley College, now Bentley University, with an accounting degree. Callahan worked for two Big Eight accounting firms—Ernst & Ernst (now Ernst & Young) and Arthur Andersen—before leaving to start his own consulting business and then to head World Jai Alai.

On paper, Callahan looked respectable enough, maybe even a bit boring. It was what he was doing off the clock and whom he was associating with after hours that would have shocked his peers. Unknown to his bosses, the Ivy League accountant was drinking and hanging out not at the local country club but with members of the Winter Hill Gang, including Whitey Bulger and Stevie Flemmi. Before long, Callahan started to skim money out of WJA, allegedly at a pace of ten thousand dollars a week. He set his sights on owning WJA and saw his mobster friends as a way to accomplish that.

* * * * *

When it comes to understanding the Winter Hill Gang, it is important to remember that there are the members you know—the infamous ones who might land in jail or whose names cause grown men to shudder in their shoes—and then there are the silent partners who sometimes are never known. Bulger, Flemmi, Martorano, and Halloran were widely known by law enforcement as members of the Winter Hill Gang, but what wasn't known was that three FBI agents were part of their criminal enterprise: H. Paul Rico, John "Zip" Connolly, and John Morris.

Whether Rico was corrupt remains disputed and controversial. Much of the evidence against Rico, who was never actually tried, came from the hoods themselves. Rico denied any wrongdoing. However, his defenders were former FBI agents who had served with Rico and so were biased in his favor. Detective Michael Huff found the evidence involving Rico to be overwhelming and even called Rico "the hub of the wheel" in the Wheeler case.

What was proved beyond a reasonable doubt was the criminal involvement of Connolly and Morris. According to testimony in several cases, both Connolly and Morris accepted envelopes filled with cash from Bulger and Flemmi. They also received expensive gifts. Morris liked wine and fancied himself a connoisseur—the thugs took him so many cases of fine wine that they started calling him "Vino."

The genesis of the FBI's connection with the Winter Hill Gang was an overwhelming desire by the FBI to bring down the Mafia, combined with a willingness to turn a blind eye to other graft if necessary to do so.

In the Boston area, the Italian-American Mafia was represented by the Patriarca family and the family's local boss, Gennaro "Jerry" Angiulo. Flemmi was turned to give information against Anguilo, who was eventually indicted on racketeering charges in 1983 and convicted in 1986. That conviction was based in part on recordings from bugs the FBI had placed in a Mafia-controlled Boston warehouse. Allegedly, Bulger and Flemmi gave the FBI a drawing of the warehouse showing where to place the bugs to escape detection but maximize eavesdropping.

Helping to take a local Mafia boss out of circulation was a double victory for the Winter Hill Gang. It solidified the gang's relationship with the FBI and damaged the gang's main criminal competitor. Although Bulger denied ever having been an FBI informant, he became a rat sometime in the 1970s. His connection with the FBI was through John Connolly, another Southie from the old neighborhood and a friend of Bulger's younger brother.

How valuable the information was that the FBI got from Flemmi and Bulger is questionable. Flemmi said he never shared anything that would hurt his friends and ratted only on the Mafia and its dealings. Bulger did not know much about the Mafia; instead, he made up stories to satisfy the FBI's appetite. The FBI informant file on the two men indicates that both also provided information on their own associates, but bear in mind that Connolly kept the file and undoubtedly might have doctored it.

As for any reservations Bulger might have had as far as his role in FBI doings, he insisted that Connolly and Morris were just dirty cops, bought with money and gifts. His reported purpose in dealing with the lawmen was to dig confidential information out of the FBI to protect his gang. Certainly, there is ample evidence to support the idea that Bulger profited from this association, including being left out of that 1979 indictment, and that Connolly and Morris received money from Bulger. As Bulger once said, "Christmas is for kids and cops."

The payoffs were real. Who told what to whom is more difficult to sort out given that the one constant in all these relationships was that everyone involved lied.

CHAPTER THIRTY-FIVE

The Investigation Continues

WHEN MICHAEL HUFF ARRIVED in Boston in June 1981, he was met with a cooperative and professional response from the Massachusetts State Police. Detectives filled him in on the Winter Hill Gang and helped to point him toward John Callahan as someone who connected the gang with World Jai Alai.

The reception was not the same from the Boston FBI. There was little or no exchange of information, and for the most part, the FBI refused to communicate at all with the Tulsa Police Department. Huff also went to Miami, Florida, to interview Rico. He came away believing Rico was more representative of the Mafia than of his FBI peers. The former agent treated Huff with disdain and barely answered any questions. It was clear to Huff that Rico felt superior to someone he obviously deemed a hick cop from Oklahoma.

As the evidence accumulated, Huff became increasingly interested in talking to Callahan, but before that could happen, the former accountant and WJA president wound up dead in the trunk of his own Cadillac. The car was parked at the Miami airport, and Callahan had been shot to death. The homicide investigation brought the Miami police into not only the Callahan case but also the Wheeler investigation.

The Tulsa police also finally pressured the Boston FBI into interviewing Bulger and Flemmi about the Wheeler murder. Connolly conducted the investigation, and when it was over, unsurprisingly, the FBI reported that the two hoods had been cleared. Then unexpectedly in 1982, the Boston FBI contacted Tulsa Police and asked for a joint meeting in Tulsa with the local police force as well as the Massachusetts State Police, Connecticut State Police, and Miami Police. The bureau sponsored the expensive confab, which lasted several days at a Tulsa motel. The four police forces went in hopeful that the gathering indicated a major shift in the FBI's attitude that would lead to solving the Wheeler murder, the Callahan murder, and numerous crimes in the Boston area.

At the end of the meeting, however, the cops left disappointed and disgruntled. They realized the FBI was simply blowing smoke and nothing had changed. Disappointed but undeterred, the dedicated law enforcement officers hunkered down, determined to find the clue or source or witness that would blow the cases open and help them to solve the crimes. It would be almost a decade before momentum at last shifted in favor of the good guys.

* * * * *

Meanwhile, the Wheeler investigation dragged on. In 1984, Tom Foley was assigned to the Organized Crime Unit of the Massachusetts State Police. Foley would later rise to superintendent of the state police. He was determined to build a case against Bulger, Flemmi, and their associates, and although it took him ten years to do so, he eventually succeeded.

To Huff, the period between 1981 and 1994 was a time of great frustration. Convinced that the killers were connected with WJA but unable to build a case against any individual, Huff struggled to find a way to inject oxygen into his investigation.

In 1987, he went on national television. The Wheeler case became the subject of the pilot show for the popular television series *Unsolved Mysteries*. Huff showed the composite drawings of the murder suspects created by OSBI forensic artist Harvey Pratt in 1981. Ironically, the killer saw the show and recognized how accurate the drawings were. Unfortunately, like all the other efforts to solve the crime, the show was ultimately of no help.

CHAPTER THIRTY-SIX

Breakthrough

A FTER TEN YEARS OF work, Tom Foley and the Massachusetts State Police finally accumulated enough evidence to support racketeering charges against Whitey Bulger, Stevie Flemmi, and several other hoods associated with organized crime in the Boston area. In the end, the police went around the corrupt Boston FBI and took their case directly to the U.S. district attorney.

In 1994, sealed indictments for racketeering were issued by a federal grand jury against Bulger, Flemmi, and other defendants, including Johnny Martorano's brother, Jimmy Martorano, Frankie Salemme, and Robert DeLuca. The indictment included charges of extortion, loan-sharking, bookmaking, and murder. But before the accused men could all be brought in, Bulger and Flemmi were tipped off by Connolly, who, although no longer with the FBI, still had contacts there.

Flemmi decided not to run, figuring his friends at the FBI would take care of him. Bulger, who as usual did not trust anybody but himself, disappeared. He would avoid arrest for sixteen years.

In the move against the Winter Hill Gang, Johnny Martorano was arrested in Florida in January 1995 for that old indictment of horse-race fixing from 1979. After he was released briefly on those same charges, he was indicted for racketeering along with Flemmi and the other defendants.

All the defendants employed competent defense lawyers, and those lawyers quickly fired a barrage of motions. The issues raised led to lengthy hearings in federal court in Boston. What tipped the case in favor of the prosecution and led to the solving of numerous crimes—including twenty murders—was, oddly, a motion filed on behalf of one of the defendants.

The prosecution had filed a lengthy witness list with the court, and the lawyer for Salemme filed a motion asking that the prosecution be ordered to reveal which of the witnesses had acted as informants for the FBI. In 1997, U.S. Magistrate Judge Mark Wolf granted the motion, and the prosecutors were forced to reveal that Bulger and Flemmi were informants.

This information inflamed the other defendants, particularly Martorano, to whom a rat remained the lowest form of existence. It was fine to steal, lie, torture, or kill, but you did not turn on your friends. In Martorano's world, the sentence for doing so was death.

The informant revelation also made it clear that Flemmi intended to testify against the other defendants. He tried to argue that he gave information to the FBI only about the Mafia, but he had lost the trust of his fellow hoods. His life was also clearly in danger.

In a criminal case with multiple defendants, it is often said, "The first rat gets the cheese." Martorano decided he would be that first rat. He had plenty of information to bargain with, and as he told author Howie Carr, the well-known Boston reporter and talk-show host who wrote a book on Martorano's life, "You can't rat on a rat."

Martorano made a deal, offering to testify against Bulger, Flemmi, and, most important, Connolly and Rico. When he was shown the FBI informant file on Bulger and Flemmi, Martorano was even more convinced that the two gangsters were informants. There was information in the file that only Bulger or Flemmi could have known.

Martorano knew because he was there when the crimes had occurred.

CHAPTER THIRTY-SEVEN

The Wheeler Case

MARTORANO SANG LIKE a bird and admitted to twenty murders. One of the twenty was Roger Wheeler. According to Martorano, the man who fingered Wheeler was John B. Callahan. In 1981, Wheeler was closing in on Callahan's skimming operation. Wheeler was investigating and auditing the WJA operations, and it looked as though Donovan and Rico might be fired.

Callahan went to Bulger and Flemmi and told them he wanted Wheeler killed. At first, Bulger was reluctant. Wheeler was clean, outside the world of crime, and a reputable and rich citizen, the kind of victim that attracted attention. Bulger was worried that killing Wheeler would generate too much heat. His concerns proved well founded. Callahan, however, was persuasive. He talked about the weekly ten thousand dollars being made off the scam.

Eventually, greed prevailed.

Callahan's next mistake was suggesting they use Brian "Bubblehead" Halloran as the hit man. Personally, Bulger thought Halloran drank too much and talked too much to be trusted with such a job, and, to make matters worse, Halloran's brother was a cop. Again, however, Bulger gave in, and Halloran was summoned to a meeting with Bulger, Flemmi, and Callahan.

The meeting did not go well. Halloran was nervous about killing someone he had never heard of in a place he had never been. He also raised the issue of the Oklahoma target being an honest, respected citizen. When Bulger saw Halloran's reaction, he cut off the meeting. Later, Halloran was paid twenty thousand dollars to keep his mouth shut about what he had heard that day.

The next man up for the job was that old reliable hit man, Johnny Martorano. Callahan and Martorano were good friends; Martorano was even known to stay at Callahan's condo in Fort Lauderdale, Florida, from time to time and to drive Callahan's car when Callahan was out of town. Martorano said he needed Bulger and Flemmi's approval before he would consider the hit. He got it and geared up to go to Tulsa.

Everyone agreed that this hit was a two-man job, and so Callahan came up with a second: Joe McDonald, also known as "Joe Mac." McDonald was another trusted killer. As Martorano understood it, McDonald was taking the job because he owed a favor to Rico, who was calling in a chip.

Although Martorano never dealt directly with Rico, he was convinced that Rico was involved in the Wheeler hit. But he could have been seeing Rico through the bias of Rico's supposed involvement with Bulger and Flemmi. Callahan described Wheeler's house, office, and schedule to Martorano, details supposedly provided by Rico.

Martorano was also given a description of Wheeler that described the businessman as having a "ruddy" complexion. In Martorano's mind, only a cop would use such a term—an ordinary person would have said Wheeler was "red-faced."

Under assumed names, McDonald and Martorano flew from Miami to Oklahoma City, sitting separately on the plane. In Oklahoma City, they rented a car and drove to Tulsa, where they spent several days moving from cheap motel to cheap motel, planning the hit. They determined that there was too much open space around Wheeler's mansion and too much security at Telex. They had been told about Wheeler's weekly golf game and, after taking a look at Southern Hills, decided it was the best place to kill Wheeler.

Then they waited for the murder kit to arrive from Boston via bus. The kit arrived addressed to "Joe Russo." It was an inside joke. Russo was the name of Boston's most notorious Mafia hit man. The murder kit contained

Roger Wheeler's Bad Investment

handguns, a carbine, a grease gun, silencers, bulletproof vests, ski masks, and a shimmy and dent puller for stealing cars.

After the kit came in, McDonald stole a car, and the killers parked it at an apartment complex near Southern Hills. On the day of the hit, they drove the rental car to the apartments, where they picked up the stolen car. They then drove it to the Southern Hills parking lot.

Both McDonald and Martorano wore disguises—full beards, sunglasses, and baseball caps. They located Wheeler's Cadillac, and they waited.

As was Wheeler's routine, at about half past four, a man who looked to be Wheeler came walking out of the clubhouse to the parking lot. Martorano stepped out of the stolen car and started to walk toward Wheeler's vehicle. If the man got into the Cadillac, Martorano would whack him; if the man went to another car, Martorano would just keep walking.

The decision would be made in an instant.

The man got into the Cadillac.

Martorano grabbed the door, threw it open, and shot Wheeler between the eyes with a snub-nosed .38 revolver.

When the gun went off, it flew apart, and the unfired shells fell out. Martorano picked up the cylinder and hustled back to the getaway car that McDonald had pulled up behind Wheeler's. Martorano wasn't worried about the shells because, like the professional he was, he had wiped them down before loading them.

The two killers then drove to the apartment complex, picked up their rental car, and returned to their motel. McDonald sawed the gun up, and they threw it into the Arkansas River. They shipped some of the remaining contents of the murder kit back to Boston and took separate flights to Florida.

Martorano received fifty thousand dollars from Callahan for "expenses." He gave half to McDonald and split his remaining twenty-five thousand three ways with Bulger and Flemmi.

Wheeler was dead, but the killing was far from over.

CHAPTER THIRTY-EIGHT

Cleaning Up the Witnesses

BRIAN HALLORAN WAS ALWAYS nervous, but after the Wheeler case, he became paranoid as well. When somebody took a shot at Halloran near his apartment in Boston, he was sure a hit had been put out on him.

Shortly thereafter, he shot a drug dealer named George Pappas in the back of the head in a Chinese restaurant but still managed to get out on bail. In fear for his life, he decided to go to the FBI.

Halloran knew about Zip Connolly's relationship to Bulger and Flemmi, so he opted to talk to two other FBI agents—a big mistake.

Connolly heard that Halloran was talking and tipped off Bulger. Kevin Weeks, a young mobster close to Bulger, was assigned to find Halloran.

On May 11, 1982, Weeks found Halloran drinking in a bar on the South Boston waterfront and contacted Bulger.

Down on the waterfront, Halloran had run into a neighbor, Michael Donahue, who was there to pick up fishing bait. Donahue knew Halloran only casually, but offered him a ride home. They pulled away from the club in Donahue's car but had not gone far when Bulger and another gunman, both armed with rifles, showed up in a car driven by a third man.

The two shooters blasted Donahue's car with a barrage of bullets, killing both Halloran and his innocent neighbor. Later, Weeks would testify that Bulger was wearing a brown Afro wig and that the other shooter, whom Weeks couldn't identify, had on a ski mask. Weeks's testimony about the ski mask was likely a lie to protect a friend, but whoever the other shooter was, he was never identified.

With Halloran out of the way, the chance of solving the Wheeler murder through his testimony had disappeared, but that still was not good enough for Bulger. From his standpoint, Callahan also knew too much. It was learned through Connolly that the FBI and Tulsa Police were set to quiz Callahan about the Wheeler case. Bulger's response was to decide Callahan could not be trusted to keep his mouth shut.

Martorano was summoned again, this time to a meeting in New York City. Bulger did all of talking, persuading Martorano that Callahan was already talking about the Wheeler hit to the FBI. As Bulger saw it, John Callahan needed to be killed, and—because of the heat over the Halloran killing—this murder needed to be done in Florida. Martorano reluctantly agreed.

Martorano's reluctance arose not from any sudden moral twinge but out of his friendship with Callahan—and simple convenience. The two men hung out together in Florida, and Callahan was also the courier who ferried money between Boston and Florida from the Winter Hill gang to Martorano. Martorano truly considered Callahan a good friend as well, but once again, killing a rat trumped everything, even friendship—if John Callahan was talking to the FBI, he had to die.

In July 1982, Mortorano decided to kill Callahan the next time he came to Miami. Once again, Martorano called on Joe McDonald for help in carrying out the hit.

Whenever Callahan returned to Miami, it was customary for Martorano to pick him up at the airport in Martorano's Dodge van. Ideally, Martorano wanted to stash Callahan's body in Callahan's own car, but he did not want to alert Callahan by picking him up in the Cadillac. He decided he would kill Callahan in the van.

As part of their plan, Martorano and McDonald stashed Callahan's car in a rented storage garage before Martorano met Callahan at the Miami airport.

Roger Wheeler's Bad Investment

Martorano spread plastic on the floor of his van and put beach towels on the seats to soak up any blood. He also hid a .22-caliber pistol under a towel on the passenger side of the back seat.

Martorano parked his van in the short-term parking garage at the airport and met Callahan inside the terminal at about eleven o'clock on the night of July 24, 1982. Martorano picked up Callahan's suitcase and headed to the van. He waited until Callahan got into the front passenger seat before opening the back passenger door, putting Callahan's bag inside, and picking up the .22 and shooting Callahan in the back of the head. He pushed Callahan's body onto the floor and drove away, followed by McDonald, who was driving his own car.

The storage garage where the Cadillac was parked would not open until 7:00 a.m. the next day, so Martorano parked the van in the lot of an Albertsons grocery store until the next morning. When the garage opened, he drove the van to the garage, and he and McDonald moved Callahan's body from the van to the trunk of the Cadillac.

At one point, McDonald thought he heard Callahan make a sound—so he took the .22 and shot him two more times.

Martorano and McDonald then wiped down the Cadillac, and then Martorano, followed by McDonald and wearing rubber gloves, drove Callahan's car back to the Miami airport. He left the Caddy in a parking lot there.

The body was discovered a few days later when the smell became overpowering and blood was spotted under the car.

CHAPTER THIRTY-NINE

The End of the Gang

WHEN MARTORANO STARTED to talk, the prosecutors had the perfect witness. Soon they would have more. Flemmi flipped, and so did Salemme. Kevin Weeks was dragged into the case, and he also copped a plea in return for his testimony.

This had a domino effect. Once nearly all of the defendants started to roll over, new cases were filed, guilty pleas entered, and sentences handed down.

Yet one could not say justice was served. Almost none of the guilty parties, particularly Wheeler's murderers, paid much of a price for their crimes.

Considering the nature of his crimes, no one ended up getting off easier than Martorano—thanks to a sweetheart deal cut by his Boston attorneys, Marty Weinberg and Frank DiMento. Although Martorano went to jail in 1995 and entered a guilty plea in 1999, he would not be sentenced until 2004, after he had testified against Connolly. It was a sentence that would have put Weinberg and DiMento in the Criminal Defense Hall of Fame if such a place had existed.

In 2004, Martorano appeared before Judge Mark Wolf for sentencing. The U.S. district attorney, apologetically, recommended twelve years. That's right—twelve years for twenty murders and assorted other crimes. The D.A.'s rationale was that the government could not have solved any of the murders without Martorano's testimony and that his cooperation had brought a guilty plea out of Flemmi and helped to convict Connolly.

Wolf handed down a fourteen-year sentence, which included a promise not to prosecute Martorano in Oklahoma or Florida for the Wheeler and Callahan murders. Martorano was also allowed to use property seized by the government to settle a judgment his ex-wife had against him. Including time served, Martorano served twelve years and was released in 2007. Offered the witness-protection program, he turned it down and returned to the Boston area, figuring his enemies were all dead or in prison.

The government reportedly gave him twenty thousand dollars of walking-around money on his release from prison. Martorano sold the movie rights to his story and his biography to a publisher. The latter became the book *Hitman* by Howie Carr, a *New York Times* best seller released in 2011.

The other Wheeler hit man, Joe McDonald, was arrested in Boston in 1984 as he stepped off a train from Florida—a felon in possession of firearms, three Uzis to be exact. McDonald did three years, got out in 1987, and died a free man at the age of eighty in 1997.

Stevie Flemmi was the last rat to plead, so he got the worst deal. In 2004, he was sentenced to life without parole. His deal included pleading guilty to the Wheeler murder in a Tulsa court and to the Callahan murder in a Miami court. He was sentenced to life in the Wheeler and Callahan murders but was allowed to serve his time in a federal prison.

The only person slated to stand trial in Tulsa for Wheeler's murder was H. Paul Rico. Michael Huff even got the pleasure of putting the cuffs on Rico in Florida in 2003, but Rico never made it to trial. Seventy-eight years old and in bad health, he died while under guard at a Tulsa hospital.

As for Connolly, he did not go unpunished. In 1999 in Boston, he was charged in federal court with bribery, leaking information to Bulger and Flemmi, and falsely altering FBI reports. He was convicted in 2002 and sentenced to ten years. In 2008, he was convicted of second-degree murder in Miami for his role in the Callahan case. He was sentenced to forty years on a murder charge and is serving time in a Florida prison.

John Morris, a particularly poor excuse for a law officer, was granted immunity, testified against Connolly, and admitted to having taken bribes from

Roger Wheeler's Bad Investment

the Winter Hill Gang and passing information to the gang. At least a dozen other Boston mobsters either pleaded guilty or were convicted as a result of the collapse of the Winter Hill Gang and its FBI partners. When it was disclosed that Billy Bulger had communicated with his brother Whitey while he was on the run, Governor Mitt Romney forced Billy Bulger to resign as president of the University of Massachusetts.

Only one question still remained—where the hell was Whitey Bulger?

CHAPTER FORTY

On the Run

FOR YEARS, WHITEY BULGER had known that a time might come when he had to flee Boston. No matter how many cops he paid off or how many people he killed, he could never be completely sure he would not be prosecuted for at least one of his many crimes. So he planned. He established a false identity under the name Tom Baxter, and he stashed cash all around the United States and in London and Dublin as well.

When Bulger first got news that he was going to be charged, just before Christmas in 1994, he didn't take it too seriously. His response was to take a vacation trip with one of his girlfriends, Teresa Stanley, to New York and Florida. When nothing happened, he decided to return to Boston the first week of January 1995. Driving home, he heard a radio report about the indictment and changed his mind.

Bulger and Stanley went on the run—moving around the country, staying away from Boston until February, when Stanley became tired of life on the lam. Bulger made arrangements to meet Kevin Weeks near Boston. Weeks had taken over control of the Winter Hill Gang in Bulger's absence.

Bulger dropped off Stanley and picked up another girlfriend, Catherine Greig. This being prior to Internet dating, Bulger had met Greig, a dental hygienist, the old-fashioned way, after he killed her brother-in-law. The two would stay together until they were finally caught in 2011.

Bulger and Greig had lived for a while in Grand Isle, Louisiana, where they rented a house and maintained the appearance of a normal couple. Back in Boston, however, Stanley was talking, and the police soon had Bulger's alias. Because Bulger was not around to solve the problem by killing Stanley, as he probably would have normally done, he had to move and change identities again.

In 1996, Bulger and Greig relocated to Santa Monica, California. Bulger paid a homeless man for his identification and with the transaction, became known as Charles Gasko. Greig became Carol Gasko, and the couple took up residence in the Princess Eugenia Apartments about two blocks from the beach in Santa Monica.

The Gaskos' new life was anything but glamorous. The Princess Eugenia was a modest, somewhat run-down facility. Bulger's life was spent mostly reading or watching television, with an occasional walk in the park. Greig took care of all the shopping, laundry, and other family chores, and the two pointedly stayed away from most of their neighbors.

Bulger figured such a life was better than prison. Why Grieg, who was some twenty years younger than Bulger, stayed with him, only she knows.

Although their life might have been dull, their cover worked for a long time, but the FBI never stopped looking for them. In 2010, the reward for Bulger's capture was up to one million dollars. The FBI also started an advertising campaign, running both Bulger's and Grieg's photographs on national television shows. The strategy paid off.

One of the few people that Grieg had befriended in Santa Monica was a neighbor at the Princess Eugenia by the name of Anna Bjornsdottir. The two women shared a mutual concern for a stray cat that frequented the apartments. An aging model, Bjornsdottir was from Iceland, where she still spent part of her year.

In June 2011, Bjornsdottir was watching the news on CNN in Iceland when photographs of Bulger and Grieg flashed on the screen. She recognized them as her neighbors in Santa Monica. Bjornsdottir contacted the FBI, and on June 11, 2011, agents from the Los Angeles office of the FBI arrested Bulger in the parking garage of the Princess Eugenia Apartments.

Roger Wheeler's Bad Investment

The FBI agents also arrested Grieg in the couple's apartment. When the agents searched the apartment, they found thirty guns, more than eight hundred thousand dollars in cash, and about a hundred pages of a memoir Bulger was writing.

Bulger was returned to Boston, where he had been previously charged in U.S. District Court with racketeering. The indictment contained thirty-two counts, including nineteen for murder, one of which was Roger Wheeler's.

The indictment also contained charges of drug dealing, extortion, money laundering, and illegal possession of machine guns.

CHAPTER FORTY-ONE

Bulger Goes Down

WHITEY BULGER WAS IN deep trouble. For one, he was guilty of the crimes of which he was charged. Moreover, many of his old pals who had helped him commit those crimes were prepared to testify against him. But Bulger had had sixteen years to think up a defense, and he had done just that.

Bulger claimed he had been granted immunity from all his crimes by Jeremiah O'Sullivan, the U.S. district attorney in Boston during much of Bulger's reign of terror. O'Sullivan was conveniently dead, so there was no danger that he would refute Bulger's claims.

But why would a district attorney grant immunity to a criminal for crimes, including murder, simply because he was an informant? Bulger had an answer for that as well. He claimed that O'Sullivan had feared for his life, and Bulger had agreed to protect both the D.A. and his family from a mob hit in exchange for immunity.

There was no corroborating evidence to support Bulger's outrageous claim, and he and his lawyers declined a judge's offer to present evidence in support of it. Furthermore, the very idea of such an agreement flouted not only reason but standard procedure: O'Sullivan had had no legal authority to grant immunity—that had to be done by a judge or by way of a non-prosecution agreement approved by O'Sullivan's superiors in the U.S. Justice Department in Washington, D.C.

The court denied Bulger's creative defense and ruled that he would not be allowed to raise the defense at trial. Without the shield of immunity, Bulger had no defense.

Yet he still wanted a trial.

Bulger's insistence on a trial was motivated by three desires. He wanted to prove that he was not an informant. He wanted to prove that he did not kill women—two of the charges alleged that he had killed Debbie Davis and Deborah Hussey. And he wanted to discredit the government by exposing and proving FBI corruption.

The trial began on June 4, 2013. The prosecution called sixty-three witnesses, including Martorano, Weeks, Flemmi, and Morris.

Martorano spent hours on the witness stand, matter-of-factly detailing murder after murder. His recitation of the murders was both chilling and unemotional. On cross-examination, he denied being a hit man and testified that the killings were not motivated by money but rather by loyalty to his criminal friends, the purpose being to eliminate rats. He said he was shocked to learn that his best friends Whitey Bulger and Stevie Flemmi were the biggest rats of all.

Whenever a witness accused Bulger of being a rat from the stand, Bulger would lash out, yelling and cursing as though he were in a rowdy Irish bar rather than a federal courtroom. One typical exchange came during Weeks's testimony.

Weeks: "I had the biggest rat next to me."
Bulger (shouting): "You suck."
Weeks: "Fuck you."
Bulger: "Fuck you, too."

Weeks went on to describe how Bulger would participate in a killing only to take a nap, while Weeks and others disposed of the bodies, usually in shallow graves, after the victim's teeth had been pulled to deter identification.

Flemmi became a particular recipient of Bulger's wrath and curses in the courtroom after he testified that Bulger had strangled Debbie Davis and Deborah Hussey. Flemmi was also involved in the murders.

Roger Wheeler's Bad Investment

Davis was Flemmi's girlfriend and Hussey, the daughter of another Flemmi girlfriend. Being Flemmi's girlfriend was a terminal condition if Flemmi and Bulger decided you knew too much.

Morris tearfully testified he had taken bribes from Bulger and Flemmi and that they were FBI informants. He also admitted the two hoods had been told Halloran was talking to the FBI. On cross-examination, Morris refused to concede that telling Bulger about Halloran amounted to giving the man a death sentence, even though it clearly did.

During the trial, one of the prosecution's witnesses, a man named Stephen Rakes, was murdered. It was found later that Rakes's murder was not done by anyone connected to the Bulger trial, but the killing put an already nervous courthouse even more on edge.

Of all the witnesses called for Bulger's trial, perhaps the one who gave the most devastating testimony against the FBI was a fifty-year employee of the Boston office. Desi Sideropoulos had been the secretary for a succession of agents in charge, and she knew of secret files kept in a safe accessible only to the agent in charge. She testified she had been instructed by an agent to destroy a document "or we'll all be fired."

When it came time for Bulger to testify, he declined. His last statement to the court was "I didn't get a fair trial. This is a scam. Do what youse want with me."

Left with virtually no defense for their client, Bulger's lawyers argued that the jury should not believe the bunch of felons and known liars who had testified against him and that he should be exonerated because the FBI was corrupt. Fred Wyshak, the lead prosecutor, told jurors to keep their eyes on the ball, reminding them that the question of FBI corruption, although unfortunate, had nothing to do with Bulger's guilt.

The jury deliberated for five days and found Bulger guilty on thirty-one of the thirty-two counts. They found him guilty of eleven murders, including the Wheeler murder in Oklahoma and the Deborah Hussey murder. They made "no finding" as to the Debbie Davis murder, perhaps figuring Flemmi had had more to do with that crime than he had said.

As Bulger left the courtroom, ever the cocky mobster, he gave a thumbs-up sign. A woman sitting with the victims in the gallery called after him, "Rat-a-tat Whitey."

On November 13, 2013, the judge sentenced the eighty-three-year-old Bulger to two life sentences plus five years. He was ordered to pay $19.5 million in restitution to his victims and to forfeit $25.2 million in assets.

The judge also awarded Wheeler's family a bit more than six million dollars of that restitution total. The family had claimed a loss of $810 million. The monetary part of the verdict was largely symbolic because Bulger's only known assets by then were the cash, guns, and other personal property found in his Santa Monica apartment.

Bulger appealed the verdict on the grounds that the question of immunity was a question of fact for the jury, about which he should have been allowed to testify. He argued that the failure to allow him to testify about immunity effectively deprived him of his right to take the stand and defend himself.

In March 2016, the U.S. Court of Appeals for the First Circuit affirmed the trial judge's ruling on the immunity issue and affirmed the verdict. Bulger appealed to the U.S. Supreme Court. His appeal was rejected by the Supreme Court in October 2016.

Now eighty-eight years old, he is serving his time in federal prison in Florida, where he has a reputation as a talkative old pest.

CHAPTER FORTY-TWO

Aftermath

THE WINTER HILL GANG HAD BEEN effectively destroyed. Perhaps more important, the FBI's corruption had been made public, and the cancerous Boston FBI office had been cleaned out. Roger Wheeler's murder had also been solved, but had the murderers been properly punished?

Michael D. Kendall, a former federal prosecutor who had investigated Bulger's associates, had this to say about the FBI's role in the matter. "This was the worst case of corruption in the history of the FBI. . . . It was a multi-organizational crime, where the FBI was actively participating in murders of government witnesses or at least allowing them to occur," Kendall said.

Tom Foley, in his book *Most Wanted*, in referring to the FBI, observed, "I'll just say that I have never known any other organization, or any individuals, who what they said and what they did had so little to do with each other."

Roger Wheeler's son David appeared at Bulger's sentencing and read a prepared statement to the court: "My family and the families of many other victims of this man were victimized by the FBI. . . ."

He then referenced a quote from court documents filed by the U.S. Justice Department: " 'The record establishes that by this date . . . a reasonable person would have had sufficient facts to form a belief that the FBI bore some responsibility for the death of Roger Wheeler and the subsequent cover-up.'"

"Where was the Justice Department in all of this? Was there no oversight at all?" Wheeler asked.

It should be pointed out that although the investigation and prosecution of Whitey Bulger and the rest of his associates revealed a cancer in the FBI, it also took the dedication of a lot of honest cops and prosecutors to bring Whitey Bulger in and his gang down.

The Massachusetts State Police, the Connecticut State Police, the Miami Police, and the Tulsa Police never gave up, and ultimately the U.S. Justice Department did its job. In spite of the work of these lawmen, it bears remembering that Wheeler's killers were never tried or punished in Tulsa.

Flemmi did plead guilty to Wheeler's murder but had already cut a deal to serve his time in federal prison. Bulger is also serving a life sentence, but Martorano is walking around, a free man after little more than a decade in prison. Both McDonald and Rico died before they could be prosecuted, and Callahan was killed by his coconspirators.

Yet at least the Wheeler murder was solved, and some price was paid by the perpetrators.

The outcome, however, never did satisfy David Wheeler, who felt that Bulger should be tried in Tulsa and made to answer for his father's murder. David's sister, Pamela Wheeler Norberg, who testified at Bulger's trial, felt otherwise. "He's an old man. He's going to die in prison at U.S. taxpayers' expense. Let him die there," she said.

Michael Huff, who retired from the Tulsa Police Department in 2011, agreed with David Wheeler. He said a crime was not only perpetrated on Wheeler but also "on the city of Tulsa." He believed Bulger should be tried in Tulsa and given the death penalty because "he deserves it."

David Wheeler and other members of his family felt so strongly about the FBI's corrupt involvement in the matter that they filed a wrongful-death case against the U.S. government. That case was dismissed for being filed after the statute of limitations had passed.

All these years later, it seems clear that Bulger will die in prison, the perpetrator of many crimes for which he was convicted and no doubt

Roger Wheeler's Bad Investment

countless more that we will never know about. No punishment, however, can adequately compensate the families of the murder victims, including the family of Roger Wheeler, a man who was killed for nothing more than making a bad investment.

The Geronimo
Bank Case

"Man is the cruelest animal."

—**Friedrich Nietzsche**

CHAPTER FORTY-THREE

Case #4: The Geronimo Bank Case

VIOLENT CRIME IN OKLAHOMA is not confined to just the big cities. One of the worst crimes in the state's history happened in Geronimo, a small town with a population of about eight hundred people in the southwestern corner of the state.

The robbers of a local bank were not satisfied with merely committing a robbery. Before they were done, they had stabbed three female bank employees to death and shot four bank customers in the head, killing one and injuring the other three.

Fortunately, thanks to quick and decisive action by the Federal Bureau of Investigation, the perpetrators were quickly captured, although the wheels of justice ground slowly after their apprehension.

Eventually, however, the two men involved were convicted, and one of them executed.

CHAPTER FORTY-FOUR

The Crime

THE CRIME TOOK PLACE on the afternoon of December 14, 1984, at a small branch of the First Bank of Chattanooga, temporarily housed in a prefabricated building on the main street of Geronimo in Comache County. The bank had no surveillance cameras, silent alarm, or security guards.

At about half past one, Pamela Matthews walked into the bank to withdraw some Christmas shopping money. As Matthews recalled, "I walked into the bank, and there wasn't any one there. It smelled funny. I heard a baby crying and followed the noises and looked in the room, and a bunch of bodies were lying on the floor."

Matthews ran outside to tell Roger Lammers Jr., who had driven her to the bank, what she had found. Lammers and another man entered the bank to the strong, acrid smell of gunpowder. Proceeding to a back room, they found four people dead and four alive, three of whom were injured.

One of the survivors was a crying fourteen-month-old baby who appeared to be unharmed. Another was a young man who said he had been shot in the head. A young woman, also shot in the head, was overheard to say, "I told you they were robbing the bank."

The room was a sea of bloody carnage. Three women, all of whom were bank employees, had been stabbed to death. Four other victims had been shot in the head. The deceased were Kay Bruno, a forty-three-old bank manager; Jeri Bowles, a nineteen-year-old teller; Joyce Mullenix, a twenty-five-year-old teller; and Ralph Zeller, a thirty-three-year-old customer. Mullenix was six months pregnant.

Autopsies would later reveal that Bruno had been stabbed thirty-four times; Bowles, fourteen times; and Mullenix, twenty-seven times. The stab wounds included attempted decapitations.

The stab wounds to the back of Bowles's neck penetrated so deeply they had caused bruises on the front of her neck. Other wounds penetrated a lung, a kidney, and the large intestine. The stab wounds to Mullenix were so deep as to strike her spine and pierce a rib. Both of Bruno's lungs had been pierced numerous times.

All the women had lost substantial amounts of blood. Bowles was found to have lost two of the seven quarts of blood in her body, and Mullenix had lost four quarts. The extreme loss of blood indicated that the women were alive and their hearts beating while they were being stabbed to death. Zeller, a local farmer, had been killed by two gunshots to the head.

Photographs from the scene and of the autopsies are almost too graphic to view, yet it is essential to see them to appreciate the horrific nature and magnitude of the crime. Why or how any human could do this to others is incomprehensible.

Wounded but still alive were Marilyn Roach, age thirty; Reuben Robles, twenty; and his fifteen-year-old wife, Bellen Robles. All of the wounded had been shot in the head. Roach, who had been shot twice in the head, was in critical condition and was rushed to Oklahoma Memorial Hospital in Oklahoma City by helicopter. As Roach was being carried to the ambulance, she had only one question: "Are they gone?"

The Robleses were taken to Comanche County Memorial Hospital in Lawton. Their child, Marie Robles, was unhurt.

Quickly, the FBI, the Oklahoma State Bureau of Investigation, the Oklahoma Highway Patrol, the Geronimo Police Department, and the Comanche County Sheriff's Office converged on the scene, and law enforcement officers began to reconstruct the story from the evidence they

The Geronimo Bank Case

gathered there and through interviews with the Robleses, who were able to communicate.

It appeared that a robber or robbers had entered the bank, herded the three female employees into a back room, and made them get down on the floor. Bellen Robles entered the bank unaware of what was going on, but seeing no tellers and noticing the back of someone leaning over something in the back room, she returned to her car and told her husband, Reuben, that she thought the bank was being robbed.

He dismissed her concerns and accompanied his wife and child back into the bank as Zeller, a local farmer, was entering. A gun-wielding robber confronted them inside, forced them into the back room, and ordered them to lie on the floor. Roach, who owned the Blue Jay Drive-In Restaurant next door, came into the bank next to make a truck payment and was also forced into the back room and down on the floor.

The robber then fired point-blank into the back of all four customers' heads. He pointed the gun at baby Marie Robles and pulled the trigger only to have the gun click harmlessly several times. He was out of ammunition. The robber fled the bank with what turned out to be about seventeen thousand dollars in loot.

In the aftermath, the suspect was described as a white male, nineteen to twenty years old, five foot nine or five foot ten, with a blond mustache, shoulder-length dirty blond hair, green eyes, and a slight build. He had worn a plaid shirt, blue jean jacket, blue jeans, and a blue cap with lettering on it. He carried a blue steel automatic handgun. It was believed that he was alone and had fled in a blue or silver car, possibly an Oldsmobile or Dodge.

But then, looks can be deceiving.

CHAPTER FORTY-FIVE

The Man for the Job

IT WAS DIFFICULT TO IMAGINE WHAT kind of person could be filled with so much hate that he could carry out such a brutal crime on his fellow man, but that is what the investigators needed to figure out. The investigation was coordinated by the FBI, which had jurisdiction because the crime included a bank robbery.

The person charged with leading the investigation was Granville Long, special agent in charge of the FBI office in Lawton, Oklahoma. There could not have been a better man for the job. Long had been assigned to the Lawton office in 1978 after serving as the bank-robbery coordinator for seven years in the FBI's San Francisco office. In that city, he had worked on or reviewed hundreds of bank robberies.

A long tall Texan, Long, who looked like Central Casting's idea of an FBI agent, had fifteen years' experience as an FBI agent and had received advanced training in behavioral science. But Long also appreciated the role serendipity could play in an investigation. He would one day admit that when it came to solving the Geronimo bank case, "there was a series of events that were almost divine intervention." Other people, however, would insist that one of those lucky breaks was Long's own experience. As Lawton District Judge Jack

Brock, who presided over the trials of the perpetrators, observed, "(this) was the best investigated case" he had ever seen.

The crime was no more than discovered when Long received a call at his Lawton office from the Oklahoma Highway Patrol reporting a bank robbery in Geronimo with casualties. Long rushed to the bank, which was less than ten miles away. Meanwhile, at the bank, Oklahoma Highway Patrolman Robert Morales was managing the crime scene. Long arrived on scene just in time to see an ambulance leaving the bank with one of the wounded survivors.

Inside, Long found two men whom he assumed were bank employees standing in the bank lobby. They motioned him toward the back of the building, where he came on four bodies in a small room that appeared to be a supply room. At that point, Long realized one of the victims was pregnant. His first thought was whether the unborn baby could be saved. Unfortunately, the emergency medical responders had already ruled that out. Recounting the story more than thirty years later, Long still has trouble controlling his emotions. Yet he recites the facts with the focused clarity of a trained and disciplined investigator.

Realizing the enormity of the crime from almost the moment he set foot on the scene, Long called his supervisor in the Oklahoma City FBI office and requested "all the help he could send." Twenty-three additional FBI agents soon descended on Geronimo and Lawton to assist in the search for the killer or killers.

After taking in the crime scene, Long returned to the lobby and began to question the two men he presumed to be bank employees. He asked them routine questions about surveillance cameras, a silent alarm, and the number of employees working that day. When neither man could answer his questions, Long became more forceful until he learned to his chagrin the men were Calvin Bowles, father of the victim Jeri Bowles, and Kirk Mullenix, husband of the victim Joyce Mullenix.

Long immediately apologized to both men and then changed his line of query. He asked whether Jeri or Joyce had ever mentioned seeing any strange or unusual characters around the bank. This was a routine question in a bank heist because most robbers case a bank before robbing it. Both men answered in the negative.

The Geronimo Bank Case

But then on reflection, Bowles said he thought he remembered his daughter saying something about an unusual customer to her mother one evening as they were setting the table for dinner, but Long would have to ask his wife because he couldn't be sure.

Janie Bowles, Jeri's mother, was on her way home to Lawton from Oklahoma City at the time and unaware of the tragedy that had just unfolded in Geronimo. Long had the highway patrol intercept her, prepare her for the worst, and bring her to the bank.

On Janie Bowles's arrival, Long raised the question of her daughter's remarks. Like her husband, she at first could not recall any such conversation. Long urged her to think harder. In doing so, Mrs. Bowles did recall her daughter mentioning two "funny" young men that had come in the bank. Jeri had given a little wave of her hand as she told her mother about the pair. Long confirmed that Jeri had thought the young men were gay. It was something a young woman in southwestern Oklahoma in 1984 might have found unusual.

Long made note of Mrs. Bowles's story. At that point, it was still unclear if the crime was the work of a solitary killer or not, so it was difficult to say if this information had any relevance to the case.

*****

The scope of the investigation did, however, lead Long to set up a command post in the Geronimo Town Hall that would be used by all the law enforcement agencies working the case. One of the first courses of action had been erecting roadblocks at various points within a seventy-five-mile radius of Geronimo. The next move was a search of the area by ground and air.

Another standard procedure in a bank-robbery investigation is to interview any bank employees absent from the bank on the day of a robbery to determine whether they might have been complicit in the heist. In the Geronimo case, Long sent an agent to interview Shirley Boggess, who worked at the bank but was absent the day of the robbery.

Boggess was quickly cleared of any involvement in the crime. During her interview, however, she confirmed seeing two men whom she thought fit the description of the young men that Jeri Bowles had mentioned to her mother.

Boggess thought one of the men had a car loan that might be in arrears at the bank. Armed with that information, Long returned to the bank to review files kept in the manager's small office. He found a file pulled out that referenced a loan in default on an Oldsmobile Firenza. The debtors were Jay Wesley Neill and Robert Grady Johnson, both of Lawton.

Long's training then kicked in. While working as an agent in Lawton earlier in his career, Long had been sent to the Specialized School of Advanced Criminology at the FBI training facility in Quantico, Virginia. The intense two-week course had covered behavioral science or what is often now called "profiling." One of Long's instructors at Quantico had been a veteran New York City homicide detective with thirty years' experience. At one point during the course, the detective had asked his students if they had ever heard of *piquerism*. His question had been met with blank looks.

The textbook definition of *piquerism* is sexual arousal from the sadistic piercing, stabbing, or wounding of another person, especially in the breast, buttocks, and groin. Long recalled the detective saying that in his experience, the people most likely to commit such a crime were homosexuals, although the detective admitted that his theory was based not on scientific evidence but on personal or anecdotal experience. In fact, both heterosexuals and homosexuals can exhibit piquerism. But in 1984, his former instructor's words were enough to make Long think of the viciousness of the stabbings of the four women in the Geronimo bank and Jeri Bowles and Shirley Boggess's descriptions of the recent bank visit by the two young, apparently gay men with the loan on the Oldsmobile. At that point, Neill and Johnson became the focus of the investigation.

The FBI was looking for not one killer but two.

Long dispatched FBI agents to interview Neill and Johnson at the address found in the car-loan file. The agents learned that Neill and Johnson had moved several times since receiving the loan, but the agents tracked them to their current residence at the Tanglewood Apartments in Lawton. The suspects were not home when the agents arrived. A neighbor told the agents that the men were out of town. Based on that, Long sent agents to the Lawton bus and plane stations to look for the suspects or their car.

The investigators struck pay dirt at the airport. The Oldsmobile Firenza was parked in the airport lot. The vehicle was locked, but a knife was visible

From the Archives

Case 1: Valentine's Day Murder

Susan Hamilton and Dr. John Hamilton appeared to be a loving couple during their thirteen years of marriage.

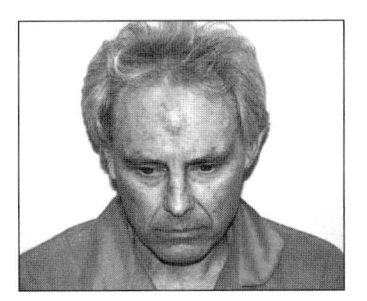

Dr. John Hamilton at the Oklahoma City Police station on the day of Susan Hamilton's murder. Dr. Hamilton testified that the bump on his head occurred when he fell outside the police station.

Tom Bevel, a blood-spatter expert, testifies at a trial. Bevel, called as a defense witness in Dr. John Hamilton's trial, gave surprise controversial testimony damaging to Dr. Hamilton.

Case 2: Clara Hamon, a Woman Scorned

In 1920, Jake Hamon was reportedly the richest man in Oklahoma and certainly was one of the crookedest. Jake Hamon met Clara Smith when she was only nineteen years old. His affair with Clara not only changed his life, it finally ended it.

The Randol Hotel in Ardmore, Oklahoma, as it looked in 1920 when Clara Hamon shot Jake Hamon. The couple lived in adjoining rooms at the hotel for many years. (Photo courtesy of the McGalliard Collection, Ardmore Public Library)

Case 3: Roger Wheeler's Bad Investment

Roger Wheeler was a multi-millionaire businessman when he was murdered in 1981.

Tulsa police examine the car in which Roger Wheeler was killed.

Whitey Bulger's mug shot November 16, 1959. Bulger ordered the hit on Wheeler in 1981.

Case 4: The Geronimo Bank Case

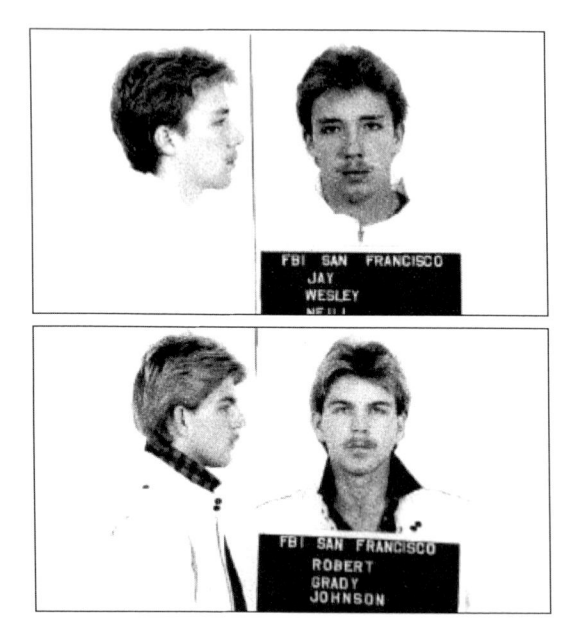

Jay Wesley Neill and Robert Grady Johnson were apprehended by the FBI three days after the Geronimo Bank robbery in Oklahoma. Their similarity in appearance, as seen in these FBI mug shots, led to some confusion as to who was actually in the bank at the time of the crime.

In 1984, the First Bank of Chattanooga in Geronimo, Oklahoma, was a temporary building with no security cameras, alarm, or guards.

Case 5: The Death of Bill Tilghman

In the 1880s, Bill Tilghman was the proprietor of a saloon in Dodge City, Kansas. At the age of seventy in 1924, he took on the job of policing the boomtown of Cromwell, Oklahoma, which led to his death. (Left photo courtesy Boot Hill Museum; right, courtesy University of Tulsa.)

Prohibition officer Wiley Lynn killed Tilghman in 1924.

In 1893, Tilghman (far right with rifle muzzle down) was appointed as a U.S. marshal and sent to Perry, a boomtown in Oklahoma Territory. (Courtesy Oklahoma Historical Society)

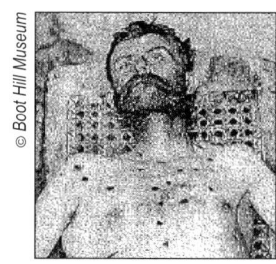

In 1896, Bill Tilghman captured Bill Doolin, the elusive leader of the Wild Bunch Gang in Arkansas. Doolin was brought to Guthrie, Oklahoma Territory, and jailed. He escaped and was hunted down. U.S. Deputy Marshal Heck Thomas shot and killed him, and his body was put on display in Guthrie—a measure to assure citizens that a killer was no longer a threat.

Case 5: The Death of Bill Tilghman

Wiley Lynn, the man who shot Bill Tilghman, with a still he raided while serving as a federal Prohibition officer in 1924. (Courtesy Oklahoma Historical Society)

Case 6: The Case of the Talking Pharmacist

Jerome Ersland poses in the Oklahoma City pharmacy where he shot Antwun "Speedy" Parker. Ersland's love for telling tall tales was his undoing.

District Attorney David Prater uses a security video to show why he is filing murder charges against Ersland.

Antwun "Speedy" Parker was sixteen years old when Ersland shot him.

Case 7: Death, Oklahoma Style

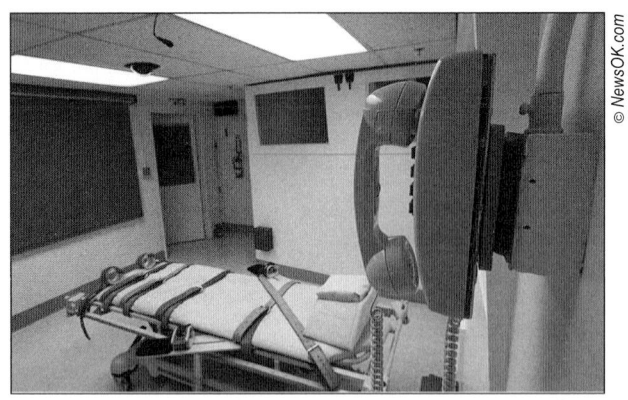

Death chamber at the Oklahoma State Penitentiary at McAlester.

Sister Helen Prejean (right) noted death-penalty opponent, celebrates the postponement of the Richard Glossip execution outside the Oklahoma State Penitentiary at McAlester.

From left, Clayton Lockett's execution was botched; Charles Warner was killed with an unauthorized drug; and Richard Glossip still awaits execution.

The Geronimo Bank Case

sticking out from under the front seat. A warrant was obtained for a search of the car, and a hunting knife with blood on it was retrieved. Papers found in the car led the agents to a Lawton travel agent, Denise Donahue of A-1 Sundown Travel Agency.

Donahue said Neill had contacted her on December 13 about arranging a flight to Nassau in the Bahamas for 6:00 p.m. December 14, but when he learned that no seats were available, he reserved two tickets to San Francisco at 5:00 p.m. on the same date. However, on the day of departure, Johnson called and reserved an earlier flight, leaving at 2:45 p.m. Neill and Johnson paid fourteen hundred dollars in cash for their tickets. Donahue also arranged for a limousine and hotel reservations in San Francisco, California.

Oklahoma FBI agents had this information by Sunday, December 16, just two days after the bank robbery, at which time the search for the suspects moved to San Francisco. Long was still well acquainted with many of the agents in the FBI's San Francisco office, and he quickly supplied them with information about the suspects.

By Sunday night, December 16, the agents had located the limousine and the driver, J. J. McDonagh, who had met Neill and Johnson at the airport. The agents interrogated McDonagh, who told them he had driven the suspects around San Francisco, helping them to buy cocaine and go on a shopping spree at a series of luxury shops.

The pair had partied hard, going to gay bars in the Castro, a section of San Francisco that by the 1980s was one of the world's most famous gay neighborhoods. Neill and Johnson picked up a third man at one point who accompanied them back to their hotel, the downtown Holiday Inn. Neill and Johnson had an expensive suite at the hotel, which they had also paid for in cash.

That cash, along with a tip they gave their cabby, included bait money from the Geronimo bank. Banks record the serial numbers of certain bills and keep them in a log to aid in the tracing of bank robbers. When the bait money leaves the bank, it becomes known as "hot money."

In San Francisco, the agents also learned the suspects had told McDonagh they were interested in looking for a permanent residence in the city. As a result, McDonagh had set them up with an appointment for the next day with his daughter, who was a local realtor. Now the question became how to carry out an arrest as safely as possible. The agents had to assume that Neill and Johnson were armed and, having mercilessly killed four people, certainly dangerous.

A plan was devised to use a female FBI agent to stand in for McDonagh's daughter. The agent would lure the pair out of their hotel room so they could be surprised and arrested.

After locating the suspects' room, the agents set up surveillance outside. For safety's sake, the entire floor of the hotel was cleared of occupants, including the hotel owner, who had a suite on the same floor.

The sting was set up for the night of December 16.

The next morning, the agents waited, covering the room. At 11:00 a.m., Johnson stepped out of the room and into the hall. Seizing the opportunity, the agents rushed into the hall, captured Johnson, and then arrested a surprised Neill as he exited the suite. The two suspects were unarmed, but more of the hot money, along with money wrappers from the Geronimo bank, was found in the suite.

CHAPTER FORTY-SIX

The Timeline

THE FBI AGENTS WERE convinced that they had the Geronimo bank killers but wanted to sew up the case. The agents separated Neill and Johnson and attempted to question them.

Neill wasn't talking, but Johnson opened up and admitted to being involved in the planning of the bank robbery. However, Johnson denied being at the bank that day or taking part in the murders. He claimed Neill had pressured him into buying the gun and that he was told no one would be harmed.

The Oklahoma agents followed up the Johnson leads and began to put together a short timeline of events starting two days before the robbery.

On that Wednesday, Neill had gone to a pawnshop in Lawton to buy a handgun. He said he needed a gun for protection after having received some threatening phone calls. He was told the purchase would require a gun permit from the Lawton Police Department. However, being only nineteen, Neill was too young to obtain one. Instead, the next day, December 13, twenty-two-year-old Johnson applied for a permit.

Lawton police informed him the permit could not be picked up for twenty-four hours.

Neill and Johnson then went together to the Geronimo bank, where they were seen looking around inside. They spoke only to each other during the visit. The pair then went to the Lawton Kmart, where they considered a selection of knives. After some discussion, they purchased two six-inch hunting knives, paying for them with a check from their joint account signed by Neill. Both Neill and Johnson furnished identification for the check.

On Friday, December 14, Neill and Johnson returned to the pawnshop at about ten o'clock in the morning. They again looked at guns and asked where they could purchase ammunition. They were shown a used .38 as well as how to load and fire the gun. They told the clerk they would return with a permit and pick up the gun at about half past two that afternoon.

At about eleven-thirty, Johnson picked up the permit at the police department. At about twenty-five minutes after noon, the two men appeared at the pawnshop, hurriedly filled out the necessary forms, and purchased the gun. Johnson put a false post-office box number for his address on the forms.

The two men then went to Gibson's Discount Store. Again, because Neill was too young to purchase ammunition, Johnson purchased the .38 shells. They left the store but quickly returned. In attempting to load the gun, they had found it was actually a .32 caliber, and so they returned to Gibson's for the appropriate ammunition. The fact that the gun was a .32 instead of a .38 probably saved the lives of three of their subsequent victims, Marilyn Roach, Reuben Robles, and Bellen Robles, who all survived gunshots to the head from the smaller caliber gun.

About a quarter to one, Johnson used a neighbor's phone to change the pair's plane reservations to San Francisco to a 2:45 p.m. flight. He left the neighbor's apartment at about one o'clock. The bank robbery took place between 1:00 p.m. and 1:30 p.m.

During the investigation, agents found all the weapons involved in the crime. One knife was found at the crime scene underneath one of the dead bodies; the other knife was retrieved from inside the car left at the airport.

Johnson's directions also led to the recovery of the gun from a pond at Eighty-Second Street and Gore Boulevard in Lawton, where Johnson had thrown it at Neill's direction. The .32 pistol contained six fired cartridges.

By then, as often happens in highly publicized cases, rumors and stories were circulating in the media about the case, many of which were untrue. A

The Geronimo Bank Case

member of law enforcement not directly involved in the case told Comanche County District Attorney Dick Tannery that the killings were incited by a derogatory remark made by a bank employee about Neill and Johnson's homosexuality. According to Long, there was no factual basis for the story, but Tannery repeated it to the press more than once, and it has become memorialized as though it were true.

It would not be the first time gossip and speculation led to historical misconceptions, nor would it be the last.

CHAPTER FORTY-SEVEN

Bank-Robbery Charges

AFTER THEIR ARREST, Neill and Johnson were immediately hit with federal charges because bank robbery is a federal crime. Neill was charged with bank robbery resulting in death and Johnson with aiding and abetting in a bank robbery resulting in death.

Tannery also filed charges in Lawton against Neill and Johnson. Both defendants were charged with four counts of first-degree murder, three counts of shooting with intent to kill, and one count of attempted shooting with intent to kill. Tannery sought the death penalty against both defendants.

Johnson was voluntarily returned to Oklahoma from San Francisco by federal authorities. On December 21, a federal grand jury in Oklahoma City issued indictments on the robbery charges. U.S. District Attorney Bill Price announced that the indictments would expedite the return of Neill to Oklahoma without the need for what could be lengthy extradition proceedings on the state charges.

Tannery was concerned about the prosecution of the federal charges for fear that they might provide the defendants a defense in the state's murder case. The federal charges carried a maximum of a life sentence, and Tannery did not want the defendants to avoid prosecution for the death penalty.

What concerned Tannery was not only the constitutional defense of double jeopardy but also an Oklahoma statute specifically prohibiting the trial of a defendant if the defendant had been acquitted or convicted of a crime at a trial in another court "founded upon the acts or omissions in respect to which he is on trial. . . ."

Price publicly disagreed with Tannery. He made it clear that he thought the federal cases could be tried without harming the prosecution of the state's cases. Both Price and his assistant, John Green, believed the federal cases could be tried without evidence of the murders of the three bank employees being introduced, which would avoid a double-jeopardy defense in the state murder cases.

After Neill was returned to Oklahoma to face the federal charges, the conflict between the state and federal prosecution continued. On December 28, the day Neill was to return, Tannery obtained writs of habeas corpus for both defendants from State District Judge Jack Brock. The writs would allow the defendants to be transferred to Lawton and held in state custody.

On the same date, however, Johnson's attorney, David Booth, a federal public defender, attempted to plead Johnson guilty to the robbery part of the charge to U.S. Magistrate Judge Ron Howland. Johnson wanted to also plead not guilty to the charge that a person had been killed. The prosecutors objected to the attempt to plead not guilty and guilty to two parts of the same charge.

Howland ruled that he did not have authority to accept the plea, and Booth renewed his attempt to enter the plea to the Chief U.S. District Judge Luther Eubanks. Eubanks set the matter for hearing on January 4, 1985, but stated to the press that he felt the defendants should be tried in Comanche County for the "revolting and brutal" slayings.

At that point, Price consented to the state's writs of habeas corpus and moved to dismiss the federal charges. He pointed out that the charges could be refiled depending on the outcome of the state trial. The defendants were then transported to Lawton and arraigned before Special Judge Allen McCall, who set a preliminary hearing for January 28, 1985.

On January 4, Eubanks addressed the status of the state and federal prosecutions. A tough old trial veteran, Eubanks, now deceased, had been an Oklahoma district judge in Lawton before his appointment to the bench, and

The Geronimo Bank Case

he had a definite opinion as to which case took priority. "Believe you me, I will not do anything that will interfere with the right of the State" to try Neill and Johnson, he made clear.

Eubanks acknowledged the presumption of innocence but could not resist adding, "If any case called for the supreme penalty, this is it."

At another point in the proceedings, Eubanks addressed Green, saying, "It is in the interest of the public that the State be given right of way. I don't criticize you, but it's time to keep your mouth shut and give the State its right." The judge then set a hearing for January 10 to consider Johnson's plea and the pending motions.

In addition, William J. Skepnek, Neill's court-appointed lawyer, raised the question of Neill's competency, asking for a psychological evaluation.

At the January 10 hearing, Booth revealed that Johnson would admit to being involved in planning the bank robbery and buying the gun, but his testimony would be that he was in his apartment in Lawton at the time of the crime and not at the bank. Booth then pressed to have the judge accept Johnson's guilty plea only to the charge of aiding and abetting a bank robbery.

Judge Eubanks denied the request to enter a guilty plea and postponed all federal court proceedings until after a state trial and any appeals. That ruling effectively ended the controversy over jurisdiction and established that the state case for murder would be tried first.

CHAPTER FORTY-EIGHT

The Killers

CRIMES SUCH AS THE Geronimo bank slaughter have always engendered a certain morbid fascination among the public with the criminals and their motives. This was particularly true with Neill and Johnson, who looked more like choirboys than mass murderers.

What drove two seemingly harmless young men to commit such a brutal crime? The answer was not entirely clear. The basic motive for the bank robbery was a shared desperation over debts. But they could have robbed the little bank in Geronimo and not hurt a hair on anyone's head. Their motive for the murders was less apparent.

Neill and Johnson were lovers. They lived together and shared a joint bank account. Each had thus far lived an unremarkable and unsuccessful life and had unremarkable and unsuccessful careers, the latter of which had left them in debt and unable to pay their bills. Their solution was to rob the bank.

What was inexplicable was what caused one or both of them to stab and shoot the victims, especially because there was nothing in either's background to indicate such a propensity for violence.

Neill had grown up in small towns in Missouri. Adopted by his stepfather, who was a deputy sheriff and policeman, Neill was described by his high school principal as a "quiet kid with no discipline problems." He graduated from high school in Bolivar, Missouri, population five thousand, in May 1983. In those days, he had a girlfriend and worked at the Country Villa Café as a busboy and part-time cook. After graduation, he worked briefly at Porter's Seed House, unloading trucks. Owner Marvin Porter recalled him as "a pretty good kid. We never had a minute's trouble out of him."

Neill joined the U.S. Army and began active duty in August 1983. In February 1984, he was transferred to Fort Sill, adjacent to Lawton in southwestern Oklahoma. His army career, however, was short, and he was discharged in less than a year for unspecified reasons in July 1984.

While stationed at Fort Sill, Neill had met Johnson in Lawton. Johnson was a local who, after high school, attended Oklahoma Baptist University in Shawnee, from 1980 to 1982. He returned home to Lawton for the fall semester at Cameron University in 1983 but withdrew, reportedly because students made fun of his sexuality.

After the pair got together, they proved uniformly unsuccessful in their work. Johnson got a job as a waiter at El Chico restaurant but was fired after two weeks. On the day he was fired, he claimed to have fallen down some steps and hurt his back. The restaurant paid some of his medical bills but then refused to pay any more, despite complaints from Johnson.

Johnson found work at J. Riggins, a men's clothing store, but was fired after a few days because the manager learned he had previously written the store a hot check. Although the manager described Johnson as "a good worker and a very quiet polite boy," the combination of the check incident and some involvement of Johnson with a stolen credit card was too much to ignore.

Neill had no more success in keeping employment than Johnson. He sold home-improvement supplies door to door for Pacesetter Products from October through December 3, 1984. He was then fired for inadequate sales. A manager described him as "such a quiet person. He was always friendly and cooperative."

At the time of the murders, Neill was not employed but was attending real-estate school in preparation for obtaining a real-estate license. His last class was on December 12, two days before the crime. An instructor at the school described Neill as "a nice, clean-cut student that sounded like he was ambitious."

The Geronimo Bank Case

Yet at least once before, Neill's dark propensities had boiled to the surface. In that instance, what prompted the outburst was a phone message left by Kay Bruno—the Geronimo bank manager and one of Neill's eventual victims—at Neill's job at Pacesetter Products. She had been seeking collection of his delinquent loans. Neill was overhead to mutter after listening to the phone message: "That bitch better lay off me."

Bruno's attempts at debt collection were not the only financial pressure weighing on Neill and Johnson. They admitted to a friend that they owed seven thousand dollars to various creditors and were four hundred dollars behind on their apartment rent. Those debts were placing a strain on their relationship, and Neill, who by all accounts was the dominant partner, decided to deal with them by robbing the bank.

Picking the Geronimo bank was an obvious choice.

Both Neill and Johnson were familiar with the bank and its lack of security. They had been in the bank many times and as problem customers might have harbored animosity toward at least some of the employees. In particular, there was Bruno, who besides placing dunning calls to Neill at his job had also refused to cash a third-party check for more than five thousand dollars drawn on a Florida bank for him. In the end, this toxic mixture of financial desperation and personal animosity might have triggered Neill's previously unknown violent temper.

Johnson's assertions of innocence when it came to the murders might have been true, but the agents could not overlook that he had taken part in buying the knives, gun, and ammunition. He had also joined Neill in casing the bank and, of course, had proved more than happy to spend the stolen money. Johnson was without a doubt guilty of bank robbery, but to what extent he was involved in the murders remained and still remains in doubt.

CHAPTER FORTY-NINE

Preliminary Hearing

BACK IN LAWTON, DICK TANNERY was determined to press the case to a speedy trial. Judge Brock appointed Linda Clark, who practiced in Ardmore and Lawton, to represent Neill and a Lawton attorney named Rodney Bassel to represent Johnson.

The defense lawyers then had to scramble to prepare for the preliminary hearing, in which more than seventy witnesses were supposed to testify.

The preliminary hearing began as scheduled on January 28, 1985, and Tannery ended up calling more than fifty witnesses for the prosecution.

Far more evidence was presented than was necessary to show cause for a jury trial. Tannery said he could have presented the state's case with only eight or ten witnesses, but he decided to call more witnesses because of an Oklahoma Court of Criminal Appeals decision that a preliminary hearing should "allow the defendants to discover all the evidence that the prosecution has." Ironically, Tannery later would object when the defense lawyers called additional witnesses, accusing them of a "fishing expedition."

The highlight of the hearing was the testimony by the surviving victims. Still recovering from various head wounds, Marilyn Roach had had her hair cropped short to accommodate the surgery that had saved her life. She still carried a bullet in her head, yet she bravely took the stand and tearfully testified as to what had happened that day at the bank.

Shot in the head, she said her only thought in the moment was, "Jesus, help me, Jesus." She heard other shots and then two men's voices. The first voice, which sounded "upset," said, "I thought you weren't going to shoot anybody." A second voice, which sounded "casual," replied, "They moved."

Prior to the hearing, Johnson and Neill had been seated in the jury box, along with five other young men, to facilitate an in-court lineup requested by Tannery. When asked to identify the man who had shot her, Roach looked at the men and broke down in tears, saying, "I'm not sure but . . ."

Two subsequent victims—Bellen Robles and Reuben Robles—had no such trouble identifying the man who had shot them. Both of them positively identified Neill as the person who held them at gunpoint and pulled the trigger. On cross-examination, Reuben Robles admitted that he had previously identified Johnson as the person who confronted and shot the victims. Robles explained that the two men looked somewhat similar, but he was sure that Neill was the gunman in the bank. Bassel had Robles approach the lineup of men in the jury box so that he could see their height and then asked him again to identify the gunman. Again, Robles pointed to Neill.

Debbie Hernandez, a friend of Neill and Johnson's, testified that while visiting her in November, Neill had said he and Johnson were "thinking about robbing a bank." Hernandez said she would not have taken him seriously, but Neill persisted, remarking that the Geronimo bank did not have any security cameras.

The prosecution also introduced into evidence the written statement Johnson had given to the FBI agents in San Francisco. The statement was signed by Johnson and admitted his role in the planning of the robbery, but it also included a denial as far as having taken part in the actual robbery. Johnson admitted he had bought the gun and ammunition and admitted to disposing of the gun after the robbery. He denied, however, being present at the bank, claiming he had remained in their Lawton apartment during the commission of the crime, only learning of the murders from Neill after his return from the bank.

San Francisco FBI Agent Dan Knowlton testified that Neill had refused to talk and, strangely, had asked questions about the crime he was accused of

The Geronimo Bank Case

committing. At one point, Neill did begin to cry, saying, "I wish I could turn back the hands of time."

Neill's attorney used every opportunity on cross-examination to establish that the real killer that day was Johnson. He recounted how Reuben Robles had originally identified Johnson and how the drawing created from Bellen Robles' description looked like Johnson. This line of questioning, along with Johnson's denial of being at the bank, made it clear that the defendants intended to blame each other for the crime.

And it was a defense with merit. More than one person had looked at Neill and Johnson's mug shots and thought they were looking at the same person. All Clark needed was reasonable doubt. Had the survivors seen one man? Or had they seen two? Had they seen Neill? Or had they seen Johnson?

The prosecution's parade of witnesses established all the fundamental aspects of the crime and the defendants' involvement. The only evidence missing was the results of the FBI's ballistic and forensic testing, which were not yet complete. Even without that evidence, Judge McCall ordered both defendants to go to trial on all the charges.

All future proceedings, including the trial, were assigned to Judge Brock, who set the trial date for May 13, 1985.

Defense attorneys for both defendants predictably raised a question as to their clients' mental competency. Brock ordered that both men be evaluated at the state mental health facility in Vinita. The conclusion of the psychiatrists at Vinita was that Johnson and Neill were both mentally competent to assist their lawyers and stand trial. The written reports including these conclusions became part of the case file, but no competency hearing was demanded or conducted.

The defendants' attorneys did file a wide array of motions seeking to suppress testimony. The motion that intrigued the press and public most was an attempt to suppress the statement of one defendant about the other under the marital privilege, barring spouses from having to testify against each other.

The basis of this motion was that a common-law marriage existed between Neill and Johnson, given that they had lived together, had sexual relations, and shared a joint bank account. The idea that a same-sex relationship could amount to a marriage was unheard of in 1985. It would be another thirty years before the U.S. Supreme Court ruled in *Obergeffel v. Hodges* in

203

2015 that the fundamental right to marry is guaranteed to same-sex couples by both the Due Process Clause and the Equal Protection Clause of the Fourteenth Amendment to the U.S. Constitution. Whether a gay couple can be involved in a common-law marriage remains an undecided legal issue.

In any event, Brock denied that motion.

The motion that would come back to haunt the judge and the prosecutor was the motion to sever the two defendants and try Johnson and Neill separately. By then, Neill was particularly concerned over a joint trial because he feared Johnson's statement to the FBI in San Francisco would not only be used against him in a joint trial but could be excluded if he were tried separately.

After reviewing the law on separate trials that was applicable at the time, Judge Brock overruled the motion for separate trials.

Johnson and Neill would be tried together.

CHAPTER FIFTY

The Trial

THE TRIAL BEGAN AS SCHEDULED on Monday, May 13, 1985. Michael Clark had replaced his wife, Linda, as the attorney for Neill. The Clarks practiced law together, and the change of counsel was done with the court's approval. Assistant District Attorney John Landon now took an active part in the prosecution of the case. Jay Walker of Lawton joined Rodney Bassel in representing Johnson. An original panel of 350 jurors was summoned for the case. Of those, 198 were excused for various reasons.

Because the state was seeking the death penalty, each potential juror had to be questioned on that issue, and the voir dire dragged on for more than two-and-a-half days before twelve jurors and two alternates were finally seated.

The jurors included a Lawton civics teacher who had taught Johnson's half sister, a man who had been a criminal-justice student, and a woman whose father had been a sheriff's deputy. One of the last jurors seated was a member of the same church as Joyce Mullenix's husband and had sent flowers to Joyce's family after her murder.

The opening statements by the defense lawyers previewed the finger-pointing to come between Neill and Johnson. The onetime lovers were both hell-bent on saving their own necks and pinning the crime on the other guy. Speaking on Johnson's behalf, Bassel told the jury, "Johnson was never in the bank on December 14 nor was he outside the bank."

Bassel went on to describe Johnson as "a victim of Jay Neill, used unknowingly and unwittingly by Neill." Bassel confirmed to the juror that "one of these two young men were in the bank on December 14," but he declared, "It certainly wasn't Robert Grady Johnson."

When it was his turn, Clark argued that Johnson was the dominant figure who had bought the gun and the ammunition, changed the airplane tickets, and thrown the gun in the pond. He compared the appearance of the two defendants with the descriptions given by eyewitnesses and concluded that the description fit Johnson, not Neill. He also told the jury that the evidence would prove Neill had acted at the direction of Johnson.

In fact, the evidence would show there was little doubt that Neill was in the bank and wielded the knife. When it came to Johnson, ample proof existed to prove he was all-in on the bank robbery, but it was less certain as to whether he was in the bank and took part in the murders.

In an effort to make it clear that both men were in the bank during the killings, Tannery pointed out that the three women bank employees had showed no signs of resistance. Why not? Why would two of the women not have run or fought once Neill started to stab his first victim? The obvious explanation was that Johnson had been present and was holding the women at gunpoint.

Although the other surviving victims saw only one man, Marilyn Roach testified that she had heard two voices. And Johnson could easily have fled the bank after Neill stabbed the women victims and before the four customers arrived. The conflict between the two defendants would color the whole trial, pitting their attorneys and stories against each other. Because Tannery was seeking to convict both Neill and Johnson, his case became the beneficiary of the defendants' accusations and counteraccusations.

The battle between the two defendants erupted during the testimony of Dan Knowlton, the San Francisco FBI agent who had questioned Johnson after his arrest.

To avoid legal error, Tannery elected not to place Johnson's statement in evidence because it did directly implicate Neill. Instead, Tannery asked

The Geronimo Bank Case

Knowlton four carefully worded questions. The answers were designed to show Johnson's admission of participation in the bank robbery without mentioning Neill.

The attempt to avoid evidence given by Johnson identifying Neill as the perpetrator did not last long. On cross-examination, Bassel elicited testimony from Knowlton that Johnson had said Neill planned and carried out the robbery and the killings. Knowlton's notes and Johnson's statement were offered into evidence. Initially, Judge Brock admitted the notes and statement, over the objection by Neill's counsel. However, before the jury saw the statement, Brock reversed himself and instructed the jury that Johnson's statement implicating Neill was hearsay "without evidentiary worth" and "should not be considered by the jury for any purpose whatsoever."

Overall, the trial progressed much like the preliminary hearing, with Tannery relentlessly calling a long list of seventy-one witnesses to set up the defendants' motives and tie each of them to the crime. Numerous witnesses testified as to the defendants' financial problems and their status as problem customers of the bank. Once again, Marilyn Roach recited the terror of being shot, and Bellen Robles steadfastly identified Neill as the gunman. Reuben Robles also identified Neill and described how he had not only shot the four customers but also had attempted to kill the Robleses' child.

Janie Bowles, the mother of the victim Jeri Bowles, was allowed to testify about a conversation with her daughter before the robbery.

According to Mrs. Bowles, her daughter had told her that "two blondish, good-looking customers" had been coming into the bank and that they had made her "feel creepy." Jeri thought the two men were "looking things over more than conducting business."

The prosecution also had the benefit of the testimony of an FBI forensic expert, William Eubanks, a serologist in the FBI's Washington, D.C., laboratory. He had examined the knife found in Neill's car at the Lawton airport and concluded that the blood found on the knife was consistent with the blood of Jeri Bowles and Kay Bruno. It bears noting that this testimony was before the advent of DNA testing, so the amount of certainty in blood matching was limited.

For reasons that remain unknown, twice during the trial, the proceedings were interrupted by bomb threats. Both times, the threats were made to the

Lawton office of the OSBI. In each instance, the courthouse was cleared and searched, but no bomb was found.

When the prosecution finally rested, no witnesses were called on Johnson's behalf and only one witness was called on behalf of Neill. Neill's witness testified only as to a hallway conversation by another witness during the trial. The testimony concluded on May 23, but the tension did not.

The conflict between the two defendants continued right through the closing arguments of their respective attorneys on May 24. Counsel for both defendants argued that it was not their client who committed the crime but rather the other defendant. As Assistant District Attorney Landon said in his closing remarks, "What that equals is the State's case pure and simple."

As it turned out, the jury was not fooled by the defendants' tactics. It took the jurors one hour thirty-seven minutes to render a verdict of guilty on four counts of first-degree murder and four counts of attempted murder. On the attempted-murder counts, the jury recommended a sentence of twenty years for each count.

During the sentencing phase of the trial to consider the death penalty, Johnson called two witnesses on his behalf. His mother, Joyce Cook, tearfully pleaded for her son's life, saying, "Spare his life because he has a life to give to people."

In support of Johnson's theory throughout the trial that he had been dominated, intimidated, and manipulated by Neill, a San Francisco psychiatrist named Roger Freed testified that Johnson had an "inadequate personality or dependent personality" that would tend to make him submissive to a stronger person.

In his closing arguments, Bassel argued there was "no direct evidence that Robby Johnson was in the bank . . . nobody said they saw him."

Clark simply reasserted Neill's trial story that he was never in the bank that day. Meanwhile, Tannery took the opportunity to point out the cruel and heinous nature of the crimes. He referred to the photographs of the crime scene, reminding the jurors that the stills proved "crimes beyond words."

Given the brutal and needless nature of the killings, the jurors needed little prompting. True to their oath, they took only eighty minutes to rule that both Johnson and Neill should receive the death penalty.

CHAPTER FIFTY-ONE

The First Appeal and Related Foolishness

IN THE STATE OF OKLAHOMA, all cases in which the death penalty is assessed are automatically appealed to the Oklahoma Court of Criminal Appeals for review. Neill and Johnson's convictions were thus appealed. It would be seven years before the court ruled on the merits of the appeal. In the meantime, unusual and bizarre events continued to dog the case.

Norman's David Autry, an assistant appellate public defender, represented Neill on the appeal, and Alan Rosenbaum of Lawton represented Johnson. Assistant Attorney Generals Tomilou Gentry Liddell, Susan Stewart Dickerson, and Sandra D. Howard represented the state.

While their appeal was pending, Neill and Johnson raised a postconviction defense regarding the handling of the defendants' pretrial request for a competency review.

Based on a recent decision interpreting a 1980 Oklahoma statute, the appeals court ruled that the defendants had been entitled to a jury trial on the issue of their competency at the time of the crime and at the time of their murder trial. The appeals court ordered the case to be returned to the district court to ascertain whether the defendants' competency as of the date of the trial could still be determined, and if so, whether a jury believed they were competent.

In 1986, a new district attorney, Robert C. Schulte, had been elected. He had to pick up the ball and run with it, and that's exactly what he did. A competency trial was conducted in front of Judge Brock on the first two days of September 1987. At the competency trial, Dr. Edward Norfleet, a state psychiatrist at Eastern State Hospital in Vinita who had examined Neill and Johnson in 1985, testified that both young men had been competent at that time.

Although Norfleet had reached the conclusion that both Neill and Johnson were competent during his initial interview, he and other doctors at the facility had conducted a series of tests to confirm his opinion. The tests confirmed his first impression, and Norfleet was thoroughly convinced that both defendants were competent in 1984 and 1985. During his fourteen-day stay at Eastern State Hospital, Neill had banged his head against the wall and talked in a loud belligerent manner, but Norfleet had discounted this behavior as an attempt to look crazy. He described Neill as "a little guy who wants to pout and put on a show."

Schulte and his first assistant, Fred Smith, also called two other doctors from the Vinita facility, two Comanche County jailers, a registered nurse who had had contact with the two defendants, and Judge McCall, the special judge who had conducted Neill and Johnson's preliminary hearing. All of those witnesses said they believed Neill and Johnson had been competent at the time of the trial.

The defendants called one witness, Dr. Hans Von Brauchitsch, a psychiatry professor at the University of Oklahoma. He criticized the testing done at Vinita and concluded that it was impossible to tell whether Neill and Johnson had been competent based on the testing.

Once again, the trial—this time the competency trial—was interrupted by a bomb threat. Only this time, it was real. Electricians working in the ceiling of the courthouse found a professionally constructed bomb that had failed to explode only because of a flaw in its triggering mechanism. However, the bomb appeared to have been in place for some time and might have been the source of the bomb threats during the defendants' trial two years earlier, in 1985.

The Geronimo Bank Case

The bomb scare interrupted the trial, but it did not distract the jurors who, after a little more than an hour of deliberation, found that both Neill and Johnson had been competent when they committed the crime and at the time of their trial. This decision returned the case to the appeals court.

The next five years would see many extrajudicial events involving the two jailbirds and other miscellaneous do-gooders, meddlers, and profiteers who involved themselves in the case.

Faced with their impending executions, both Neill and Johnson found God. Neill in particular associated himself with religious groups, going so far as to give interviews to the Christian Broadcasting Network and *The 700 Club*. In his interview with *The 700 Club*, Neill admitted to the crimes and pleaded for forgiveness.

Finding Jesus did not keep Johnson from acting like the rat he was. In an attempt to exonerate himself, Johnson began to claim that he was innocent and that Neill's real accomplice was Reuben Robles, one of the victims. The assertion was outlandish and unsubstantiated, but nonetheless the *Daily Oklahoman* published it as a result of a conversation between Johnson and a reporter. The accusation against Robles was quickly denied by Tannery, who was now in private practice in Lawton, and by the FBI. Neill also publicly disavowed any participation by Robles in the crime.

Aiding and abetting Johnson in this farce was a rogue Lawton police officer named Ann Lord.

Lord had become acquainted with Johnson and Neill during a 1984 credit-card fraud investigation she had conducted that resulted in Neill's being arrested and charged. Johnson was never charged in that investigation, but both men remained in touch with Lord after their Geronimo bank convictions, even writing and calling her from the Oklahoma State Penitentiary in McAlester. Lord was also in touch with Johnson's mother, Joyce Cook.

Ann Lord took it upon herself to investigate the accusation against Robles, even though the crime was outside the jurisdiction of the Lawton police department. She did not inform the FBI, the Lawton police, or either Johnson or Neill's attorneys about her investigation. Instead, she struck out on her own witch hunt for no clear or justifiable reason.

At one point, Lord aggressively tracked down and questioned Bellen Robles, who was divorcing Reuben. Lord's questions so alarmed Mrs. Robles that she contacted the FBI, who hastily intervened by informing Lawton Police Chief Robert Gillian about what Lord was up to.

Lord resigned from the Lawton police force, and Johnson's groundless accusations against Reuben Robles were rejected by both the district attorney and the FBI.

During that time, another character surfaced. This one was a Dallas dentist, Paul Dunn, who professed to be writing a book about the case. Dunn was assisted by a Lawton talk-show host named Francie Ford. Dunn befriended both Neill and Johnson, visiting them at McAlester on numerous occasions. Both men wrote lengthy letters to Dunn, which he later shared with the authorities. It does not appear that Dunn ever published a book on the case, but his correspondence with Neill and Johnson became the subject of subsequent court proceedings.

In 1992, more than seven years after the murders, the Court of Criminal Appeals finally issued a decision. It was an unconscionable delay as far as both sides of the case were concerned. If the defendants had been determined to be innocent, they would have spent seven years in prison for a crime they did not commit. And if they were guilty, should the families of the victims have had to wait so long for justice?

But it was about to get worse. The appeals court did not rule on the merits of the case. Instead, the court found that Neill and Johnson were entitled to separate trials and returned their cases to district court so that each could be tried separately. The appeals court more or less adopted a new standard relative to the joint trial of two or more defendants. The court made a previously unrecognized distinction between "inconsistent" defenses and "antagonistic" defenses. The court decided that in the case of antagonistic defenses, the parties were entitled to separate trials. In this case, the court said, "The two defense strategies inexorably clashed as the sole defense of each defendant was the guilt of the other."

Mark Henricksen of El Reno, one of the attorneys who represented Johnson in his second trial, pointed out that this distinction has been largely ignored in subsequent cases. In Henricksen's experience, the Neill decision is often raised by defense lawyers but is rarely followed. Regardless, it was the law of the land when it came to the Geronimo bank case.

There would be two more separate trials.

CHAPTER FIFTY-TWO

Neill's Trial

ROBERT SCHULTE WAS ANXIOUS to get Neill to trial and eager to again assess the death penalty. Stung by the reversal of the first verdict, Judge Brock, who clearly thought Neill was guilty, set the trial to begin on September 21, 1992.

This trial would differ from the first one because Neill had decided to admit his guilt and throw himself on the mercy of the court. Now represented by Jim Pearson and Don Gutteridge Jr. of Oklahoma City, the defense goal was simple: Try to save Neill's life. Starting with the opening statement, the lawyers set the theme as they worked to establish that Neill sought only to be sentenced to life without parole and had no intention of denying his guilt any longer.

Given the posture of Neill's defense team, the guilt phase of the trial proceeded very quickly. Schulte called most of the witnesses who had been called in the first trial. The evidence against Neill was supplemented by Neill's previous admissions of guilt. The prosecution played Neill's interview on *The 700 Club*. During this unedited ninety-minute tape, Neill admitted his guilt and described his feelings before and after the murders. He explained that his crimes were committed because he was a slave in a homosexual relationship with Johnson. Johnson forced Neill to support both men and to buy Johnson drugs and clothing, Neill said.

As far as the stabbings, Neill said in the interview that he had "never had such a horrible feeling. All I can do is pray to the Lord that they didn't feel it." Neill also professed that he was no longer afraid to die because the Lord had forgiven him, and "I know I'm not going anywhere but into His arms."

The most controversial testimony at this trial came from would-be author Paul Dunn. He had received several letters from Neill. One described the crime at length and put the blame for all the murders on Johnson. In that correspondence, Neill told a tale in which Johnson did all the killing and Neill was repulsed and shocked by Johnson's acts. Subsequently, Neill recanted this story in another letter to Dunn exonerating Johnson.

Given the uncontested evidence, the jury took only ninety minutes to find Neill guilty of four counts of first-degree murder, three counts of shooting with intent to kill, and one count of attempted shooting with intent to kill. They recommended a twenty-year sentence on each of the charges of shooting with intent to kill and a ten-year sentence on the attempted-shooting charge.

The trial then entered the sentencing phase. The prosecution called Kirk Mullinex, Joyce's husband; Jerry Bruno, Kay's husband; and Calvin Bowles, Jeri's father. The three witnesses described their ongoing and inconsolable grief for their murdered loved ones. Known as victim-impact statements, their stories were both real and touching.

In the ultimate Hail Mary, Neill took the stand and pleaded for his life. In fact, his lengthy testimony probably only inflamed the jury more. Under oath, Neill said that he alone had gone to the bank and committed the crime while Johnson remained behind at their apartment in Lawton. Neill described forcing the women employees and the customers into the back room at gunpoint. He said he stabbed the customers simultaneously and tried to cut off their heads only because "I remember thinking I have to get these ladies out of this pain. . . . After the initial moans and screams I was somewhat concerned and wanted it to be over."

The only criminal act Neill denied was attempting to shoot the Robleses' baby, Marie.

At the end of his direct testimony, Neill tearfully told the jury and the

The Geronimo Bank Case

families of his victims that he was sorry for his crimes. He stated that if he was sentenced to life without parole, he would not appeal, and the case could be closed for all involved.

Taking the stand, of course, subjected Neill to cross-examination. Under Schulte's questioning, Neill admitted that Kay Bruno had pleaded for her life and that when he began stabbing her, she screamed in pain, "I'm dead! I'm dead! I'm dead!"

Unmoved by Neill's professed remorse and after hearing and, more important, seeing the graphic photographs of the brutality of the victims' deaths, the jury took only ninety minutes to return four death sentences. One juror wept in open court while Neill, without visible emotion, received his sentence.

CHAPTER FIFTY-THREE

Johnson's Trial

NEILL HAD NOW BEEN convicted, but Johnson still needed to be tried. Unlike Neill, Johnson continued to assert his innocence. He approached his new trial prepared to fight for a not-guilty verdict. He was helped by a small inheritance that had come his way on the death of his grandmother. The funds enabled him to employ a private attorney. He chose Don Ed Payne of Idabel, Oklahoma.

Payne had served as a county judge and as the county attorney of McCurtain County. He had also been district attorney for Oklahoma's Seventeenth District, composed of McCurtain, Choctaw, and Pushmataha counties. He had been in private practice largely devoted to criminal defense, including death-penalty cases, since 1971. Later, Payne would serve as associate district judge in McCurtain County from 1995 until his death in 2006.

Payne chose to associate Mark Henricksen in Johnson's defense. Payne and Henricksen had become close friends while serving together on the board of directors of the American Civil Liberties Union. Henricksen had experience as a trial lawyer, but this would be his first death-penalty case. Since the Johnson case, Henricksen has handled dozens of death-penalty cases at various stages of the proceedings.

The two Oklahomans were joined by Michael Barta of Washington, D. C. Barta, a young lawyer who worked for a prestigious Washingtonian law firm, had begun to represent Johnson pro bono when Johnson filed a Freedom of Information Act request with the federal government seeking information about his case. The request ended up before a federal judge in the District of Columbia who appointed Barta to represent Johnson. That representation led to his further involvement on Johnson's behalf.

When the case went to trial in July 1993, Robert Schulte was assisted in the prosecution by Assistant District Attorney Eddie Valdez. The prosecution was again seeking the death penalty, and Jack Brock was the presiding judge.

The witnesses called by the prosecution replicated those called at the joint trial and Neill's own trial. Significantly, the surviving victims could identify only Neill as the one robber they had seen in the bank. Marilyn Roach, however, repeated her testimony that after she was shot, she heard two distinct voices discussing the crime. There was much actual evidence to prove that Johnson was involved in planning the bank robbery but only circumstantial evidence that he was inside the bank when the crimes occurred.

During the guilt phase, Johnson took the stand in his own behalf. Some parts of Johnson's story were downright unbelievable, and these hard-to-swallow assertions worked to undermine his credibility.

Johnson admitted obtaining the gun permit, purchasing the gun and knives, changing the travel plans, and spending the stolen money in San Francisco. However, he contended that he only learned of the robbery when Neill returned from the bank with the cash and told him about it.

Johnson denied casing the bank the day before the robbery and taking any part in the crime. He said he obtained the gun for Neill because Neill was underage and that he did not know Neill was going to use it in a robbery. He said the knives were purchased as Christmas gifts for Neill's nephews.

It might have sounded all well and good to Johnson, but he did not hold up on cross-examination. Schulte called to Johnson's attention the statement he had given to the FBI in San Francisco in which he had said Neill told him about plans for the robbery on December 13. Schulte also asked Johnson why he didn't turn Neill in after Neill told him he had killed six or seven people. Johnson's weak answer was that he did not feel that he could leave Neill.

The Geronimo Bank Case

Although Johnson's testimony was less than perfect, he could not be shaken on one important point—that he did not personally rob or murder anyone. On that point, he had an alibi. A neighbor had been with Johnson in her apartment at about one o'clock that day. Neill was not with Johnson at the time. The bank robbery occurred in Geronimo between 1:00 and 1:30 p.m., when the victims were discovered.

Geronimo was about twelve miles from Johnson's Lawton apartment. Johnson's argument was that it would have been impossible for him to have driven to the bank and taken part in the crime in the available time frame.

To support Johnson's alibi, the defense lawyers called Gilbert "Dub" Armstrong, a private investigator who had previously served as the police chief of El Reno, Oklahoma. Armstrong drove from Johnson's apartment to the Geronimo bank via three routes, three or four times each, and testified that the fastest the route could be driven was seventeen minutes. Brock did not allow Armstrong to testify as an expert witness and give his opinion but did allow Armstrong's testimony about the timed drives to the bank.

That did create a reasonable doubt as to whether Johnson was at the bank when the robbery took place.

In his closing argument, Schulte said about Johnson, "For him to come in and tell the jury he didn't know the bank was robbed is inconceivable."

The district attorney also continued to pound on the circumstantial evidence that showed Johnson was indeed in the bank that day. "I tell you why nobody fought," Schulte said. "While they was being stabbed someone else held a gun to their head. What's your choice? Either fight this knife or be shot."

When it was Henricksen's turn, he emphasized that no one saw Johnson at the bank and that Johnson's location at 1:00 p.m. precluded his presence during the crime.

Before deliberating the verdict in the penalty phase, the jury was instructed on the elements of felony murder. According to the law, a person who takes part in a felony is guilty of a murder that results from the felony even if the person did not commit the murder himself. Whatever doubts the jury had about Johnson's guilt were reconciled against him.

After seven hours of deliberation over two days, the jury found Johnson guilty on all eight charges, including four counts of first-degree murder.

The jury recommended twenty-year sentences on each count of attempted shooting with intent to kill as well as a ten-year sentence on the attempted-shooting charge. Those convictions triggered the second phase, in which the state would seek the death penalty.

Prior to beginning the punishment phase of the trial, the prosecution asked the court to remove one of the jurors, Karen Nobis. Schulte alleged that Nobis had not candidly answered some voir dire questions and that she had violated the court's order not to discuss the case with third parties.

He called as a witness Nobis's mother-in-law, Evelyn Nobis, who testified that Karen had talked to her about the case after the jury found Johnson guilty. According to Evelyn Nobis, Karen had stated that the prosecution had not proved Johnson was in the bank, and he would likely be sentenced to life or life without parole. Schulte was so fixated on the death penalty that it was probably more Karen Nobis's attitude than her violation of the rule that drove his request to remove her as juror. Brock, whom Henricksen remembers as tyrannical, went along with Schulte's request. Nobis was dismissed without being called to testify. She was replaced with a male alternate. In an interesting aside, Nobis would later appear in *Playboy* magazine.

During the argument over Nobis's dismissal, Payne argued that the prosecutor had been listening to the jurors' deliberations. Because of a quirk in the location of the jury room, lawyers could sit in a spot outside the room and hear some of the conversation among jurors. Unfortunately for Payne's argument, one of the defense lawyers had seen what Schulte was doing and joined him in listening to the jurors' deliberations.

Brock, aware of this unique feature of the courthouse, had chosen to ignore it. Later, Nobis told the press that she had initially voted for a not-guilty verdict, but the vote was eleven to one for guilty, and after hours of further deliberation, she changed her vote to guilty.

During the punishment phase, the prosecution called family members of the victims, as had been done in Neill's trial. Jerry Bruno, who had been married to Kay Bruno for twenty-four years at the time of her murder, testified, "I couldn't handle my job and retired. I sold the home. There are too many memories." Kirk Mullenix, who had lost his wife and unborn daughter, admitted, "I feel a lot more angry." Calvin Bowles tearfully observed, "Holidays have never been the same. One time, I almost didn't make it."

The Geronimo Bank Case

On Johnson's behalf, his lawyers pulled out everything they could think of to save his life. Both Johnson's mother and grandmother testified, trying to portray Johnson as a reformed man, a good, religious person. Johnson openly wept during that testimony.

The defense also called Fred Cook, the manager of the death-row unit at McAlester. He described Johnson as a model prisoner who was even used as an inmate counselor. Three ordained ministers told of their contact with Johnson and their belief that he was sincere in his religious conversion.

Johnson retook the stand and testified that God had visited him at the McAlester prison. He said a light had appeared in his cell one night, and a voice told him that he did not have to be a homosexual and then quoted a Bible verse. Johnson said he then began to spread the Gospel. Johnson asked the jury to spare his life so he could help others.

During closing arguments, Payne did everything but rend his garments. He emotionally quoted Scripture and Shakespeare and described in detail how Johnson would be executed. Schulte, intent on getting the death penalty, pointed out that Johnson had had eight years to practice his story while the "victims pled their case to the executioner . . . and their trial only lasted three to five minutes."

Whether it was the testimony and arguments offered during the punishment phase or the fact that reasonable doubt existed in some minds as to whether Johnson was in the bank, the jury, after nine hours of deliberation, chose to spare his life. They recommended life without parole on all four murder counts.

Johnson was thirty-one at the time. He would not be executed, but he would sit in jail for the rest of his life. He would have plenty of time to think about whether that was better than a swift execution. Although in Johnson's case, he might have held out some faint hope that somehow, someday, he would walk away a free man.

At the request of the defendant, Judge Brock sentenced Johnson immediately so that he could be returned to McAlester. Payne and Henricksen's job was done, and they withdrew from the case. The lawyers waived a motion for a new trial; both were convinced that Johnson would be ill served by an appeal because a reversal would again expose him to the death penalty.

Regardless of their advice, Johnson decided to appeal.

CHAPTER FIFTY-FOUR

Further Appeals

THE APPEAL PROCESS FOR BOTH Neill and Johnson was unnecessarily lengthy and complicated. The FBI, the judge, the prosecutor, the defense lawyers, and the jurors had all done their job expeditiously, but now justice crept to a final solution over the course of many years.

Neill's case was first considered by the Oklahoma Court of Criminal Appeals. The court had seemingly cleaned up its docket since the first appeal, and it took only two years to render a decision affirming Neill's guilt and his death sentence.

That decision did not stop Neill from pursuing legal relief. He resorted to the federal courts by filing a writ of habeas corpus in the U.S. District Court. His request for a writ was turned down, and so he appealed again to the Tenth Circuit Court of Appeals. When the appellate court rejected his arguments, he sought certiorari in the U.S. Supreme Court, which rejected his request. Neill's execution finally took place on December 12, 2002, eighteen years after commission of the crime.

Because of a change of counsel, Johnson's appeal was originally dismissed for failure to file a brief in the Court of Criminal Appeals. It then took a series of independent appeals in federal court to reinstate his case.

Thus, Johnson's appeal on the jury verdict was not ruled on until 2002, nine years after his trial. The appeals court affirmed the verdict and sentence. Specifically, the appeals court affirmed the concept of felony murder as it applied to Johnson. Based on that ruling, Johnson could be convicted of murder whether he was at the bank or not because he was involved in the robbery. The ruling effectively disposed of Johnson's best argument for acquittal.

Like Neill, Johnson then went to the federal court to seek relief. His appeals were exhausted in 2007, and he remains in prison, where he should stay for the rest of his life.

On appeal, both Neill and Johnson attacked their respective verdicts on many grounds. One argument was that the prosecutor unfairly cross-examined them on their homosexual relationship and in his closing arguments, inflamed the jury against them by remarks about their gay behavior. Given the enormity of the crime, the jury likely would have reached the same decision had the two been heterosexual or had sexual congress with goats. The defendants also conveniently overlooked the fact that each had raised the subject of their relationship as part of their defense.

The appeals courts uniformly rejected the gay defense argument, with one exception. Tenth Circuit Court of Appeals Judge Carlos F. Lucero wrote a hand-wringing dissent in Neill's case, speculating that the gay references were the cause of his receiving the death penalty. Judges Deanell Tacha and Bobby R. Baldock outvoted Lucero, and Neill's conviction was again affirmed. Lucero's dissent was picked up by some gay activists and judicial critics as having validity. Those people made it the cornerstone of their arguments about antigay discrimination in the judicial system. Johnson has fostered this sentiment in press interviews to this day.

The heirs of Ralph Zeller, one of the murder victims, filed a civil suit against the First Bank of Chattanooga alleging that the bank was negligent in not providing adequate security for its customers. The bank had no security at all, so the suit was well grounded. John Norman, the lawyer for the plaintiffs, remembers that the bank was no more than "two double-wide trailers." The suit was settled without a trial.

The Geronimo bank case continues to weigh heavily on the minds of not only those involved but also some older citizens of southwestern Oklahoma. Many vividly remember the horrific crime that happened in a place where

The Geronimo Bank Case

such violence was not supposed to occur. It shook their views on safety and security, particularly in small rural communities in that part of the state. To those people, the Geronimo bank case is as real now as it was then.

The Death of Bill Tilghman

"He died with his boots on."

—**Old Western saying**

CHAPTER FIFTY-FIVE

Case #5: The Death of Bill Tilghman

THE HISTORY OF THE American West is as much a state of mind as a retelling of actual events. We demand good guys and bad guys, cowboys and Indians, sheriffs and outlaws, white hats and black hats. In reality, most of our heroes should have worn gray, given how often they crossed the line back and forth between the law and lawlessness.

Good reasons exist for this behavior.

The American West was a harsh and brutal land. Survival took courage, tenacity, and a strong sense of self-preservation. If on occasion this meant stealing horses or rustling a few cows or running a saloon or brothel, so be it. Making do was a way of life. If you survived heat, cold, thirst, and starvation, someone might still shoot you if you did not shoot him first.

As the frontier was tamed, many famous rough-and-tumble heroes softened along with it. Some of them also developed selective memory, remembering their heroic achievements while conveniently forgetting any checkered past. In many ways, Bill Tilghman fit that picture.

When Tilghman was shot to death in 1924, he was a law enforcement icon—a status built not only on his remarkable achievements but also on years of shameless self-promotion.

CHAPTER FIFTY-SIX

Frontier Days

THE FACTS OF BILL TILGHMAN'S early life on the plains of Kansas, Colorado, and New Mexico remain obscure, but without a doubt, he had an adventurous time. Tilghman worked through the years as a buffalo hunter, rancher, gambler, saloonkeeper, horse thief, and ultimately a legendary lawman.

Born in Fort Dodge, Iowa, in 1854, William Matthew Tilghman left home in 1870 at the age of sixteen, traveling to southwestern Kansas to become a buffalo hunter. A crack shot, he learned to hunt with the popular .50-caliber Sharps rifle. The Sharps weighed sixteen pounds and was accurate to seven hundred yards or more. From 1870 to 1874, Tilghman hunted American bison—first for their hides and later for meat, helping to feed workers on the Atchison, Topeka and Santa Fe Railway.

It was a time of change. At the beginning of the century, the buffalo numbered some fifty million strong, moving the explorers Lewis and Clark, who encountered a herd in 1806 at White River in what later became South Dakota, to observe, "The moving multitude ... darkened the whole plains." By the end of the nineteenth century, only a few hundred bison would remain. Tilghman found himself in the last hurrahs of an era when buffalo were still plentiful, but the end was in sight. He estimated that in his years as a buffalo hunter, he single-handedly killed about twelve thousand bison.

During that period of time, Tilghman also befriended and rode with the famous horse thieves "Dutch Henry" Born and "Hurricane Bill" Martin. By Bill Tilghman's own admission, he participated in the theft of horses from various Indian tribes, hunted illegally on Indian land, and sold whiskey and ammunition to Indians illegally.

During that same period the Plains tribes—Cheyenne, Arapaho, Apache, Kiowa, Sioux, and Comanche—clashed with hunters and other white settlers. Tilghman's brother Dick was killed in such a clash, and Tilghman took part in several skirmishes with the tribes. Most notably, he escaped two Cheyenne war parties in an epic race that left both him and his famous horse, Chief, exhausted and near death from thirst. Tilghman recovered, but Chief never did, broken down by his long run without water.

In 1874, while roaming the plains, Tilghman was arrested for suspicion of murder in southeastern Colorado. A knife found near the body of a young boy was identified as Tilghman's, but Tilghman proved the knife had been stolen from him and that he was nowhere near the scene when the crime occurred. He was released after questioning and never prosecuted for the murder.

In 1874 at Adobe Walls, Texas, the Cheyennes, Arapahoes, and Comanches made one last attempt to drive off the buffalo hunters, only to be beaten back by a heavily armed group of hunters. A subsequent campaign against the Indians by the U.S. Army, combined with starvation brought on by the demise of the buffalo, drove most of the tribes to surrender to reservation life in 1875. Indian uprisings continued for several years thereafter, but the constant threat that the tribes had posed to white settlement of the area diminished greatly.

During Tilghman's time as a hunter, his operations were based around Dodge City, Kansas, and in 1875, with most of the once magnificent buffalo herds slaughtered and gone, he decided to make his home there. This was the Dodge City of western lore, a wild frontier town built on saloons, gambling, and prostitution and home to the likes of Bat Masterson and Wyatt Earp, both of whom befriended Tilghman.

Tilghman settled on acreage near the town and became partners in a saloon. In 1875, he and Flora Kendall began what was most likely then a

The Death of Bill Tilghman

common-law marriage, given that records of the union do not exist. In any event, he and Flora stayed together until her death in 1900 and had three children. Flora, a young widow, also had a child from a previous relationship.

In 1878, Tilghman was arrested yet again—this time in connection with an attempted robbery of a Santa Fe train in Kinsley, Kansas. The charges against him were ultimately dismissed for lack of evidence, and some accounts attribute the arrest to the fact that one of the real suspects was named Tilman. Despite Tilghman's various brushes with the law, Bat Masterson named him deputy sheriff of Ford County. This marked the beginning of a career in law enforcement that Tilghman would pursue on and off until his death, although not always in Kansas.

The year 1880 found Tilghman in New Mexico working for the Arizona and Pacific Railroad. Returning to Dodge City, he was once again appointed deputy sheriff in 1882 and was named town marshal in 1884. His brother Frank took over the saloon, but Tilghman remained involved in other businesses, including interests in a restaurant, a dairy farm, and a cattle-trading company.

In 1888, acting in his capacity as deputy sheriff, Tilghman shot and killed Ed Prather in Farmer City, Kansas. Prather, who had been a friend and associate of Tilghman's, had started drinking on July 3 in anticipation of the Fourth of July holiday. He then proceeded to terrorize the town over the next two days, kicking in doors, demanding service, and brandishing and firing a gun. He also repeatedly threatened and insulted Tilghman. Tilghman finally confronted Prather in a saloon and demanded that he turn over his gun. Prather refused and then made the mistake of placing his hand on his weapon. Tilghman shot Prather twice, killing him.

About a year later, Tilghman was involved in another shoot-out. This one stemmed from a dispute over whether the town of Cimarron or Ingalls would become the county seat of Gray County, Kansas, which was adjacent to Ford County. In 1889, a judge ruled Ingalls the winner in court, but the county records were in Cimarron, and the clerk refused to give them up.

The Gray County sheriff deputized Tilghman, along with Bat Masterson's brother Jim and several others, and the group proceeded to Cimarron to retrieve the documents. The citizens of Cimarron took exception to the intrusion and opened fire on the sheriff's party as it left town. A wild gun battle ensued. One resident of Cimarron was killed, several others were wounded, and three deputies were trapped in the temporary courthouse by a mob but were rescued later. The culprits in the battle were charged with murder but exonerated at trial when the source of the fatal shots could not be determined.

Such colorful incidents, along with the routine arrests Tilghman made as marshal, established his reputation as a lawman. And despite the questionable fanfare that accompanied some of his altercations, he became known far and wide for his levelheadedness and a propensity to use as little force as possible in dealing with a situation.

CHAPTER FIFTY-SEVEN

The Three Guardsmen

ALTHOUGH TILGHMAN WAS succeeding in law enforcement, he was not so lucky in business. None of his many endeavors was prospering, and in 1889, he decided to sell what little property he had acquired and join the first land run in Oklahoma Territory.

Tilghman was not only there when the town of Guthrie instantly sprouted from the Oklahoma prairie, but he also became one of its first saloonkeepers as a co-owner of the Alpha Saloon. Like most establishments of its kind, the Alpha Saloon featured whiskey, gambling, and women.

Tilghman's stake in it was his ticket into Guthrie's business community. He also pursued his lifelong love of horses by operating a racetrack on the outskirts of town. It was the saloon, however, that would bring him both acceptance and trouble. Tilghman would eventually be charged with several municipal crimes involving gambling and prostitution.

In 1891, when the Sac and Fox tribal lands were opened to settlers, Tilghman claimed a 160-acre plot near Chandler. He called it Bell Cow Ranch and developed a facility there to raise and train horses that he would operate for the rest of his life. In spite of his many business interests through the years, Tilghman's true vocation was law enforcement.

In 1893, he was appointed deputy U.S. marshal, serving under the new U.S. Marshal E. D. Nix. This was the post that would bring Tilghman his greatest public notoriety. He soon became associated with two other notable deputies, Heck Thomas and Chris Madsen. Together, the three were dubbed the "Three Guardsmen," and they were given credit for clearing the outlaws out of Oklahoma Territory. In retrospect, some of their fame was well deserved, but much was fueled by tall tales, not true accomplishments.

Thomas and Madsen had both served under the previous U.S. marshal, William C. Grimes, in the U.S. District Court in Fort Smith, Arkansas, where cases were presided over by the famous "hanging judge" Isaac Charles Parker.

Both Madsen and Thomas were colorful characters, but they came from vastly different backgrounds. Madsen was a Dane born in 1851 in Denmark. He claimed to have served as a soldier in the Danish-German War and in the French Foreign Legion and to have fought on the side of the French in the Franco-Prussian War of 1870. No historian, however, has ever found record of any of that service.

Madsen came to America in 1876, possibly fleeing criminal charges in Europe, and immediately joined the U.S. Army. From 1876 to 1891, he served in the Fifth Cavalry, taking part in the Indian wars in the western United States. Much of Madsen's military service was in the Quartermaster Corps. At one point in his career, he did six months in prison for the illegal sale of government grain. In 1891, he was appointed a U.S. deputy marshal, in spite of his record.

Of the Three Guardsmen, Heck Thomas had the most experience and credibility as a lawman. Born in 1850 in Athens, Georgia, he was twelve years old when he accompanied his father, an officer in the Confederate Army, to the Battle of Second Manassas. Heck's father resigned from the army in 1863, and the family settled in Atlanta, Georgia.

After the war, the elder Thomas became the city marshal of Atlanta, and Heck served as a policeman under his father. In 1876, Heck Thomas moved to Texas, where he worked as a cowboy and then as a messenger for the Texas Express Company, guarding money and securities shipped by the railroad. In that capacity, he was involved in a train robbery carried out by the infamous Bass Gang. Although the robbery succeeded, Thomas

The Death of Bill Tilghman

received a commendation for hiding most of the money he was guarding from the unsuspecting robbers.

In 1885, Thomas was involved in his first notorious incident. Working as a bounty hunter out of Fort Worth, Texas, he and Deputy U.S. Marshal Jim Taylor hunted down and killed the Lee brothers, cattle rustlers wanted for the murder of another deputy U.S. marshal. In 1886, Thomas himself became a deputy U.S. marshal assigned to the court in Fort Smith. In 1888, he was wounded in the line of duty. Thomas also shot and killed Bill Doolin after Doolin had escaped from the Guthrie jail in 1896. Along the way, Thomas built a reputation for bravery in the face of danger.

CHAPTER FIFTY-EIGHT

The Wild Bunch

ONE OF THE PRINCIPAL TARGETS of the Three Guardsmen was the outlaw gang known as the Wild Bunch, or the Doolin Gang. The gang worked out of the lawless town of Ingalls, just east of Stillwater in Oklahoma Territory.

After robbing banks and trains in Kansas, Missouri, Arkansas, and Oklahoma Territory, the outlaws were known to sometimes hide out in the Osage Nation near Pawhuska, in Indian Territory, until things cooled off.

Led by Bill Doolin, the son of a sharecropper, the gang included at various times Bill Dalton, Charlie Pierce, William "Tulsa Jack" Blake, Charles Daniel "Dynamite Dick" Clifton (also known as Dan), William "Little Bill" Raidler, Roy "Arkansas Tom Jones" Daugherty, George "Red Buck" Waightman, and George "Bitter Creek" Newcomb.

The gang also had two teenage girls who gathered information and spied for the gang and went by the aliases of "Little Britches" and "Cattle Annie."

The Wild Bunch was a spin-off from the old Dalton Gang, which had been largely wiped out in a shoot-out in Coffeyville, Kansas, in 1892.

* * * * *

KENT FRATES

Before Bill Tilghman could get involved in hunting down the Wild Bunch, he was sent to bring the peace to Perry, a boomtown formed by the opening of the Cherokee Strip in a massive land run in Oklahoma Territory in 1893. It was not unusual for law officers of that period to hold more than one job. In his case, Tilghman was appointed town marshal of Perry while still remaining a deputy U.S. marshal. His time in Perry lasted only a few months, but combined with his previous tenure in Dodge City, it solidified his reputation as lawman known for taming wild frontier towns. He soon returned to Guthrie to concentrate on his duties as a U.S. deputy marshal.

When U.S. Marshal E. D. Nix gave his marshals the order to bring in the Wild Bunch, he authorized his men to do so "alive if possible—dead if necessary." Although the letter containing his directive might have been created years later for publicity purposes, history does support the sense of that order.

The first major effort to capture Doolin and his gang took place at Ingalls on September 1, 1893.

Deputy Marshal John Hixon had learned that the gang was openly staying in Ingalls and frequenting the hotel and saloon. Hixon gathered a force of fourteen lawmen, deputized them, and proceeded to Ingalls by horse and wagon. They found the gang drinking in the saloon, and the lawmen opened fire. A wild gun battle erupted. Three of the deputies were killed, along with a young bystander.

All the outlaws except Arkansas Tom Daugherty shot their way out and escaped on horseback. Arkansas Tom, who had been firing a rifle from the upper floor of the hotel, was captured and later tried and sent to prison. Bitter Creek Newcomb was badly wounded but escaped with the rest of the gang. Although most of the Wild Bunch escaped that day and continued to rob banks and trains in the months and years to come, they would all eventually be hunted down and captured or killed.

Tilghman was personally involved in the capture of Little Bill Raidler and Bill Doolin. In 1895, Tilghman learned that Raidler was hiding out in the Osage Nation just south of Elgin, Kansas. Along with two other deputies, Tilghman set up an ambush on a ranch where Raidler was sometimes known to eat his meals.

Tilghman was armed with a double-barreled shotgun, and when Raidler appeared on foot, Tilghman ordered him to put his hands up. Raidler drew

The Death of Bill Tilghman

a pistol and fired in Tilghman's direction instead. Tilghman knocked Raidler down with a load of buckshot, wounding him in six places. The outlaw survived long enough to be tried and imprisoned but died in 1903 because of complications from the shotgun wounds.

By late 1895, Bill Dalton, Tulsa Jack Blake, Bitter Creek Newcomb, and Charlie Pierce had all been killed either by deputy marshals or bounty hunters, but the leader of the gang, Bill Doolin, was still on the loose. That might well have been because Doolin had been lying low, spending time in New Mexico working as a cowboy and not out breaking the law. He had not taken part in any reported crimes since 1894.

Most historical sources have Tilghman capturing Doolin in Eureka Springs, Arkansas, in January 1896. According to Tilghman's account, he tracked Doolin to Burden, Kansas, where he learned that Doolin had moved on to Eureka Springs in hopes that the town's famous mineral baths would help heal an old gunshot wound.

Tilghman returned to Guthrie and then proceeded to Eureka Springs by train. There he found Doolin reading a newspaper in the waiting room of a local bathhouse. The element of surprise worked in the lawman's favor. Tilghman drew his gun on Doolin and captured him without firing a shot. In later years, Tilghman often recounted how he had asked the bathhouse proprietor to disarm Doolin while Tilghman continued to cover the outlaw with his gun, but the proprietor was so scared that he ran out of the building instead.

Tilghman brought Doolin back to Guthrie, arriving by train on January 16, 1896. More than two thousand people gathered to see Doolin brought in by the lawman. Interestingly, Doolin was neither handcuffed nor chained, and later there was speculation about whether he might have surrendered peacefully and Tilghman and Nix had concocted the story of the capture to make themselves look good. Doolin's subsequent acts would tend to refute the theory that he surrendered of his own free will.

While awaiting trial, the outlaw was jailed in Guthrie. Dynamite Dick Clifton, who had been apprehended recently in Texas, was also there.

On July 5, 1896, Doolin and Clifton led a jailbreak, assisted by other prisoners. The two outlaws overpowered and disarmed two guards and fled the jail. Doolin was on the loose again and had to be recaptured.

Heck Thomas figured that Doolin would go to see his wife and child. Edith Doolin was living near the small town of Lawson, Oklahoma Territory, at the time.

Thomas formed a posse and arrived in Lawson on August 24. Sure enough, about midnight, Doolin showed up and started to pack a wagon for a trip. The wagon with his family's belongings headed out, and Doolin commenced down the trail on foot, with his Winchester at the ready.

The outlaw had not gone far when Thomas yelled at him to surrender. Instead, Doolin fired in Thomas's direction, getting off two shots before the lawman cut him down with a single fatal shotgun blast.

Doolin's body was taken to Guthrie and, as was the custom of the day, photographed and put on public display.

The capture of Doolin made Tilghman a national hero. He had already gained recognition for bringing in Raidler, for civilizing rough frontier towns, and for many other arrests and shoot-outs, but it was the Doolin case that solidified his image as a lawman and established his reputation as an American hero for the rest of his life.

Tilghman's most notable achievement during his remaining tenure as a deputy, which ended in 1900, was being part of the posse that found and killed Little Dick West in 1898. West, the last member of the Doolin Gang still on the loose, was found hiding on a farm not too far from Guthrie. When the posse discovered him, he resisted arrest, firing at the officers. The outlaw was shot and killed by Deputy William Fossett and Logan County Sheriff Frank Rinehart.

CHAPTER FIFTY-NINE

Sheriff and Police Chief

SINCE ACQUIRING THE Bell Cow Ranch in 1891, Bill Tilghman had made his home in Lincoln County, Oklahoma Territory, where he bred and trained racehorses, some of which had success at tracks around the country. Given his local address and national reputation, it was no surprise when Tilghman was elected sheriff of Lincoln County in 1900.

In the same year, Tilghman's wife, Flora, became ill and died. Tilghman married Zoe Agnes Stratton in 1902, and the couple had three children. Zoe Tilghman would later gain fame as an author of thirteen books and numerous stories and articles. At one time the literary editor of *Harper's Weekly*, she also served as assistant director of the Oklahoma Writers' Project. Her writings, both fiction and nonfiction, were based on western stories, usually involving lawmen and outlaws.

By all accounts, Tilghman did a good job as sheriff for Lincoln County, handling lots of cases and making many arrests. His most sensational case involved the murder of an eighteen-month-old child. The two women suspected of the crime fled the area, but Tilghman tracked them to Gainesville, Texas, arrested them, and returned them to Lincoln County, where they were tried and found guilty of murder.

But all was not as it should have been for a lawman.

In 1904, Tilghman was faced with accusations regarding fees and travel expenses that he had charged to the county. He decided not to run for reelection, although he reversed that decision a few years later, running again in 1907. He was defeated by only 176 votes.

If he was not wanted at home, the same could not be said of the country. Still commissioned in 1905 as a deputy U.S. marshal, Tilghman was given a special assignment to travel to Mexico in hopes that he could find and bring back J. L. Fitzpatrick, who had been charged with embezzling money from the Frisco Railway.

Tilghman found Fitzpatrick working for a railroad in Mexico and arrested him in Aguascalientes. He transported Fitzpatrick to Mexico City and later brought him to the United States after the extradition formalities were completed.

In 1909, Tilghman was pressed into service to help look for the Creek renegade Chitto Harjo, popularly known as "Crazy Snake." Neither Tilghman nor the Oklahoma National Guard, which Governor Charles N. Haskell has called in to lead the search, ever found Crazy Snake, who is believed to have died in 1911 either in the Choctaw Nation or in Mexico.

Although Tilghman liked to dismiss any idea of becoming a politician, he did in fact run for the Oklahoma state senate in 1910. He was elected to represent Lincoln and Pottawatomie counties but did not stay long in that office—his first love came calling. By 1911, he had taken his next job in law enforcement as chief of police of Oklahoma City.

The city had been operating as a wide-open home to saloons, gambling, and prostitution. Whit M. Grant, the new mayor, had won office on a pledge to clean up the town. Grant chose Tilghman as his police chief because of his experience in other unruly communities, such as Dodge City and Perry, and his reputation as a U.S. deputy marshal.

Given free rein to clean house, Tilghman started off with a bang, raiding gambling houses and busting bootleggers and prostitutes. The cleanup campaign faltered only when Grant received political pushback from the local businessmen who profited off the illegal entertainment. Relations between Grant and Tilghman became strained, and in 1913, Tilghman resigned as police chief.

The Death of Bill Tilghman

Tilghman's next move was to make an all-out campaign to be appointed U.S. marshal for the Western District of Oklahoma. Tilghman used every bit of political influence he could muster but fell short of his goal when President Woodrow Wilson appointed Dr. J. Q. Newell. Although Newell, a medical doctor, had no qualifications as a marshal, he had what it took to get the job—political influence, having served as a state senator from Noble County.

CHAPTER SIXTY

The Three Guardsmen Go Hollywood

WHILE BILL TILGHMAN HAD BEEN serving off and on in law enforcement, the other two Guardsmen had continued their careers as lawmen without interruption.

In 1901, Heck Thomas had moved to Lawton, Oklahoma Territory, where he served as the first chief of the Lawton Fire Department and then police chief until 1909. He went on to serve as a deputy game warden and again as a deputy U.S. marshal until his death in 1912. Chris Madsen continued to hold a position as deputy U.S. marshal.

When Teddy Roosevelt formed the Rough Riders during the Spanish-American War, he called on Madsen to act as his quartermaster. Madsen put together the supplies for the group but never left Florida, staying behind while the Rough Riders fought in Cuba.

As for Tilghman, after his stint as Oklahoma City's police chief, he largely stayed out of law enforcement until his last job, in 1924. In the interim, he took up a new career, this time as a filmmaker, once again trafficking on his reputation as a frontier lawman.

In 1914, Tilghman joined forces with Nix and Madsen to make *The Passing of the Oklahoma Outlaws*. The silent motion picture was inspired at least partly by the success of a movie made by Al Jennings, a convicted train robber who had received a presidential pardon from Teddy Roosevelt and become famous after a series of articles about his outlaw days appeared in the *Saturday Evening Post*. In what could only be called a sign of the times, Jennings not only made a movie but also ran for governor of Oklahoma. He would not have been the only crook ever elected to that position, but he came in a sad third in the Democratic primary in 1914.

The Three Guardsmen took another lesson from Jennings's success in Hollywood. Believing that his film gloried outlaws, the three ex-marshals announced that their movie would tell the "real truth" behind the notorious crimes of Oklahoma outlaws. They planned to film in the locations where events had occurred and to use some of the former deputies and lawmen and even an outlaw who had been involved. In fact, the final result was a combination of fact and fiction, often embellishing the involvement and bravery of the Three Guardsmen.

The movie was shot in and around Chandler and completed in 1915. For the next few years, Tilghman supported himself by traveling the country with the film and giving talks before and after it was screened. The movie was accompanied by a display of firearms and memorabilia connected to the three marshals' fight against crime. No complete version of the film exists, but a twenty-minute segment of very poor quality can be found in the Library of Congress and has been transferred to video.

Hollywood, in the end, provided no happy ending. The outlaw movie made by the three lawmen was only mildly successful, although it did provide Tilghman with a badly needed source of income at the time.

By that point in his life, Tilghman had experienced more change than most people—from the day of the buffalo to the age of the automobile, from the lawlessness of frontier towns to the rise of big-city, anticorruption police forces.

Thus far, he had managed to make a place for himself wherever he landed. But with his horse ranch producing little revenue and his movie income on the wane, Tilghman could have been forgiven if he had begun to wonder if there was still a place for an old ex-lawman like him in the world. His doubts would be resolved by one last job.

CHAPTER SIXTY-ONE

Cromwell

NEEDING WORK, TILGHMAN CALLED in some political chips. The result was a new job for Tilghman as a special investigator for Governors James B. A. Robertson and Martin E. Trapp, but it was Tilghman's relationship with Trapp that led to his last, fatal assignment in Cromwell, Oklahoma.

A town spawned by the Seminole oil boom, Cromwell sprang from nowhere in a matter of weeks in Seminole County in 1923. Catering to oil-field workers, most of whom were transients, Cromwell was soon a den of sin and corruption where gambling, drugs, prostitution, and alcohol flourished.

How Tilghman ended up in Cromwell, the authority under which he was there, and the real reason for his being there remain obscure. For sure, his presence was related to his association with Governor Trapp and the local district judge, George C. Crump.

Something of a Boss Hogg character, George Crump was the decider-in-chief when it came to political matters in Seminole County. He used his judicial and political clout to influence local politics and often clashed with both County Attorney Walter Billingsley and Sheriff Blanch Doyle. Evidence also suggests Crump himself had financial interests in some of Cromwell's less than legal businesses. That might explain why it seemed that while Crump was cracking down on some establishments, his enforcement of the law appeared to be selective, leaving plenty of illegal businesses to operate freely.

Legend has it that Tilghman was approached by a group of honest Cromwell businessmen, an oxymoron, and asked to clean up the town. The group had supposedly formed a local chamber of commerce headed by W. E. Sirmans, an oil and gas lease broker. That assignment would have been consistent with Tilghman's work in Dodge City, Perry, and Oklahoma City, and there might be some element of truth to it.

In the end, Tilghman was in Cromwell for only a few weeks, so it is difficult to know for sure what his purpose for being there was. What is known is that sworn testimony at the trial of Wiley Lynn indicated that Tilghman's enforcement of the law in Cromwell, like Crump's, appeared to be highly selective and might have been influenced by graft.

A clue to the source of Tilghman's motivation for taking the job can be found in an article in the Cromwell newspaper dated September 12, 1924. According to this front-page story, Tilghman was named chief of police "with authority to act also in the surrounding district. His authority for taking charge comes from Governor Trapp and commissions from Judge George C. Crump of the District Court and Sheriff Blanch Doyle."

Cromwell was not an incorporated town, so no one had the legal authority to appoint Tilghman to act as its chief of police. Crump, as district judge, also had no power to "commission" Tilghman as Cromwell's police chief, and Trapp later disclaimed that Tilghman was acting as his agent. Doyle later testified that he had appointed Tilghman as a deputy sheriff, and because Tilghman did make at least one arrest during that time, this was apparently the source of his authority.

Whatever the purpose of the people who convinced Tilghman to take the job, his own motivation was clear. He was seventy years old and in poor health. Madsen had advised him not to take the job, but Tilghman needed the money, which reportedly included a salary of four hundred to five hundred dollars per month, making him the highest-paid law enforcement officer in the state.

Taking the job would be more a matter of necessity than of choice, and it led to his ultimate demise. But who is to say Tilghman would have wanted

The Death of Bill Tilghman

it any other way? To go out with his boots on rather than withering away in a hospital bed is likely the way the legendary lawman would have chosen to die. In the end, Tilghman's death would only add to the many legends about his life.

CHAPTER SIXTY-TWO

Bloody Death

ON HIS ARRIVAL IN CROMWELL, Tilghman quickly crossed paths with Wiley Lynn, the local U.S. Prohibition officer. Historic accounts often portray Lynn as corrupt, but no actual evidence has been found to support such claims. In fact, Lynn was in good standing on his job and made numerous arrests for violation of liquor laws during 1924.

A resident of the Madill, Oklahoma, area with a father who was a policeman, Lynn was a former deputy sheriff in Marshall County and might have served on the Madill police force. There is no record that he had any problems in either of those jobs. Evidence was presented at Lynn's trial that he and Tilghman had had trouble with each other and that bad blood existed between the two men. Tilghman had accused Lynn of dealing with bootleggers and drug dealers, and Lynn had accused Tilghman of selling confiscated whiskey. This animosity no doubt played a part in what happened when Lynn and Tilghman confronted each other in front of "Pop" Murphy's Dance Hall in Cromwell the night of November 1, 1924.

The details from that night remain in question, but the final result of the confrontation between the two men is not in dispute: Lynn shot Tilghman to death at close range.

Wiley Lynn would go on trial for killing one of Oklahoma's most famous lawmen. No transcription of the Wiley Lynn trial exists or was likely ever made, so newspaper reports of the trial—some including sworn statements—are the principal source of information about what happened in that courtroom. According to contemporary news accounts, the testimony of eyewitnesses was varied and conflicting. The following version is based largely on these newspaper accounts—discounting much of Zoe Tilghman's book *Marshal of the Last Frontier*, which was a compilation of hearsay and speculation, and Oklahoma historian and former police officer Glenn D. Shirley's book *Guardian of the Law*, which appears to have relied mainly on Mrs. Tilghman's recounting of the event.

* * * * *

It all began with a doomed road trip.

At 10:00 p.m. on November 1, 1924, Wiley Lynn arrived in Cromwell in a Ford touring car accompanied by some rather suspect company: Rose Lutke, Eva Caton, and David Thompson, an army sergeant on furlough from Fort Sill, Oklahoma.

Lutke and Caton were both proprietors of what they claimed were rooming houses in Wewoka, Oklahoma. And maybe on some nights the businesses were just that, but Judge Crump had already closed Lutke's business for operating as a bawdy house, and conventional wisdom held that Caton's establishment was a house of prostitution.

Although it was the era of Prohibition, Thompson and Caton were said to have been drinking heavily that evening, and Caton appeared to have been drunk. Thompson later testified that, in fact, Lynn had furnished the booze, and all four people in the car had been drinking.

Lynn was driving the foursome, and he parked the car across from Murphy's Dance Hall on Shawnee Street, the main drag in Cromwell. He had no more than stepped out of the car than the pearl-handled .45-caliber automatic gun he was carrying fired into the ground. The pistol could have fired accidentally because it had reportedly been malfunctioning or it could have been a test. No one could say for sure. The only thing not in dispute was that the gun did go off.

The Death of Bill Tilghman

With gun still in hand, Lynn approached the front door of Murphy's, followed by Lutke. Thompson and Caton remained in the car. Tilghman, who was inside the dance hall, heard the shot and stepped out onto the porch with his own gun drawn.

It all happened very quickly. When Lynn approached him, Tilghman jammed his gun into the Prohibition officer's side and pushed him up against the wall. Lynn's gun was in his right hand, and Tilghman grabbed that wrist and pushed Lynn's hand above his head.

Tilghman then called for help in disarming Lynn, and Hugh Sawyer, a deputy working with him, stepped up and twisted the gun from Lynn's hand. In the instant that followed, Lynn, using his left hand, pushed Tilghman's hand away and drew a second gun from a holster and fired three shots, two of which hit Tilghman in the stomach, fatally wounding Tilghman.

In Lynn's version of the incident, Tilghman also got off a shot intended for Lynn as Lynn pushed Tilghman's hand away.

Without stopping to see what damage his shots had wrought, Lynn turned his second gun on Sawyer and demanded the return of his .45 automatic. Sawyer turned the pistol over to Lynn, and Lynn ran to his car and, along with his companions, left town immediately.

Tilghman was carried into a nearby store but died in a matter of minutes. Some two hours later, Lynn turned himself in to U.S. Commissioner Park Crutcher in Holdenville in Hughes County, about twenty miles away. Lynn and his companions were placed in the Hughes County jail. Both Crutcher and Hughes County Sheriff Sam Turner later testified Lynn did not appear to have been drinking and was not intoxicated.

Although it might have initially seemed as though Lynn was fleeing the scene of a crime, he might have just been concerned for his own life. Rather than take his chances with Tilghman's friends and associates in Cromwell and Seminole County, he instead surrendered to federal jurisdiction, which he and later his lawyers deemed proper in view of his status as a U.S. Prohibition officer. Leaving Cromwell could well have been a quick-witted decision to protect himself and his companions rather than an attempt to flee from justice, as it had been portrayed.

The matter grew murkier when Lynn produced a search warrant issued by Commissioner Crutcher authorizing a search of Murphy's Dance Hall.

Lynn claimed he had been attempting to carry out a raid on the dance hall when Tilghman blocked him and threatened his life. Lynn contended that the shooting was in self-defense. As for his merry crowd of fellow travelers, Lynn said Lutke was accompanying him to search the women who worked at the dance hall and were known to conceal liquor under their dresses.

The testimony of eyewitnesses as to what had occurred was varied and confusing. Three sworn statements, by Lutke, Sawyer, and A. I. Sinclair, were published in the November 3, 1924, edition of the *Oklahoman*.

Lutke's statement supported Lynn's version of the incident. Indeed, she was quoted as saying that Tilghman yelled, "You—bleep—we got you now" and fired off a shot before Lynn did.

Sawyer's statement, however, differed from everyone else's account of what had happened that night. He testified that he was around the corner at Carroll's Drug Store when the altercation began:

"I came back around the corner. I saw the captain and Lynn struggling in front of Murphy's place. Uncle Bill had Lynn locked up against the wall, and both of his, Lynn's hands were up over his head. He had a pearl-handled six-shooter in his right hand, and Uncle Bill said, 'Hugh, get his gun.' I ran up and wrenched the gun out of Lynn's hand, and Uncle Bill crumpled at the edge of the sidewalk. I had heard two or three shots before I came around the corner and think Uncle Bill was shot before I got there."

Because the gun that killed Tilghman was a revolver and Lynn's other gun was an automatic, Sawyer appears to have been wrong on which gun he removed from Lynn's right hand. And no one else thought Tilghman had been shot before Lynn was disarmed.

The third sworn statement was by A. I. Sinclair of Ponca City, who was in Cromwell looking for work. Sinclair, who said he was standing across the street from Murphy's at the time of the altercation, claimed to have seen the whole thing:

"I saw someone across the street come up to the man (Lynn) and they began scuffling. This was on the sidewalk in front of the dance hall. I don't know whether the man who was scuffling with him had a gun or not. I saw their hands go over their heads and the gun which looked like the same gun the man had when he got out of his car, was in one of their hands. I couldn't tell which. I heard someone say, 'Get the gun,' and saw another man grab the

The Death of Bill Tilghman

pistol, but just before he got the gun I heard two shots. The crowd began to gather in and I didn't see anything else."

News of Tilghman's death swept across the state.

Governor Trapp called Judge Crump to the capitol and reportedly discussed declaring martial law in Cromwell. No such action was taken, but Attorney General George Short did begin an investigation, sending Assistant Attorney General Edwin Dabney to Cromwell. Dabney was also assigned to assist County Attorney Walter Billingsley in prosecuting Lynn. Newspapers across the state landed on the same side, portraying Tilghman as a law enforcement hero and publishing accounts of his legerdemain, some of which were true and some of which were highly exaggerated or even fanciful.

Tilghman's body lay in state in the state capitol rotunda for two days, attended by a guard of honor.

A funeral was held in Oklahoma City at First Presbyterian Church, with some eight hundred people present. Tilghman's pallbearers included Governor Trapp, former Governor Robertson, General Roy Hoffman, and Alva McDonald, U.S. marshal for the Western District of Oklahoma.

After the funeral, Tilghman's body was taken by train to Chandler, where he was buried.

CHAPTER SIXTY-THREE

Legal Maneuvering

THE FIRST LEGAL PROCEEDING involving Wiley Lynn took place on November 7, 1924, when Commissioner Crutcher held a bond hearing in Holdenville. Crutcher was acting under the authority of a statute giving the federal court jurisdiction over Lynn's actions, if Lynn was a federal officer acting under the authority of his office at the time of the shooting.

Hugh Sawyer, Roscoe Lutke, C. B. King, and W. E. Sirmans all testified at the hearing. Contrary to his prior statement, Sawyer now claimed he had heard no shots at all. Sirmans, aka Sermans or Seirmans, testified that he had stood within three feet of the men during the entire affair and that no shot was fired by Tilghman. It should be noted that Sirmans had been inside the dance hall with Tilghman and had gone outside after he heard the first shot.

According to Sirmans, he did not hear either of the men speak to each other, but Tilghman did shove his gun into Lynn's side and call for help in taking his gun. With that done, Tilghman released Lynn, who pulled another weapon and fired three times.

The report of King's testimony, on the other hand, is conflicting. In one instance, it says that King "was not certain whether Tilghman fired one of the shots." In another, it says, "Tilghman ran out when the shot was heard, grappled with Lynn, fired one shot."

After hearing the evidence, Crutcher determined that Lynn was subject to federal jurisdiction and set his bond at ten thousand dollars. The bond was signed by Lynn's father, brother, two bankers, and two leading businessmen of Holdenville.

In spite of the claim of federal jurisdiction, Billingsley filed murder charges against Lynn. Lawyers for Lynn quickly obtained an injunction against state prosecution from U.S. District Judge F. E. Kennamer of Muskogee. Billingsley and Edwin Dabney, the assistant state attorney general assigned to the case, vowed to fight for the right to try Lynn in state court all the way to the U.S. Supreme Court.

Before any further proceedings occurred, however, Kennamer disqualified himself from the case at the request of the prosecution. He was a personal friend of Lynn's family and had helped Lynn obtain his job as a Prohibition officer. The question as to whether a state or federal court had jurisdiction had yet to be determined.

The hearing on this issue was conducted in early January 1925 by U.S. District Judge A. S. Van Valkenburgh of Kansas. Lynn testified along with Sergeant Thompson, Sirmans, Sinclair, and Mr. and Mrs. John H. Striff of Slick, Oklahoma.

Thompson testified that Lynn had been drinking prior to the shooting. Sirmans reiterated the testimony he had previously given before Commissioner Crutcher. Sinclair said he had heard Lynn say he was going to test his gun before he fired the shot into the street that attracted Tilghman's attention.

The Striffs, who had lived in Cromwell at the time of the shooting, said they had heard Lynn fire the shot into the street and then yell out, "Get out of the road you narcotic—bleep—" as Lynn started across the road to the dance hall. Lynn's lawyers called Hughes County Sheriff Sam Turner and Holdenville druggist Carl Stanfere, both of whom testified that Lynn did not appear drunk when they saw him later on the night of the shooting.

In the end, Judge Van Valkenburgh ruled that Lynn must stand trial in state court. He gave Lynn thirty days to appeal to the U.S. Circuit Court, but Lynn declined. On February 25, 1925, he surrendered to the sheriff of Seminole County. Once again, Lynn was released on a bond of ten thousand

The Death of Bill Tilghman

dollars and continued in his job as a Prohibition officer, pending trial. Judge Crump disqualified himself from hearing Lynn's case, and District Judge Frank Mathews of Mangum was appointed to preside over the trial.

Lynn was represented by W. W. Pryor, a prominent Holdenville attorney; W. M. Stokes of Wewoka; and George L. Sneed of Madill. The state's case would be made by Billingsley, Dabney, and two special prosecutors, S. P. "Prince" Freeling and Roy Hoffman.

The two special prosecutors were especially notable. Freeling was a former Oklahoma attorney general known for his courtroom prowess. Hoffman was an interesting historical character in his own right. He had served as an assistant U.S. attorney and state judge but was best known for his military career. After serving in the Spanish-American War as a captain, he had remained in the National Guard and rose to the rank of colonel. During World War I, he became a brigadier general and commanded the all-black 93rd Division in France in 1918, seeing frontline combat. After the war, he commanded the 45th Division, Oklahoma's National Guard unit, and retired in 1933 as a major general. Hoffman and Charles Tilghman, one of Tilghman's sons, were married to sisters.

CHAPTER SIXTY-FOUR

The Trial of Wiley Lynn

WILEY LYNN'S TRIAL WAS HELD in Wewoka and began on May 21, 1925. The Prohibition officer claimed that he had acted in self-defense while trying to carry out his official duties.

In keeping with Lynn's plea of self-defense, it was clear from the very start of the trial that the defense planned to try to discredit Tilghman and impugn his motives for being in Cromwell.

Beginning with the voir dire of the jury, W. W. Pryor implied that a corrupt conspiracy involving Tilghman existed, one that went all the way to the governor's office.

As the trial progressed, much of the defense's evidence in regard to Tilghman's alleged graft was excluded by Judge Mathews, who at one point admonished Pryor by saying, "I thought you were too good a lawyer to try to introduce this kind of testimony. You must think you can prove to me the moon is made of green cheese. … Even if you could prove all of this it wouldn't justify Lynn for killing Tilghman."

Most notable about the state's case was the witnesses that were not called: Eva Caton, W. E. Sirmans, and Hugh Sawyer. The sheriff could not find Caton and Sirmans to be served with subpoenas, and it was rumored that

Sirmans was in Florida. Although present, Sawyer was not called, probably because of the confusing nature of his original testimony.

However, in a bizarre legal ruling, Judge Mathews allowed Sawyer's prior testimony at one of the previous hearings to be read to the jury. The judge also allowed Sirmans's prior testimony to be read to the jury, presumably because of the state's inability to find the witness and subpoena his appearance in court.

The state did call several witnesses whose testimony proved damaging to Lynn. Sheriff Doyle affirmed Tilghman's appointment as a deputy sheriff, establishing that Tilghman was acting with legal authority that night in Cromwell. Sergeant Thompson testified with regard to the drinking on the trip to Cromwell and how Lynn had obtained liquor for the group.

Sinclair once again testified, although what he had seen was not definitive. J. J. Narral also stepped forward as an eyewitness, confirming that what he had seen was similar to Sirmans's version of the shooting. Albert B. "Blackie" Jones, who was serving time for possession of narcotics, testified that Tilghman had ordered Lynn to "drop the gun" and that instead of doing so, Lynn had made "a profane oath" before shooting Tilghman.

When the defense began its case, the temperature in the courtroom ratcheted up as a dispute over the admission of evidence regarding bribes supposedly paid to Tilghman immediately erupted. Judge Mathews excused the jury and listened to three witnesses give testimony about the alleged corruption.

J. H. Morgan, whose son had been previously arrested by Tilghman, testified that Tilghman had offered to "fix things" for a ten-dollar bribe. Mrs. B. A. Williams, a Wewoka widow, testified that Tilghman had told her not to invest in a building in Cromwell "till we get rid of Wiley Lynn" and said, "We are going to skid Mr. Lynn over." Marcelle Tucker, a former dancer at Murphy's from Slick, Oklahoma, testified that Tilghman returned her and two other girls to the dance hall after they had run away. Judge Mathews ruled all this testimony inadmissible, along with the testimony of fourteen similar witnesses.

The defense then proceeded with Lynn's theory of self-defense. Several witnesses tried to establish a motive for Tilghman to have killed Lynn. A deputy sheriff from Carter County, who had been in Seminole County to return a prisoner, testified to having heard Tilghman say in reference to Lynn

The Death of Bill Tilghman

that "if he doesn't quit fooling around me I'm going to get shut of him." A Cromwell druggist testified that he had heard Tilghman say Lynn wanted "to close up the town," and that if Tilghman could "get rid of Lynn," he could "make some money." The proprietress of a Cromwell rooming house testified that Lynn had raided her establishment and that Tilghman had threatened Lynn in her presence.

The most dramatic witness, however, was Lynn himself, who took the stand on his own behalf.

By all accounts, Lynn made a believable witness. Even an intense cross-examination by Dabney failed to shake him. Lynn recreated his version of the shooting, at one point physically demonstrating what had happened that night using his own gun, with Dabney playing the part of Tilghman.

According to Lynn, he had identified himself to Tilghman, declaring, "This is Lynn, Uncle Bill." Nonetheless, Tilghman still had pressed the gun into his side. Lynn said that he only prevented Tilghman from pulling the trigger by inserting the little finger of his left hand behind Tilghman's trigger finger. He then shoved Tilghman's hand away as Tilghman fired, drawing his other gun and shooting Tilghman. Lynn also pointed out that his right hand was crippled as a result of a threshing-machine accident and that he could not have fired a gun with that hand. Lynn's right index finger was gone, the middle finger stiff and extending upward, and the thumb stiff and extending straight. These defects were apparent to the jury.

Called again to the stand, Lutke affirmed Lynn's version of the event, testifying that Tilghman had grabbed Lynn by the throat, thrown him against the wall, and shot once, while Lynn shot three times. During the trial, Judge Mathews learned that Lynn had brought his loaded .45 automatic with him to court. Enraged, the judge refused to accept Pryor's explanation that the gun was going to be used as an exhibit in the trial and had Lynn disarmed.

The closing statements of the attorneys were more about Tilghman, Lynn, and the politics surrounding the case than about the facts. Freeling portrayed Tilghman as a frontier hero.

Billingsley and Hoffman assailed Lutke's character and the hypocrisy of Lynn's drinking and providing the "hellish liquid that he was supposed to stamp out" as a Prohibition officer.

As for the defense, W. M. Stokes and George Sneed attempted to portray Lynn as an honest underdog railroaded by the governor, implying Dabney had been ordered to "hound down a man regardless of his guilt."

The jurors deliberated for four hours on May 25 and were sequestered by the judge at 9:30 p.m. when they failed to reach a verdict. The next morning, they began deliberation at 8:30 a.m. At 10:45 a.m., after the fifth ballot, the jury returned a unanimous verdict of "not guilty."

Reportedly, the jurors on the first day of deliberation favored finding Lynn guilty by a vote of seven to five, but on the morning of the second trial day, they voted ten to two for acquittal. The vote changed to eleven to one for acquittal and finally to the unanimous verdict of not guilty.

What changed the jurors' votes is unknown, but it should be noted that at the time, and for years thereafter, Seminole County had a reputation for dubious jury conduct. The verdict entered, Judge Mathews managed to have a last say of sorts, finding Lynn guilty of contempt of court for having brought a loaded gun into the courtroom. He sentenced Lynn to ninety days in jail. Lynn was released on a bond of one thousand dollars and appealed the sentence. The final disposition of the contempt charge is unknown.

CHAPTER SIXTY-FIVE

Shoot-out in Madill

THE PUBLIC WAS GENERALLLY shocked by the verdict of not guilty. Oklahomans wanted to believe that their hero had been wrongfully killed and not shot in self-defense. Given the conflicting testimony of eyewitnesses and Lynn's apparently persuasive description of the event, however, it is not difficult to understand how the jury found at least "reasonable doubt" as to Lynn's innocence.

Zoe Tilghman was, of course, appalled by the verdict and quickly made her displeasure known. "The outcome of this trial has added a supreme dishonor to the law in Oklahoma," she said.

Rather than just getting mad, she decided to get even by writing a book on Tilghman's life, including her version of Tilghman's fatal shooting. Now long dead, she no doubt would be happy to know that her characterization of Lynn as a drunken, corrupt, and cold-blooded killer has been largely accepted as fact, even though clearer eyes might call such a description biased at best and largely unsupported in fact.

As for Lynn, he could have easily faded into obscurity as so many men have, but he did not. On July 23, 1925, he did resign from his job as a Prohibition officer. Later, he separated from his wife and returned home to the

Madill area, where it appears that he again served as a deputy sheriff. He was convicted or charged at least twice more with minor crimes, including public drunkenness.

In Madill, Lynn also came in contact with an old enemy and former fellow Madill deputy named Crockett Long. Tall and slim and always wearing a cowboy hat, Long looked every inch the western lawman. He hated Lynn, who it is said returned the favor. Long supposedly once even went to Lynn's house and physically beat Lynn. Long, who became the chief of police in Madill, might also have arrested Lynn at one point. The animosity between the two men had built over the years, even after Long was named an agent for the newly formed Oklahoma State Bureau of Investigation and was spending most of his time in Oklahoma City.

Lynn's animosity for Long boiled over on Sunday, July 17, 1932. Long, who frequently visited Madill, was sitting in the Corner Drug Store talking to friends when a drunken Lynn entered the store with gun in hand. Witnesses reported that Lynn yelled, "Crockett Long, throw 'em up. I'm gonna get you sometime and it might as well be now."

Long, who was hard of hearing, initially did not hear Lynn but then turned in his direction and saw the gun. Long yelled for Lynn to put down the gun, while drawing his own pistol, and both men let fly. Long was immediately shot in the leg and crawled toward his nemesis, emptying his .44 Smith & Wesson at Lynn while Lynn advanced, firing his .38 at Long.

Each man was hit five times and both died as a result of his wounds.

Tragically, two of Long's shots passed through Lynn's body and hit two innocent bystanders. One was wounded, and the other, a young boy named Rudy Watkins, was killed.

Thus, two men made their place in Oklahoma history—Wiley Lynn as the infamous killer of two renowned Oklahoma lawmen and Bill Tilghman as a classic western hero.

The Case of the Talking Pharmacist

"Loose lips sink ships."

—Slogan from a World War II poster

CHAPTER SIXTY-SIX

Case #6: The Case of the Talking Pharmacist

IN THIS ERA OF STANDING one's ground, just how far can you go in defending yourself? In 2011, one Oklahoma pharmacist found out. The question was set in play on the evening of May 19, 2009. Pharmacist Jerome Ersland was at work behind the counter of Reliable Discount Pharmacy at Southwest Fifty-eighth and Pennsylvania Avenue, in southwestern Oklahoma City, Oklahoma. Two female coworkers were at work that night in the small store.

Just prior to closing time, at about 5:50 p.m., two men wearing masks burst into the store and demanded at gunpoint money and drugs.

That was not the first time the store had been robbed, and that prior experience came into play. According to a store safety plan, the two women ran to the back of the store, and one called 911.

Meanwhile, Ersland pulled a gun.

Shots were fired.

The entire incident took place in less than one minute.

When police arrived at the scene, they found a young black man lying dead in a pool of blood on the pharmacy floor, with Ersland and the other employees safe and apparently unharmed.

Ersland would initially be hailed as a hero for protecting his coworkers and himself, only to be charged later with murder for the killing of the sixteen-year-old armed robber, Antwun "Speedy" Parker.

The controversy over whether Ersland should have been charged with any crime at all began almost immediately and continues to this day. His case sparked strong opinions from gun owners, the local African-American community, gun-control advocates, and just plain ordinary citizens. As the case rumbled its way toward a final verdict, it was difficult to find anyone who did not have an opinion on Ersland's guilt or innocence.

Yet regardless of the facts, perhaps the single determining factor in the outcome of the case became the garrulous personality of Ersland himself and the statements he made to both the police and the media.

CHAPTER SIXTY-SEVEN

The Talking Pharmacist

IMMEDIATELY AFTER THE SHOOTING, an excited Ersland called 911. By then, the 911 operator had already spoken with Jeanne Read, one of the employees who had fled to the back of the store, and police officers had been dispatched to the scene.

In his call, Ersland identified himself as "Colonel" Jerome Ersland and then gave a quick recap of what had happened: "There was two of them; they came in with guns . . . both shooting . . . they both had guns. . . . I got one. He's dead."

The first policeman to arrive at the scene was Kevin Long, who had been on patrol only four blocks away. Long entered the pharmacy and found fifty-nine-year-old Ersland, wearing a back brace, behind the counter. A young black man lay on the floor next to the counter; he had been shot and appeared to be dead. He was later identified as Parker. Ersland told Long, "They started shooting, and I didn't want them to hurt the girls."

The crime scene was then secured, and crime-scene investigation personnel and homicide detectives were dispatched to the pharmacy. Not long afterward, a few blocks away from the pharmacy, police arrested Emanuel Dewayne Mitchell on a complaint of possessing a stolen Honda.

Mitchell was on foot when he was arrested. A witness had observed him in the Honda earlier, picking up a young black man who appeared to be running from the pharmacy. Mitchell crashed and abandoned the Honda a few blocks from the store.

Sergeant Pearl Stonebreaker arrived at the scene and was assigned to drive Ersland to the police station for an interview with homicide detective David Jacobson. Because of his bad back, Ersland requested to sit in the front seat of the patrol car.

During the short ride to the station, Stonebreaker engaged Ersland in what she later describe as "chitchat." She asked him about his back brace, and he said he had been "injured in a Humvee accident in the [Gulf] war." Noticing a bandage on his arm, Stonebreaker inquired whether he had been hurt in the robbery." Ersland blamed it on a ricocheted bullet from the incident. He also volunteered that he suffered from posttraumatic stress disorder and still had nightmares as a result of his military service.

Ersland was not a suspect or under arrest at that time. Indeed, he was being treated as a victim and a witness.

At the police station, Ersland was placed in a small room with a desk and two chairs and then was interviewed by Detective Jacobson at about half past ten. The interview was videotaped.

With more than sixteen years on the force, Jacobson had served as a patrolman for nine years, with mounted police for two years, with the assault squad for one year, and as a homicide detective for four years. A veteran himself, having served four years in the U.S. Marine Corps and then the Navy Reserve, Jacobson approached Ersland politely and with the deference warranted a veteran. He kept his questions to a minimum.

Given Ersland's personality, however, questions were hardly necessary. He launched a protracted diatribe about the robbery and himself. Much of what he said would later prove to be fanciful at best. Ersland had begun to talk his way into prison.

* * * * *

Ersland began his narrative with an apology.

He told the detective he was sorry he had to kill the young robber, but he

The Case of the Talking Pharmacist

had to do it. He volunteered that he had "killed a number of people with a .50 caliber, I was a platoon leader, Fort Bragg." Ersland also said that he had "PTSD from the Gulf War," and he had "killed a lot of people but I had to do it." He also claimed his back problems stemmed from injuries from a mortar blast. Those statements all proved later to be false, greatly eroding Ersland's credibility with the public and the jury.

From that point, Ersland moved on to how the robbery had happened. His mouth quickly overran his brain as he described events that simply had not occurred.

Ersland knew the store had surveillance cameras that would have recorded most of the happenings of the evening. Why he would tell a story contrary to the facts, which almost certainly had been recorded, remains inexplicable. Perhaps his tale was fueled by an overwhelming desire to be considered a hero or maybe he was delusional.

Ersland would later claim he had been under stress at the time of his first police interview, which is certainly a possibility given what he had just gone through. Yet police videotape shows not the slightest nervousness or indecision on pharmacist's part as he talked to Jacobson. In fact, during the interview, Ersland spoke calmly, with an almost childlike demeanor and directness. One can only speculate at what the outcome of the case might have been had Ersland simply kept his mouth shut in those first hours following the shooting.

Instead, the pharmacist provided the detective with a play-by-play description of the attempted robbery. According to Ersland, two masked robbers entered the store—both armed with cheap black handguns, probably .38 or .357 caliber—and demanded all the money and drugs.

Ersland said one robber came around the nearest end of the front counter while the other robber circled the other end, trapping Ersland behind it. The robbers began to shoot and got off two shots at Ersland. Ersland drew a Kel-Tec .38 handgun from his pocket and grabbed from the counter drawer a gun he called "the Judge." It was loaded alternately with .44-caliber bullets and .410 shotgun shells.

As Ersland told it, he then engaged in a two-handed gun battle with the robbers, shooting Parker left-handed with the Kel-Tec. Parker fell, and the other robber ran from the store. As Ersland rounded the corner of the counter to chase after the fleeing robber, Parker rose from the floor, and Ersland shot him five more times. In Ersland's words, "he (Parker) kept staying up."

Finally, Ersland said, he exited the store and fired again at the fleeing robber, who had run to a white Oldsmobile parked nearby. The driver of the Oldsmobile was armed with a shotgun, but Ersland said he pointed his gun at the driver, and the driver said, "I'm getting the fuck out of here" and sped away in the car alone. The stranded robber took off again. Ersland said he fired at and thought he hit him with a .410 shell from the Judge, but it proved to be too great a distance for the shot to fell him.

Ersland returned to the store, checked on the two employees, and called 911. He thought he had fired ten shots and the robbers two shots. Noting the bandage on his arm, Ersland told the detective he had been "nicked" there by a bullet; otherwise, he thought the robbers were "firing high."

The Ersland interview happened so soon after the attempted robbery that Jacobson had yet to see surveillance videos or receive any results from the crime-scene investigation, so he had no reason to doubt Ersland's account. Jacobson concluded the interview by assuring Ersland he had acted in self-defense, and "you had to do what you had to do."

Being the veteran policeman that he was, Jacobson also informed Ersland that the police would investigate the attempted robbery and give the results to the district attorney. He explained that the district attorney was the only person who could bring charges. Ersland ended the interview by expressing a concern about getting sued.

CHAPTER SIXTY-EIGHT

The Surveillance Videos

WHILE JEROME ERSLAND WAS being interviewed at the station, the police were at the crime scene collecting the surveillance videos and other evidence. They found two video cameras inside the store and one outside. Officer Ken McBride collected the surveillance tapes and took them back to the police station. There, Detective Jacobson, his partner Ron Porter, and McBride viewed the videos sometime after midnight. What they saw differed dramatically from Ersland's version of events.

The videos, which are easily accessed online, show an armed figure in a knitted face mask—later identified as fourteen-year-old Jevontai Ingram—entering the store. Ingram pointed a handgun at Ersland and kept it trained on him while the teen danced from side to side near the cash register.

Parker followed Ingram into the store, pulling on a mask similar to Ingram's as he entered. Parker was not armed. He settled to the right of Ingram, facing the counter and Ersland. Ersland shot Parker, who fell to the floor.

Faced with a gun-touting pharmacist, Ingram rabbited out the door, having never fired a shot. In fact, his gun was later found to have been unloaded.

Ersland stepped from behind the counter and went out the front door carrying a gun. The outside camera picked up Ersland returning to the store after only a few seconds outside. As he reentered the store, he was once again visible on an inside camera.

Ersland walked past Parker, who was sprawled on the floor but not visible on the tape. Ersland walked behind the counter again and pulled another gun from what appeared to be a drawer in the counter. He then deliberately walked around the counter and back to where Parker was lying, leaned down, and fired five shots point-blank into Parker.

That was all caught on tape. Ersland then turned and returned to his position behind the counter. At no time after he was shot the first time was Parker visible on the surveillance tapes.

The entire incident was over in less than a minute.

CHAPTER SIXTY-NINE

The Robbers

THE FIRST OF THE ROBBERS to be identified was the deceased Antwun Parker. Only sixteen, Parker was a student at Seeworth Academy who loved basketball. He had not had any prior trouble with the law and was described by one neighbor as a "typical young man."

It did not take the police much longer to arrest Jevontai Ingram. Only fourteen, Ingram was identified as the pistol-carrying robber who had accompanied Parker into the store. Ingram's mother, Natasha Spigner, said of her son, "My baby is fourteen years old. My baby goes to school faithfully; my baby's an honor-roll student. If they weren't encouraged by these older people that were involved, it wouldn't have happened."

The arrest of her son allowed the police to connect two older men to the crime—thirty-one-year-old Emanuel Dewayne Mitchell and forty-three-year-old Anthony Devale Morrison. According to Ingram, the two men planned the robbery, supplied Ingram with an unloaded gun, and told him and Parker what to demand while in the store. Mitchell also drove Parker and Ingram to the pharmacy in the stolen Honda and then picked up Ingram as he fled the scene afterward. Both Mitchell and Morrison had extensive criminal records. Mitchell had previously been convicted of robbery and kidnapping, had served thirteen years of a twenty-year sentence, and was on probation at the time of the robbery. Morrison had multiple previous convictions for armed robbery and assault and at one time had also escaped from prison. He had been out of prison less than a year before taking part in the pharmacy robbery.

Initially, Oklahoma County District Attorney David Prater announced that he would not charge the three robbers with murder because of Ersland's intervening acts, but after further review of state law, Prater changed his mind and charged all of the robbers with felony murder. Under Oklahoma law, those who help to plan a robbery in which an accomplice dies can be prosecuted for murder.

The D.A. did choose to treat Ingram as a juvenile because of his age and his willingness to cooperate in the case against Mitchell and Morrison.

CHAPTER SEVENTY

The Charge

JEROME ERSLAND'S ORIGINAL statement on the night of the crime was not his last word on the subject. As the investigation proceeded, he kept right on talking.

On May 20, 2009, the day after the robbery, he gave a television interview on KOCO Channel 5 and another interview to the state's largest newspaper, the *Oklahoman*. In both interviews, Ersland said the robbers were shooting at him. He told the *Oklahoman*, "All of a sudden, they started shooting. They were attempting to kill me, but they didn't know I had a gun. They said 'You're gonna die'—that's when one of them shot at me, and that's when he got my hand."

Ersland also claimed, as he had in his original police interview, that he had shot Parker a second time when he saw the teen getting up as Ersland was leaving the store to chase the second robber. Up to that point, Ersland's insistence on this version of Parker's shooting, although false, was at least consistent. That would soon change.

On May 27, Ersland's own status abruptly flipped from hero to accused. District Attorney Prater filed first-degree murder charges against Ersland. Relying on the security videos, the autopsy report, and an examination of the crime scene, Prater concluded that Ersland had gone too far in standing his ground and had exceeded any reasonable standard of self-defense.

Prater showed the surveillance videos to the press. He said Ersland was justified in shooting Parker in the head with the first shot, but he broke the law when he returned to the store, retrieved a second gun, and then shot Parker five more times while he lay helpless on the floor.

According to Prater, the autopsy report concluded that Parker was not yet dead at the time, but was disabled and unconscious when Ersland fired those last five shots into his prone body.

Prater seemed to realize that his decision would not play well with everyone, because he added, "I do not want the charging of Jerome Ersland with first-degree murder to have a chilling effect on any person legitimately in a position to defend themselves from an assailant."

The charging of Ersland was immediately controversial. Social media, Internet chat boards, and blogs erupted with commentary. Gun advocates damned Prater for his decision while they continued to praise Ersland for defending himself and his fellow employees. As many people on both sides pointed out, the entire incident would never have occurred if Parker and Ingram had not committed armed robbery in the first place. In the minds of many people, the robbers were fair game once they entered the store with a gun, and Ersland, who was acting with fear for his life and the lives of others, was justified in taking action.

But were there limits to the action allowed a person in such a situation?

Just what did constitute enough force or too much force?

On that point, Prater was clear: The killing of a prone defenseless person, even if he was a robber, was murder.

There was no denying that the video was damning to Ersland. On returning to the store, the pharmacist walked right past Parker, turned his back on the robber, obtained a second gun, returned, leaned over, and fired five shots point-blank into Parker's prone, unconscious body. That was clearly not the scenario that Ersland had originally represented to the police and the media.

CHAPTER SEVENTY-ONE

Bail

DAVID PRATER HAD BEEN THE district attorney of Oklahoma County since 2006, when he was narrowly elected over the incumbent district attorney, Wes Lane, in a hotly contested race. Prior to becoming district attorney, Prater had served on the Norman, Oklahoma, police force and had been an Oklahoma County assistant district attorney and an Oklahoma assistant attorney general.

At one point, Lane had fired Prater, but he returned to defeat his old boss, in part because of the backing of the Fraternal Order of Police. The FOP had issues with Lane and saw Prater as being sympathetic to police because of his law enforcement background.

Prater would later earn a reputation for prosecuting corrupt politicians, but at the time, he was still a political neophyte, and deciding to prosecute Ersland took guts and commitment on his part. He would be going against a stand-your-ground fever that had reached a boiling point in states such as Oklahoma.

Ersland hired well-known Oklahoma City criminal-defense attorney Irven Box. A former marine, Box had served as an Oklahoma City policeman, an assistant district attorney in Oklahoma County, and a legal adviser to the

Oklahoma City Police Department. In 1975, he went into private practice. An experienced and successful criminal attorney, Box was also widely known as a legal analyst for a local television station. He was easily recognizable on the street because of his preferred choice of business attire: a nice suit, a pocket-handkerchief, and distinctive running shoes. Box didn't know it yet, but he had just taken on a difficult client, one who would make his case more difficult and harder to win.

Accompanied by his lawyer, Ersland surrendered to the police and was jailed. He did not remain in jail long. The next day, a bail hearing took place before the assigned District Judge Tammy Bass-LeSure. The judge ordered bail of one hundred thousand dollars and denied Ersland access to guns, knives, or other weapons. Ersland was also ordered to wear an ankle monitor and to be restricted to his home other than for work or church, to shop for groceries or eat, or to see his doctors or attorneys.

The weapons restriction led to an unusual exchange between the judge and Prater. Prater did not oppose bail, but he thought Ersland should have access to a gun at the pharmacy for protection. The D.A. said he worried that criminals would think it was "open season" at the pharmacy if they knew Ersland was unarmed. He also suggested to the judge that Ersland could be fired if not allowed to carry a gun.

The judge asked Prater if he felt that way, why had he charged Ersland in the first place? Obviously irritated by the question, Prater responded that Ersland had gone too far in shooting Ingram five more times, but added, "I'm the one who charged him, so my butt's on the line."

When the judge refused to modify the restriction on weapons, Prater protested, "That's wrong." After the hearing, Prater told Ersland, "I want you to be treated fairly."

It was clear that Prater was conflicted about the case. As a former policeman and a prosecutor, Prater had no love for criminals, nor did he want to discourage citizens from protecting themselves legally. However, in the case of the pharmacy shooting, he believed Ersland had gone beyond self-protection.

The controversy over Ersland's guns was not over either. Another hearing was held before Judge Bass-LeSure three days later to verify to the court that Ersland had complied with the judge's order to disarm. Ersland swore he had

The Case of the Talking Pharmacist

given all his weapons to Box. Box said he had accepted the guns as down payment on his fee. The judge asked Ersland for a list of the weapons only to get an unexpected reply from his attorney.

Box claimed the guns were now his, not Ersland's, and as such, he did not have to give the judge any such list. When the judge asked Ersland how many weapons he had turned over, Box instructed his client to exercise his Fifth Amendment rights. Prater also agreed that it would be prejudicial for Ersland to answer such a question.

Infuriated, the judge threatened at first to revoke Ersland's bail if he refused to answer her question. Neither Box nor Ersland budged. Finally, Judge Bass-LeSure relented, saying that in the future, she would not let a defense attorney receive a defendant's weapons.

CHAPTER SEVENTY-TWO

Still Talking

JEROME ERSLAND WAS NOW officially charged, but that did not stop him from talking publicly about the case. In fact, he took his story national. On June 1, he was interviewed by Bill O'Reilly on the Fox News Channel. By then, Ersland's story had changed. He acknowledged shooting Parker after returning to the store as Parker lay on the floor rather than on his way out while chasing Ingram.

He told O'Reilly: "I went up to him and he started talking to me and he started turning to the right. . . . I'm crippled. And I knew . . . when he got up, if he was just dazed, that he could kill me. . . . I thought I was going to get killed in the next few seconds. . . . I still think he had a gun." He also continued to insist that Parker had brought a gun into the pharmacy and fired at him, even though the video showed otherwise.

The O'Reilly interview was not the last time Ersland would make a nonjudicial statement about his shooting of Parker.

On July 8, he inexplicably sent a letter to the Oklahoma State Bureau of Investigation telling yet another story. This time Ersland said he had shot Parker because he was trying to get up and posed a threat to him. In the letter, Ersland wrote, "As the robber in the corner began to climb up the bookcase with his right hand, he yelled, '---- you,' and slipped on the floor, so I saw my chance to end the threat and went for the backup gun and shot him just as he slid down on the slippery surface. I was experiencing a tremendous amount of adrenaline."

Such public statements created a slippery slope, handicapping Ersland's defense and sliding Ersland toward conviction.

Ersland's statements provoked the district attorney to issue a subpoena for Ersland's military records. The defense objected on the grounds that the records were irrelevant, citing concerns about confidentiality and self-incrimination as well as possible violation of the Health Insurance Portability and Accountability Act, more commonly known as HIPAA, which protects the privacy of medical information.

The prosecution argued that Ersland had raised the issue when he claimed he suffered PTSD because of his military service and that the state needed the information to prepare in case Ersland claimed he was mentally incompetent as a result of his condition. Judge Bass-LeSure ruled in favor of the request. Ersland's attorneys asked the Court of Criminal Appeals to block the subpoena. The appeals court refused and the records were produced.

The records proved damaging to Ersland's credibility. It seems that Ersland was in the U.S. Air Force, not the U.S. Army, during the first Gulf War. During the fighting in Kuwait and Iraq from August 1990 to February 1991, Ersland was safely stationed at Altus Air Force Base near Altus, Oklahoma. No record existed of his being in combat or incurring any injuries in the line of duty.

Not all of Ersland's records were damning, however. They also revealed a good record for service, including commendations and an honorable discharge. But once again, Ersland kept talking.

Despite what his military records plainly showed, he continued to insist he had been in combat and had secretly flown to Iraq from Altus. One thing is certain, Ersland served as a pharmacist in the military and not as a .50-caliber machine gunner.

There was no good explanation as to why Ersland felt compelled to exaggerate his service record, which was exemplary. It was also true that his exaggerations had nothing to do with the merits of his case. Still, it all worked to make it increasingly difficult for him to testify on his own behalf—much less

The Case of the Talking Pharmacist

submit to cross-examination on the veracity of his many statements to the police and media.

CHAPTER SEVENTY-THREE

The Preliminary Hearing

ON NOVEMBER 4, 2009, A preliminary hearing on the Ersland case was conducted before Judge Gregory J. Ryan. Ersland was charged with one count of first-degree murder. To meet the burden of proof necessary to have Ersland bound over for trial, the state called five witnesses. Perhaps the most crucial of them was Dr. Collie Trant, the medical examiner who had conducted the autopsy on Parker.

Dr. Trant testified that Parker had been hit in the head by three particles, or slugs, apparently a .410 charge from Ersland's "Judge" handgun.

One of the slugs had penetrated Parker's skull and lodged in his brain. Trant said that was not a fatal wound. The shot had disabled Parker, but it had not killed him. Trant noted that any one of the subsequent five shots could have been fatal.

In the end, it was the volley of five shots fired by Ersland that the state contended caused Parker's death and made Ersland a murderer.

* * * * *

A string of witnesses then began to take the stand.

One of the first was Megan West, the daughter of Jeanne Read. Read was the employee who had made the first call to 911. West was the other employee who had fled to the back of the store that evening.

West testified that she and her mother were working alongside Ersland that night. For security reasons, the door to the pharmacy was locked but could be opened by hitting a buzzer behind the counter. Read, seeing what she thought were two customers approaching the front door, buzzed the pair in only to watch them charge through pulling on masks.

One of the two carried a gun pointed inside the pharmacy. West and her mother rushed to the back of the store. They could no longer see what was happening out front but could hear some of what was said. West testified to hearing Ersland say, "I got it"—followed by voices other than Ersland's saying, "Oh crap, he's got a gun" and "I'm going to shoot your ass" and then gunfire. After a pause in which West heard the front door of the store open, she heard more shots and then heard Ersland call 911.

The prosecution also called Tom Bevel as an expert. He was the same witness who had been called by the defense, with disastrous results, in the Dr. John Hamilton case. In Ersland's case, however, Bevel assumed his more usual role as a blood-spatter witness for the prosecution. He had reviewed photographs of Parker's body at the scene. Presented with the photos in court, Bevel stated that in his opinion, based on blood patterns, Parker had not moved after the first shot to his head.

Detective David Jacobson testified about his interview with Ersland and his investigation of the scene. He established that there was no evidence that Parker was armed or that Ingram had ever fired a shot.

Sergeant Detective Ron Porter was the state's final witness. A sixteen-year veteran of the police force, Porter identified the three security videos—two inside the store and one outside—that had captured the robbery and shooting. The videos were played for the judge and then replayed, with Porter supplying commentary.

The defense, as is typical at a preliminary hearing, offered no witnesses, but Ersland's lawyers did vigorously cross-examine all prosecution witnesses. At the close of the state's evidence, Box sought to have the case dismissed. In moving to dismiss the first-degree murder charge against his client, Box argued that at most, Ersland's actions might warrant a charge of first-degree

The Case of the Talking Pharmacist

manslaughter. In that regard, Box had the law on his side. Oklahoma law defines first-degree manslaughter as "unnecessary killing . . . while resisting an attempt by the person killed to commit a crime or after such attempt shall have failed." However, after considering the exhibits and his notes, Judge Ryan found sufficient evidence to establish probable cause on the first-degree murder charge, and Ersland was bound over for trial.

By the time of the hearing, Box had brought his two sons, Jeff and Steve, into the case to assist him. Joe Brett Reynolds, a former wrestling champion at the University of Oklahoma and a combative criminal-defense lawyer now deceased, had also joined the defense team.

For the state, Assistant District Attorney Jennifer Chance came aboard to work on the case with Prater. Chance, who would go on to be Oklahoma Governor Mary Fallin's attorney, was a felony supervisor at that time, experienced in the prosecution of murder cases and other violent crimes. She took a prominent role in presenting the evidence for the Ersland prosecution.

During the preliminary hearing, counsel on both sides treated one another with the normal amount of professional courtesy expected in a courtroom. There was no sign of the amount of personal acrimony and courthouse politics that would soon follow.

Shortly after the preliminary hearing, Judge Bass-LeSure ordered that television cameras would be allowed in the courtroom for the trial. The trial date was set for September 13, 2010. All seemed to be progressing toward a trial to begin on that date, until courthouse fireworks began to go off.

CHAPTER SEVENTY-FOUR

There Goes the Judge

O N AUGUST 30, THE MEDIA learned that the district attorney wanted Judge Bass-LeSure to recuse herself from the case. The news came as a shock to the Ersland team. According to Box, Prater had met with Bass-LeSure and the presiding judge, Patricia Parrish, without him present.

On August 31, Bass-LeSure held a meeting in chambers—this time with both Box and Prater. The judge announced that she was recusing herself from the case but did not give a reason.

Prater refused to comment on Bass-LeSure's decision, but an obviously angry Box accused the D.A. of "intimidation." Box also announced that he would move to have Prater removed from prosecuting the case. From that point forward, the attorneys engaged in a running feud, characterized by personal accusations and perceived slights on both sides. Their mutual animosity flared up at every subsequent hearing related to the case. Time would eventually reveal that Bass-LeSure, in an unrelated case, had engaged in private extrajudicial conversations with a criminal defendant who was also a personal trainer at her health club and whose case was pending in her court. She had given the defendant, Colton Taz Ama, the names of three lawyers and suggested hiring one of them despite the fact that Ama was already being represented by counsel. One of those recommended lawyers was Joe Brett Reynolds, one of the members of Ersland's defense team.

Ama reported the conversation to his lawyer, Rich Rice, who advised Prater of the improper contact. Prater then had Ama wired for a subsequent conversation with Bass-LeSure. As a result of that, Bass-LeSure was relieved of her duties on the criminal docket, although she continued to serve as a judge. Not long afterward, Bass-LeSure was charged, along with her husband, of criminal fraud in a phony adoption scheme; ultimately, she pleaded guilty to a felony, resigned, and was disbarred.

With Bass-LeSure recused, the case was immediately assigned to Judge Ray Elliott. Elliott had presided over many murder trials, including the John Hamilton case. His assignment to the Ersland case, however, further complicated the personal relationships involved because Box's wife, Isla Rodriguez, had worked for Elliott but had quit on less than friendly terms. One of Elliott's first rulings was to reverse Bass-LeSure's order and ban television cameras from the courtroom.

The change of judges resulted in a delay of the trial, but it also precipitated more action from the defense.

Box filed a motion requesting that Prater be removed as prosecutor on the case. The motion alleged that Prater had compromised Ersland's right to a fair trial by releasing the surveillance video and making public remarks about the case. Prater called the motion "baseless." Judge Elliot overruled the motion, and Prater continued as the prosecutor. It appeared that the trial would start in December, until another surprise delay arose.

Calling into question Judge Elliott's ability to act impartially, Box requested that Elliott recuse himself during a private hearing in Elliott's chambers—the first procedural step for the removal of a judge. When Elliott refused, Ersland was then entitled to a public hearing on the motion to recuse. Such a hearing would be conducted before the judge being asked to recuse—in this case, Judge Elliott.

Box quickly obliged, filing a formal request to remove Elliott. The defense cited three reasons why Elliott should not be the judge in the Ersland case. First, Box asserted that the judge had given him advice about how to defend the case a few weeks before the case was assigned to Elliott. Second,

The Case of the Talking Pharmacist

Box noted that Elliott's wife, Sandy Elliott, an assistant district attorney, had engaged in conversations with Elliott directly related to the case. And third, Box noted that Elliott had used ethnic slurs that raised a question of bias. The third allegation was curious given that the ethnic slurs were supposedly against Hispanics, and neither Ersland nor the robbers were Hispanic.

The hearing for removal took place over two days, December 6–7. It quickly degenerated into a barrage of personal accusations and acrimonious responses. Adding to the hostile atmosphere was another new accusation. According to Prater, Jennifer Chance had been the subject of inappropriate and unprofessional remarks from both Irven Box and Joe Brett Reynolds, whom Prater had banned from the district attorney's office.

Both Box and Rodriguez testified, along with the judge's bailiff, Tarryn Henderson. Box testified that Elliott had suggested an argument he thought Box should make on Ersland's behalf at trial. Rodriguez, who was Hispanic, then recited conversations in which Elliott had referred to Hispanics as *wetbacks* along with other disparaging remarks. Evidence was also introduced to show that Sandy Elliott had furnished the judge with a copy of an Oklahoma Supreme Court opinion dealing with whether cameras should be allowed in the courtroom.

Prater called three witnesses: Judge Kenneth Watson, an African-American; Robert Ravitz, the Oklahoma County public defender; and Ron Wallace, a criminal-defense lawyer. All three said they believed Elliott to be a fair and impartial judge who had never exhibited any kind of racial prejudice.

At the conclusion of the hearing, Judge Elliot made a lengthy statement. He denied having given Box advice regarding the defense of the case. Elliott admitted using the term *wetbacks* but explained it was because he had been angry at delays and incompetence associated with the repair of the roof on his house and that the term was directed at workers on his house who were illegal immigrants, not Hispanics in general, and he harbored no prejudice against Hispanics. The judge said he had not discussed the Ersland case or any other criminal case with his wife but only had asked her to supply him with a copy of a written decision of the Oklahoma Supreme Court because he had left his own copy at home. Elliot concluded his remarks by refusing to recuse.

Ersland remarked to a member of the press, "I didn't know this was going to be about Irven and his wife. I thought this was going to be about my case."

Regardless of the merits of the attempt to remove the judge, the threat was not over yet. Box appealed Elliott's ruling to the presiding judge of the district court, Bill Graves. After argument and briefing, Graves issued a detailed written order sustaining Elliott's decision and refusing to remove him from the case.

Undeterred, Box appealed to the Oklahoma Criminal Court of Appeals, which sustained Graves's order. It was clear Judge Elliott would hear the case.

The failure to remove Elliott proved to be bad news for the defense. Trying to remove a judge by a party to a case is something like attempting to kill the king. You had better be damn sure you pull it off because if you fail, you will still have to deal with his authority.

CHAPTER SEVENTY-FIVE

Two Robbers Go to Court

BEFORE JEROME ERSLAND COULD finally be tried, Emanuel Dewayne Mitchell and Anthony Devale Morrison were brought to trial in Oklahoma County District Court.

Prior to their trial, their young accomplice Jevontai Ingram had pleaded guilty to first-degree murder in juvenile court—again, the result of his having been an accessory in a crime in which an associate was killed, even though Ingram did not do the killing. Ingram went on to be the principal witness against Mitchell and Morrison, testifying as to how the two felons had planned the pharmacy robbery to get drugs to sell in Tulsa. The two men had supplied Ingram and Antwun Parker with masks, clothes, and an unloaded gun, and Mitchell had driven the boys to the scene of the crime.

The defense lawyers argued that the robbery was over before Ersland shot Parker, and so the defendants had not killed anyone. Prater pointed out that the crime was the cause of Parker's death and that by his calculation, only one minute two seconds had elapsed between the time the robbers entered the store and the time Ersland fired the last shot.

The jury found both Mitchell and Morrison guilty of first-degree murder and sentenced each of them to life imprisonment. They also sentenced

Mitchell to thirty-five years and Morrison to thirty years for conspiracy to commit robbery. The jurors also found Mitchell guilty of stealing the Honda and gave him ten years on that charge.

The highlight of the trial, however, happened during the district attorney's closing argument during the sentencing phase. As Prater was speaking, Mitchell sprang from his seat behind the defense table and slugged Prater in the head. Prater pushed Mitchell into the spectators' gallery and landed on top of him before Mitchell could be restrained by sheriff's deputies. Prater suffered cuts on his nose and cheek and an abrasion on his jaw. Mitchell was taken to the hospital with a dislocated shoulder. It was not Mitchell's first violent outburst. Prior to the trial, he had attacked another prisoner in the Oklahoma County Jail and had threatened his own lawyer. Mitchell had also demanded that he be allowed to represent himself without a lawyer, a request denied by the trial judge, Kenneth Watson.

Assistant District Attorney Jennifer Chance recalled in a later interview that trying the robbers first had been helpful to the prosecution in the Ersland trial. For one thing, prosecutors learned that the jurors in the Mitchell and Morrison trial also believed Ersland was guilty of murder. That helped the prosecution in its jury selection in the Ersland case as well as when it came time to prepare the evidence that would be used to make the state's case against Ersland.

CHAPTER SEVENTY-SIX

The Trial

THE ERSLAND CASE FINALLY WENT to trial on May 16, 2011. The laborious task of selecting a jury took four days as prospective jurors were questioned by Judge Elliott, the prosecution, and the defense.

As often happens in high-profile cases, it was difficult to find jurors who had not heard about the Ersland case or had not already formed an opinion as to his guilt or innocence. There were also the issues regarding a person's right to own a gun and defend himself, about which many Oklahomans have strong opinions.

The jury eventually selected on May 19 included eight women and four men, along with two female alternates. None of the jurors was black.

Prior to opening statements, a hearing was conducted regarding the admissibility into evidence of Ersland's video statement to the police made on the night of the shooting. The defense challenged the statement on the grounds that Ersland had not received a Miranda warning and had been coerced. A hearing was conducted on that topic outside the presence of the jury. Detective David Jacobson testified that Ersland was not a suspect at the time of the statement, was not under arrest, and gave his statement voluntarily and willingly. After hearing Jacobson's testimony, the judge overruled the objection and declared the statement admissible. Although the ruling was not unexpected, it was yet another blow to Ersland's defense because Ersland's statement contained numerous falsehoods.

After the lawyers made their opening statements, the prosecution began a parade of witnesses designed to pin down the sequence of events that had occurred at the pharmacy that night. As she had at the preliminary hearing, Megan West testified about what she had heard and seen inside the pharmacy about the robbery.

Outside the pharmacy that same evening, Michelle Powell and her teenage son Kaleb Powell were moving a boat in their driveway, three houses down from the pharmacy on the other side of Fifty-Eighth Street. Kaleb was in his pickup in the middle of the street, and his mother was standing in the front yard helping to direct him.

Michelle Powell testified that while helping her son, she noticed a white man, whom she later learned was Ersland, standing outside by the corner of the pharmacy as a young black man fled the store. She testified that Ersland held a gun in a two-handed stance as he fired three shots at the fleeing youth. Meanwhile, she yelled to her son to take cover because he was near Ersland's line of fire, and she feared for his safety. Kaleb Powell responded by jumping out of the truck and hiding behind it.

Both Powells then saw the black teen get into a silver-colored Honda that took off going east, away from the pharmacy. They followed the car, which crashed a few blocks away. The young black man jumped out and took off running again, while the driver, an older black man, walked away from the wreck. When the police arrived, they quickly found the driver and took him into custody. The Powells' story conflicted with Ersland's account that he had confronted an armed man in a white Oldsmobile parked close to the pharmacy after the failed robbery.

A paramedic dispatched to the scene by EMSA, Levi Sutliff, testified that when he arrived on the scene that night, Ersland had asked him for a bandage for a small scratch on his wrist that did not appear to be a gunshot wound. That testimony once again debunked another of Ersland's prior statements.

Several police personnel were called to testify as to their part in investigating the crime. Each added some fact that buttressed the prosecution's case or identified an important piece of evidence, including the three surveil-

The Case of the Talking Pharmacist

lance videos. Kevin Long testified that he saw no weapon in the proximity of Parker's body. Pearl Stonebreaker testified about Ersland's talk of war injuries and being shot in the robbery during her conversation with him on the way to the police station, again establishing that more of his statements were false. Detective Jack Sullentap of the computer-forensics division of the Oklahoma City Police Department described collecting the surveillance videotapes from the store, converting them to a disc, and showing them to Jacobson and Porter at the station that night.

As the lead detective on the case, Jacobson testified as to the details of the investigation, going over Ersland's video statement and pointing out Ersland's many untrue assertions. Among them were the statements that Ersland suffered from PTSD from the Gulf War, had been injured in combat, and had killed people in the war. More important, Jacobson showed that Ersland had lied about the facts of the robbery and shooting, including stating that both robbers entered with guns, that both robbers had shot at him, and that he had returned fire with two guns, one in each hand.

Jacobson also pointed out Ersland's statement that before he ran out of the store after the second robber, he had shot Parker five times in response to Parker rising from the ground as if to attack Ersland. The claim that Parker was getting up was proved patently false by the video evidence.

One key witness when it came to supporting the prosecution's case of murder was Dr. Chai Choi. The medical examiner who had performed the original autopsy and testified at the preliminary hearing, Dr. Trant, was no longer with the medical examiner's office and so was unavailable to testify. Thus it was necessary to call another M. E. to establish the victim's cause of death, and the task fell to Choi. Choi based her testimony on her predecessor's original examination of Parker's body and Dr. Trant's autopsy report, including X-rays of the deceased.

According to Trant's report, the first shot fired by Ersland struck Parker in the head above his hairline. What was later identified as a .410 pellet fractured Parker's skull and pierced his brain. Another pellet creased Parker's head but did not penetrate the skull. In Choi's opinion, the head wound would have created "a loss of conscious probably quickly."

When asked if the first wound would have been immediately fatal, Choi replied, "Probably not." She observed that Parker might have survived the head wound, given that he was alive when he received the additional five gunshot wounds to his chest and abdomen. As to the cause of death, Choi's opinion was that Parker had died of "multiple gunshot wounds to the head and abdomen, all six together."

Choi's testimony was crucial in establishing the murder charge against Ersland. The first shot to Parker's head was clearly fired in self-defense. If the head wound was immediately fatal, then the subsequent shots fired by Ersland would have been into Parker's already dead body and not a foundation for a murder conviction.

Another significant part of Choi's testimony was her opinion that the first shot would have rendered Parker immediately unconscious. That conclusion precluded Ersland's contention that Parker remained a threat that had to be dealt with further.

Box effectively cross-examined Choi, including at one point making it clear that Choi disagreed with Trant's original characterization of Parker's head wound as "nonfatal." Box's questions also established that Dr. Andrew Sibley, the acting head medical examiner after Trant's departure, had also disagreed with some of Trant's findings. That previewed part of the defense's case that was to be based on Sibley's opinion.

On redirect, Choi testified that rather than describing Parker's first wound as "nonfatal," the appropriate description should be "potentially fatal." In other words, the head wound by itself might or might not have killed Parker. However, Choi stuck to her opinion that Parker was alive when he was shot by Ersland an additional five times.

The prosecution next called Tom Bevel, the independent blood-spatter expert who had previously testified at the preliminary hearing. Bevel testified that in his opinion, Parker had never moved after being hit by the first shot. Bevel based this in part on the undisturbed pool of blood found under Parker's head and the absence of blood on Parker's gloves. The lack of blood on the gloves indicated that Parker had never moved his hands to his injured head or raised them in defense of Ersland's subsequent gunshots.

A three-dimensional reconstruction based on that evidence and portraying the state's version of the case was then presented by crime-scene investigator Sergeant Everett Baxter. The reconstruction showed a crime consistent with the state's evidence. Although the reconstruction was not necessary to

The Case of the Talking Pharmacist

prove the state's case, it was persuasive and was another tool in the district attorney's attempt to persuade the jury to find Ersland guilty of murder.

Dr. Laura Black-Wicks was called to further discredit Ersland. A family physician, Black-Wicks saw Ersland in her office on July 22, 2009, about two months after the shooting. At that appointment, Ersland complained of a gunshot wound to his wrist that he was concerned had become infected. The doctor examined Ersland and found two wounds, one on each side of the same wrist, too far apart to be covered by one bandage. She ordered an immediate X-ray.

When the X-ray came back, the doctor examined it outside of Ersland's presence and found two metallic particles in one of the wounds. When she returned to the exam room to discuss her findings with Ersland, to her surprise, he had already removed the fragments from his own wrist. He asked the doctor not to document what had happened, but Black-Wicks told Ersland she had to include her findings in her records. She subsequently saw Ersland again, and that time, at his request, she prescribed an anti-inflammatory salve even though his wounds seemed to have healed and had not been deep enough to affect his bones.

The only possible conclusion from the doctor's testimony was that Ersland had, subsequent to the shooting, inflicted a wound on himself, going so far as to place metal fragments in it to make it appear to be a gunshot wound. Such bizarre behavior haunted Ersland throughout his trial, giving him the appearance of guilt.

* * * * *

After the prosecution rested, the defendant presented a written stipulation setting out the testimony of Dr. Andrew Sibley. His opinions were noteworthy, particularly as to the possibility that Parker could have moved after having been hit by Ersland's first shot.

Although Sibley agreed with Choi that Parker was likely rendered unconscious by the head wound, Sibley also thought that Parker could have moved spasmodically even though not fully conscious. Such movements could have led Ersland to believe Parker was still dangerous, provoking Ersland's second volley of five shots.

Jeanne Read was called on to testify as to her state of mind that night, which she did, mentioning not only her fear but also her reliance on Ersland that he would protect her and her daughter. However, like her daughter, Read had not seen what occurred after the initial invasion and their flight to the back room of the pharmacy.

In the end, Ersland elected not to testify on his own behalf.

Given his original statement to the police and his many subsequent and shifting and contradictory statements regarding the shooting, this was an understandable decision by Ersland and his attorneys. If Ersland had taken the stand, he would have been ripped to pieces on cross-examination, compliments of his own words. He also would have had to explain the mysterious "gunshot" wound on his wrist that had only appeared months after the crime. Yet despite knowing Ersland's problems and vulnerabilities, Box gave last-minute consideration to the idea of his client taking the stand. This was born out of his feeling that the trial was not going well. Box raised the possibility with his sons and Reynolds. The others were all strongly against it, but Box decided to talk with Ersland one more time to see just what his client's testimony might be if he were to take the stand. That conversation made it clear to Box that Ersland's proposed testimony would only make matters worse.

Ersland's inability to testify did hurt his defense. In many ways, the pharmacist was a sympathetic defendant: a veteran, a solid citizen, and a man who had willingly risked his own life to protect the lives of two coworkers. And in spite of the medical testimony, Ersland might have raised some doubt as to whether Parker remained a danger to him and the others after being hit by that first shot. Ersland most certainly could have taken the stand and defended himself had he not so freely spilled out fanciful stories to the police and public before the trial.

In the end, it was the defendant who destroyed his own defense.

When both sides had rested, a legal argument arose over one of the jury instructions. Neither party had purposed an instruction on first-degree manslaughter even though the facts justified such an instruction as a lesser included crime. Instead, both parties had decided to go for broke on the first-degree murder charge.

Judge Elliott, however, decided to give an instruction that the jury could find Ersland guilty of first-degree manslaughter. After reflection, Prater agreed

The Case of the Talking Pharmacist

with the judge, but Box objected. Ultimately, Elliott gave the instruction over the objection of the defense.

The punishment for conviction of murder in the first degree, when the state is not seeking the death penalty, is either life imprisonment or life without parole. The punishment for first-degree manslaughter is four years to life.

Prior to the Ersland case, Oklahoma's stand-your-ground laws had applied to people in their residences, but not in their workplaces. As a result of the Ersland case, the legislature changed the law to include places other than a residence. The change, however, was made after the pharmacy robbery and therefore too late to apply to Ersland's trial. The jury did, however, receive instruction on self-defense.

Chance made the first argument for the state. She emphasized that Parker was unconscious on the floor when Ersland was shot him five times. In her words, in that moment, Ersland made himself "judge, jury, and executioner." Although pressing for a murder conviction, Chance did allude to the first-degree manslaughter charge, stating that Ersland was certainly guilty of that crime as well.

When it was his turn, Box noted all the factors that justified Ersland's acquittal, portraying the pharmacist as a man who, while under threat to his own life, acted bravely to protect himself and his two fellow employees. He described Ersland as a veteran with a clean record who was both a victim and a hero and who had had only seconds to react to an armed threat.

At that point, Box asked the jurors to close their eyes and visualize the action in the store as the robbers entered with gun drawn. At the end of forty-five seconds, he asked the jurors to open their eyes, in an attempt to help the jurors understand the brief span of time involved and the extreme pressure Ersland had been under while dealing with the threat.

As he wound down, Box that conceded Ersland had, indeed, spouted some "goofy" statements, but Box reminded the jurors that those statements had not altered the facts.

The district attorney made the closing argument for the prosecution. During his argument, Prater played the security video for the jury again, repeatedly reminding jurors of Ersland's many lies and concluding that Ersland had lied "about everything." Prater also called attention to Ersland's acts after he reentered the store, including how he had walked near or stepped over

Parker and then turned his back on the fallen robber before returning to shoot him the second time. That evidence, Prater argued, showed that Ersland no longer saw Parker as a threat and so had no reason to inflict further deadly force.

Prater also made a revealing point about Ersland's mind-set that evening, remarking that Ersland had been prepared with three guns available and a plan as to how to "handle it" in case of a robbery at the store, almost as though he was looking forward to a chance to shoot someone. That attitude might explain Ersland's subsequent attempts to turn the shooting into what sounded like a wild gunfight, with himself as the hero.

* * * * *

After some three hours of deliberation, the jury found Ersland guilty of murder in the first degree and recommended a sentence of life imprisonment. They declined to opt for the lesser crime of first-degree manslaughter and a more lenient sentence. Some of the jurors were emotional when they announced the verdict, and it appeared some had struggled to arrive at what they felt was a just result.

The *Oklahoman* quoted one juror as saying, "It was a really hard day."

Another juror described it as "a very emotional day," noting that, "We're judged by the laws of our society. You have to live with those laws. Tough or not, you still have to live with those laws."

Given the life-threatening situation into which Ersland was thrust on the evening of May 19, 2009, as well as the actions he took to protect himself and the other employees, it seemed remarkable that the jury had reached a unanimous agreement on the murder charge and only in a matter of a few hours. No one would have been surprised if such a case at such a time in the country's history had resulted in a hung jury, leading to a mistrial.

Instead, the jury put emotion aside and followed the law. What convinced them to do so? Maybe the deliberate, cold-blooded way Ersland had walked past Parker's prone body, retrieved the second gun, returned, leaned down, and pumped five shots into the motionless Parker and then lied about it.

As for Ersland, the pharmacist received the verdict stoically. He was immediately taken into custody and checked into the Oklahoma County Jail.

The Case of the Talking Pharmacist

Apparently he had prepared for the worst, having already given away his dog, but soon the talkative pharmacist resurfaced, with Ersland telling the media he was "shocked" by the verdict and "innocent of everything."

CHAPTER SEVENTY-SEVEN

After the Verdict

THE VERDICT DID NOT END THE controversy over the case. Ersland still considered himself a hero and now viewed himself as a victim of the system. His propensity to talk to the press also continued unrestrained. Before he had been in jail long, he was complaining that he had been denied access to medicine for his back and was "suffering in misery." He also claimed he had received more than one hundred death threats since being jailed.

Oklahoma County Sheriff John Whetsel responded to those accusations by saying that Ersland was being held in a small medical cell by himself for his own safety and was receiving adequate food and health care. Whetsel also explained that it was against jail policy to allow a prisoner the opiate-based medicine Ersland used for his back pain.

Ersland, however, was not the only person outraged by his conviction. Some of his friends and supporters began to aggressively circulate a petition asking the governor of Oklahoma to grant Ersland a pardon. Their efforts succeeded in collecting seventeen thousand signatures. When the petition was presented to Governor Mary Fallin's office, Fallin released a statement that Ersland must follow the legal process for an appeal. She also punted the issue to the Oklahoma Pardon and Parole Board, saying she would review the matter only on the board's recommendation.

On July 11, 2011, at a formal sentencing hearing, Judge Elliott, as expected, followed the jury's recommendation and sentenced Ersland to life in prison. Ersland was shortly thereafter transferred to the state prison facility in the rural community of Lexington in central Oklahoma.

An appeal was filed, and the case began to wind its way through the appellate process, but as usual with Ersland, nothing proceeded in an orderly manner.

In 2012, Ersland fired Box and retained a new lawyer, Doug Freisen. Known as the "gun lawyer" for his expertise in legal matters related to the ownership and use of guns, Freisen quickly called a press conference. Before the gathered media, Freisen blasted Box's handling of the case and announced that one of Ersland's grounds for appeal would be ineffectiveness of counsel. Box retaliated by denouncing the accusation as a "publicity stunt" and calling Freisen "unethical and unprofessional." Given Box's vigorous defense of Ersland and the difficult nature of his client, his reaction was understandable.

Before the Oklahoma Court of Criminal Appeals could rule on the appeal, Ersland made more front-page news.

In February 2013, Cleveland County District Attorney Greg Mashburn charged Ersland with possession of contraband in prison. At Ersland's request, his thirty-six-year-old son, Jeff Ersland, had smuggled two patches containing fentanyl, a powerful pain reliever, into the prison. A guard had discovered the patches in Jerome Ersland's pocket after his clumsy attempt at concealment. When confronted, Jeff Ersland admitted that he had made a mistake in trying to help his dad, understandable but still against the law. The bad publicity certainly did not help Ersland's chance of securing a pardon or parole. Later, Ersland pleaded guilty in the contraband case and was sentenced to an additional two years in prison. Jeff Ersland pleaded no contest and received a sentence of two years' probation.

For Ersland, the hits just kept on coming. On June 20, 2013, in an unpublished opinion, the Court of Criminal Appeals affirmed Ersland's conviction and sentence. The court denied all the grounds for appeal. The opinion exhaustively and painstakingly rejected each specific argument Ersland had made regarding his theory that he had had ineffective counsel.

The Case of the Talking Pharmacist

* * * * *

Still, Jerome Ersland continued to fight for a new trial. In May 2014, Freisen filed an application for postconviction relief asking for a new trial, claiming newly discovered evidence.

In support of the application, Ersland claimed he had recalled evidence that he had previously been unable to remember because of his PTSD. He stated that the PTSD was a result of his reaction to a 2007 robbery at the pharmacy—even though he had not been present when the 2007 robbery occurred and even though he had previously said the PTSD stemmed from his military service. Among his new revelations about the 2009 robbery: The Kel-Tec was in his pocket rather than in a drawer, and he had heard Parker moaning and seen the teen's arm move while he was on the floor.

Freisen also claimed to have conducted a reinvestigation and recreation of the event and, in doing so, he had found that the bullets Ersland claimed to have heard buzzing past him were actually ricochets of his own shots rather than shots fired by the robbers. Ersland also produced an affidavit from a doctor claiming that Ersland might be suffering from Asperger's syndrome, which would have rendered him incompetent at the time of the shooting.

Prior to his trial, Ersland had posted photographs on his website that purported to show bullet holes in the wall of Reliable Discount Pharmacy. Assistant District Attorney Jennifer Chance sent police investigators to examine the supposed bullet holes. The police found a punchboard with holes in it hung in front of the wall. The holes possibly had been made by a pencil or other object, but no bullet holes were in the wall behind the punchboard. Contrary to Ersland's theory, the investigators also found no evidence of any ricochets from his own weapon.

Unable to produce any new evidence to support his ricochet theory, Ersland nonetheless continued to argue that if given a new trial, he would have the chance to present new evidence that could lead to his acquittal.

Judge Elliott denied the application when it was presented to him. His ruling was appealed to the Court of Criminal Appeals, which likewise denied the application.

Ersland has now filed a request for a writ of habeas corpus in the U.S. District Court. As this book goes to press, that request has not been ruled on.

Epilogue

WHILE JEROME ERSLAND SAT in jail and pursued his various appeals, the robbers who had, in a way, helped to put him there also continued to make news.

Jevontai Ingram was released from juvenile custody when he turned eighteen. Back in society, he almost immediately vandalized his mother's car, pleaded guilty to a misdemeanor, and was returned to custody for an additional four months. After his second release, he violated the terms of his probation, and a warrant was issued for his arrest. Ingram was arrested again in December 2013 when he was shot in the head at an apartment complex in Moore, Oklahoma. Police believed the shooting to be gang related.

In July 2014, Ingram kicked in the door of a Del City apartment and kneed a pregnant woman in the stomach. He was charged with first-degree burglary, assault and battery, domestic abuse by strangulation, domestic abuse committed against a pregnant woman, malicious injury to property, and first-degree robbery. In May 2015, he pleaded guilty to some charges and received a seven-year jail sentence.

Emanuel Dewayne Mitchell also resurfaced. He appealed his original robbery conviction, alleging that he should have been allowed to represent himself in court as he had requested. Never ask for something unless you are sure you want it. The Court of Criminal Appeals granted Mitchell's request and ordered a new trial. He got his chance to represent himself, and the jury rewarded him with a harsher sentence, a verdict of life without parole.

Mitchell then appealed, arguing that he was denied counsel. The Court of Criminal Appeals affirmed Mitchell's sentence, somehow managing to do so without laughing.

As for the outcome of the Ersland case, it remains hard to believe.

Oklahoma is a gun-friendly state and one that preserves the Old West tradition of turning to firearms for self-defense. Although Ersland's acts in retrieving a second gun and then firing it into an apparently helpless young man seem to go beyond reasonable self-defense, the overall circumstances themselves certainly warranted a strong response. Ersland could just as easily have ended up dead that night, along with his two coworkers. At the most, one might have expected a jury to find Ersland guilty of first-degree manslaughter, a charge that also would have fit the crime.

With that said, the only thing certain about jury trials is that they are unpredictable, and the Ersland case once again proved the point.

Some gun advocates have blamed Ersland's defense lawyers for the conviction, but the Court of Criminal Appeals found defense counsel competent in every way. Indeed, a review of the transcript of all the proceedings confirms that Box and the other defense lawyers filed motions and vigorously and competently raised objections, cross-examined witnesses, and argued their client's case.

Some people might explain the verdict in the Ersland case as a sign that Americans still adhere to a legal system that protects the rights of both the victim and the accused and that those who would tread too far in either direction should do so with caution—and be prepared to serve time if they overstep.

Still, the answer to the outcome of the Ersland case most probably lies in the personality of Ersland himself. District Attorney David Prater might well have hit on something when he argued that Ersland behaved that night as if he was looking forward to being robbed—perhaps so he could use his arsenal of guns, perhaps so he could be a hero. There is no doubt Ersland was obsessed with guns. A friend of Ersland's once told Freisen that the pharmacist's conversations "were 80 percent about guns, 15 percent about his dog, and 5 percent unintelligible."

In the end, however, the real weapon of mass destruction was Ersland's mouth. He could not keep it shut. Nearly all the parties involved in the case

The Case of the Talking Pharmacist

agree that if he had simply said nothing, the outcome could well have been different, and he might not have faced ending his life in prison. That lesson is clear.

Death, Oklahoma Style

"There are things I've done I can't erase.
I want to look in the mirror and see another face."

> —From the song "Walk Away"
> by Tom Waits, part of the score of the
> movie *Dead Man Walking*

CHAPTER SEVENTY-EIGHT

Case #7: Death, Oklahoma Style

IN OKLAHOMA, WE SUCCESSFULLY and humanely kill cats, dogs, and horses—and even giraffes and elephants when necessary. This is not the case when it comes to executing humans.

Oklahoma's problem with executions by lethal injection began on April 29, 2014, when prison personnel at the Oklahoma State Penitentiary in McAlester botched the execution of Clayton Lockett, leading to his protracted and painful death. On January 15, 2015, Oklahoma tried again with the execution of Charles Warner. Warner's autopsy would later reveal he had been given a drug that was not included in the three-drug protocol approved by the Oklahoma Department of Corrections.

Undeterred, the state pressed on, scheduling the execution of Richard Glossip for September 30, 2015. Glossip's planned execution proved particularly controversial. It drew protests from not only antideath-penalty activists, such as Sister Helen Prejean, but also religious leaders such as Pope Francis, political figures including Oklahoma's U.S. Senator Tom Coburn, and celebrities such as former University of Oklahoma football coach Barry Switzer. Glossip's lawyers filed a variety of last-minute requests for a stay of execution, but all the pleas on his behalf were rejected. The execution remained on track.

Then on the day of his execution, while Glossip was in his cell preparing for his imminent death, it was learned that the pharmacy providing the execution "cocktail" had again delivered the wrong drug. The pharmacy was unable to provide the correct drug, and so Governor Mary Fallin postponed Glossip's execution. Glossip would live another day.

Oklahoma Attorney General Scott Pruitt immediately asked the Oklahoma Court of Criminal Appeals to stay all executions until he could conduct an investigation into the problems connected with the administration of the death penalty. On October 2, 2015, the appeals court granted the stay of execution and ordered a moratorium on the death penalty in Oklahoma.

Pruitt then began an investigation that included the seating of a statewide grand jury. Before it was over, the warden at the McAlester prison, the director of the Oklahoma Department of Corrections, and the governor's own attorney would resign.

As for the moratorium, it would stay in place pending the final outcome of the attorney general's investigation and a revision of the state's death-penalty procedures. All these events served not only to revive the never-ending fight over the death penalty but also gave Oklahoma a national black eye for incompetence.

CHAPTER SEVENTY-NINE

An Oklahoma Tradition

THE DEATH PENALTY IS AN American tradition, and Oklahoma has always been a state that liked to hang 'em high. The United States acquired the territory that would comprise Oklahoma as part of the Louisiana Purchase in 1803. In 1804, the U.S. Congress applied the laws of the land to this new territory. At the time and for decades afterward, "willful murder" was punishable by death, as was rape.

Prior to 1890, capital crimes in what was then Indian Territory were prosecuted in the federal courts of Kansas, Texas, and Arkansas. Indian Territory fell largely within the jurisdiction of the western district of Arkansas, and the district court was in Fort Smith, Arkansas.

From 1875 to 1896, that court was presided over by Judge Isaac Parker. Known as "the hanging judge," Parker sentenced 151 people to death and presided over seventy-six executions.

In 1890, a territorial court was established for Oklahoma Territory, which had been formed from the western part of Indian Territory. These territorial courts had authority to assess the death penalty. By 1895, a previously established federal court in Muskogee, Indian Territory, also had jurisdiction over capital offenses in Indian Territory. The various Native

American tribes in the area also had tribal courts that assessed the death penalty. Executions were common and were typically carried out by hanging, although a few of those convicted were shot with one or more firearms.

Oklahoma became a state in 1907. Although records are incomplete, it appears that at least six people were executed by hanging between 1907 and 1911. Between 1911 and 1915, no executions took place because the governor, Lee Cruce, was opposed to the death penalty. In 1915, the electric chair became the principal means of execution. Between 1915 and 1966, eighty-two people were put to death by "riding Old Sparky." One man was hanged for the federal crime of kidnapping.

It should be noted that Oklahoma also had a taste for lynching in its early days, most notably in 1909, when a mob dragged four men from the Pontotoc County Jail in Ada and hung them in a nearby barn. That hanging was memorialized by a famous photograph, as was the subsequent lynching in 1911 of a mother and son who were hung from a bridge near Okemah in Okfuskee County in east-central Oklahoma.

In 1972, in the landmark case of *Furman v. Georgia*, the United States Supreme Court ruled the death penalty as administered by Georgia and Texas unconstitutional. The decision was by a five-to-four vote, with the judges ruling against the death penalty expressing a different rationale for the decision.

In the aftermath, many states sought to recreate their death-penalty statutes in an attempt to conform to the Furman ruling. In 1976, in the case of *Gregg v. Georgia*, the U.S. Supreme Court affirmed the new death-penalty laws adopted by Georgia, Texas, North Carolina, Florida, and Louisiana.

Those laws were crafted so that a jury rather than a judge would have the last say when it came to assessing the death penalty. The laws called for a bifurcated proceeding. First the jury would determine the guilt or innocence of the defendant, and then, after a second hearing, it would decide whether the death penalty should be imposed. The U.S. Supreme Court also required that certain specific standards be adopted so that the death penalty could be administered more consistently across the country.

Based on the Gregg decision, the Oklahoma legislature passed a death-penalty statute in 1976. The measure passed by a vote of forty-five to one in the state senate and ninety-three to five in the house of representatives. The first execution under the new law took place in 1990 and was carried out by

Death, Oklahoma Style

lethal injection. Since 1990, Oklahoma has executed 112 people, all by lethal injection. Only Texas has executed more people in that time.

When Oklahoma first began to perform executions by lethal injection, a three-drug cocktail was widely used. The first drug was an anesthetic to render the recipient unconscious. The second drug caused paralysis, and the third stopped the heart.

The most widely used anesthetic was sodium thiopental. Vecuronium bromide was the paralytic, and potassium chloride was used to stop the heart.

In 2010, the American manufacturer of sodium thiopental, at the urging of the federal Food and Drug Administration and groups that opposed the death penalty, stopped producing the drug. States then turned to foreign sources instead.

Eventually, as foreign manufacturers also began to resist having their product used for executions, sodium thiopental became difficult to obtain. Oklahoma substituted the drug phenobarbital. That anesthetic appeared to work, but before long, phenobarbital was also removed from the market.

As Oklahoma approached the execution of Clayton Lockett in 2014, corrections officials—unable to acquire phenobarbital—decided to use the drug midazolam as an anesthetic instead. Midazolam had been used by Florida in an execution in 2013 and in an Ohio execution. Some evidence existed that in both cases, the prisoners had exhibited signs of consciousness after the administration of midazolam. Witnesses said the Ohio prisoner snorted, heaved, and clenched one of his fists after he was supposed to be unconscious. Investigation by Oklahoma authorities led them to believe midazolam would render a person unconscious, and they prepared to use midazolam in the Lockett's execution.

CHAPTER EIGHTY

The Lockett Case

FOR CLAYTON LOCKETT'S VICTIMS Bobby Bornt and Summer Hair and for the relatives and friends of his victim Stephanie Neiman, Lockett's execution was a long time coming.

In June 1999, Lockett, a previously convicted felon, accompanied by Shawn Mathis and Alfonzo Lockett, burst into Bornt's house in Perry, Oklahoma. Armed with a shotgun, Clayton Lockett wakened Bornt, who had been sleeping, and beat him with the shotgun. The three assailants then restrained Bornt by taping his hands and mouth with duct tape.

When Summer Hair and Stephanie Neiman arrived there in Neiman's pickup, the attackers restrained both women, and Clayton Lockett and his cousin Alfonzo Locket raped and sodomized both women. The three victims and Bornt's nine-year-old son were then forced into Bornt and Neiman's pickups and driven to a rural area in Kay County. There, Clayton Lockett raped Hair again and then had Mathis dig a shallow grave.

Clayton Lockett told the victims he would kill them unless they agreed not to report the crimes to the police. Bornt and Hair agreed, but Neiman refused, and so Lockett blasted her with the shotgun. She fell to the ground, still alive and screaming with pain. Lockett started to shoot her again, but the shotgun jammed. He managed to fix the gun and shoot Neiman a second time. Although Neiman was still alive after the second shot, Lockett instructed Mathis to bury her anyway, and so she was buried while still breathing.

The three attackers then drove Hair, Bornt, and Bornt's son back to Bornt's house and released them. The next day, Bornt and Hair reported the crimes to the police. All three perpetrators were promptly arrested, and Neiman's body was found. Clayton Lockett eventually confessed. He was found guilty of first-degree burglary, assault with a dangerous weapon, forcible oral sodomy, first-degree rape, kidnapping, robbery by force and fear, and first-degree murder.

A jury gave Lockett the death penalty.

CHAPTER EIGHTY-ONE

Lockett's Legal Mess

IN SPITE OF HIS DISREGARD IN general for human life, when it came to his own, Clayton Lockett wanted to keep it. After all his state and federal appeals were seemingly exhausted in January 2014, it became clear that his lawyers had just begun to fight. They began proceedings that called into question the drugs the state planned to use in executing their client.

The Lockett proceedings tied the state's legal system in knots. In the words of Attorney General Scott Pruitt, it created a "constitutional crisis," a breakdown in the orderly operation of the government, in this case, pertaining to the administration of the death penalty.

Although Pruitt's assessment might have been a political overstatement, there was no doubt that the Lockett case had brought the entire Oklahoma court system to a halt and created an unprecedented standoff between the state's two highest appellate courts.

Lockett's attorneys joined with the attorneys for Charles Warner, another inmate on the schedule to be executed, to make a challenge—a last-ditch effort to prevent their clients' executions. Oklahoma statute on the administration of the death penalty made the identity of the source of the execution drugs confidential. The lawyers challenged this statute on constitutional grounds, claiming that the statute denied their clients "access to the courts." The challenge was filed in the form of a declaratory judgment proceeding in the District Court of Oklahoma County. The declaratory judgment case was accompanied by a request for a stay of execution. The combination of those two legal requests kicked off an exercise in sophistry that would have gratified the most hardened skeptics of the criminal justice system.

A declaratory judgment action is a civil proceeding, whereas a request for a stay of execution is governed by criminal law. In Oklahoma, civil and criminal cases are both handled by district courts at the trial level, but they take different paths on appeal.

The Court of Criminal Appeals decides criminal appeals, and the Oklahoma Supreme Court is the highest civil court in the state. Overlap between the two courts is rare and almost unprecedented.

In the Lockett case, attorneys Susanna Gattoni and Seth Day originally filed a petition in state court that included both state and federal claims. That resulted in the state of Oklahoma removing the case to federal court.

Lockett then dismissed the federal claims, and the case was returned to the Oklahoma County District Court and assigned to District Judge Patricia Parrish. She ruled that she had no authority in the declaratory judgment case, a civil matter, to issue a stay of execution, which was a criminal matter. Lockett and Warner appealed her ruling immediately to the Oklahoma Supreme Court and pressed their request for a stay.

The Oklahoma Supreme Court referred the request for a stay to the Oklahoma Court of Criminal Appeals, ruling that it was a criminal matter and thus not in its jurisdiction. At about that time, Attorney General Scott Pruitt had to ask for a delay in Lockett's execution because the state could not obtain the proper execution drugs. The execution was postponed until April 22, 2014.

Judge Parrish ruled in favor of the condemned prisoners in the declaratory judgment case and declared that the Oklahoma statute relating to confidentiality of the execution drugs was unconstitutional. She still declined to issue a stay. The state then appealed the judge's ruling to the Oklahoma Supreme Court.

The Oklahoma Court of Criminal Appeals denied the request for a stay, ruling that it arose out of a civil matter, putting the stay request back in the

Death, Oklahoma Style

Oklahoma Supreme Court. The Oklahoma Supreme Court disagreed and returned the case to the Court of Criminal Appeals, which again bounced it back to the Oklahoma Supreme Court.

If the stakes had not been so high—to end or not to end a human life—the whole affair might have made for an absurd comedy routine featuring a legal ping-pong game between baffled, quarrelling judges. But the question did involve an execution, and faced with that, the Oklahoma Supreme Court reluctantly, by a five-to-four vote, granted a stay on April 21, one day before Lockett's scheduled execution.

The granting of the stay elicited a firestorm of political rhetoric. Governor Mary Fallin rescheduled Lockett's execution for April 29 and openly questioned the authority of the Oklahoma Supreme Court. One state legislator vowed to impeach the five justices who had voted for the stay, and as tempers rose, the media feasted on the controversy.

To clean the legal swamp that had been created, the Oklahoma Supreme Court decided to immediately settle the matter. The court ruled the confidentiality law constitutional and lifted the stay.

Oklahoma Supreme Court Justice Steven Taylor, who had consistently resisted accepting jurisdiction over the stay issue, wrote in reference to the confidentiality aspect of the law, "I must also express my opinion that the plaintiff's Eighth Amendment and access to the courts claims are frivolous and not grounded in the law. It is my view that from the very beginning this so called 'civil' litigation had been frivolous and a complete waste of time and resources of the Supreme Court of Oklahoma. The plaintiffs have no more right to the information they requested than if they were being executed in the electric chair, they would have no right to know whether OG&E or PSO were providing the electricity; if they were being hanged, they would have no right to know whether it be by cotton or nylon rope; or if they were being executed by firing squad, they would have no right to know whether it be by Winchester or Remington ammunition."

Although the legal issues thus far had been confusing and frustrating, they would soon take a backseat to the circumstances surrounding Lockett's execution.

CHAPTER EIGHTY-TWO

You Can't Make This Stuff Up

THE DAY OF CLAYTON Lockett's execution began strangely and ended in a bizarre series of events that left him dead. The procedure also called into question the manner in which executions are conducted in Oklahoma and elsewhere by lethal injection.

When officers arrived to take Lockett from his cell on the morning of his execution, they found him hiding under his covers. He refused to get out of bed. Lockett had pulled a blade from a safety razor and made half-inch-long surface cuts to his arms near the bend below the elbow. His autopsy would later reveal that he had a higher than therapeutic level of the prescription drug hydroxyzine in his system.

Lockett had previously been prescribed the drug and apparently had hoarded the pills and taken them all at once that morning. The presence of the drug should not, however, have interfered with his execution.

There were also some reports that he had intentionally dehydrated himself to make his veins harder to inject, but that was not found in the autopsy.

Confronted with the reluctant Lockett, the officers left his cell to get permission to Taser him. By their return, he had jammed shut the door to his cell. The officers forced open the door, Tasered Lockett, and dragged him from the cell. He was then taken to a medical unit, where he was to be held until shortly prior to his execution, scheduled for 6:00 p.m. Charles Warner was scheduled for execution the same day at 8:00 p.m. While awaiting execution, Lockett declined to meet with his attorneys and declined to eat.

At 5:22 p.m., Lockett was strapped to a gurney and rolled into the execution chamber. Present in the chamber were a paramedic, a McAlester family medicine and emergency-room doctor named Johnny Zellmer, and Anita Trammell, the prison warden in charge of the execution. Other Department of Corrections personnel were also in the execution chamber. Zellmer was present only to pronounce Lockett dead and record the time of death; his Hippocratic oath forbade him from taking part in an execution.

The execution was to be carried out by three anonymous executioners from the confines of a tiny nearby room. The identity of all persons taking part in an execution is confidential under Oklahoma statutes. However, Zellmer's name later became known because of a subsequent lawsuit.

Witnesses to the execution included reporters, Lockett's lawyers, and law enforcement personnel in one viewing room. A separate viewing room was provided for Stephanie Neiman's relatives. The chamber had blinds that remained shut until execution time.

The paramedic was tasked with placing an IV in Lockett's arm for the lethal injection. Usually a routine task, it quickly became complicated. The paramedic attempted to stick a needle into Lockett's left arm three times but was unsuccessful in finding a vein. She then asked Zellmer for assistance in placing the IV. Zellmer decided to help, placing the IV in Lockett's jugular vein. At the same time, the paramedic made three more attempts to stick a needle in Lockett's right arm, all of which were also unsuccessful.

Meanwhile, blood was now spreading under the prisoner's skin where the doctor had placed the IV. Zellmer decided the needle had gone through the vein and withdrew the needle. The paramedic tried two veins in Lockett's right foot but neither of them worked either. Zellmer then attempted to place the IV in a vein running near Lockett's collarbone. That also failed.

Zellmer next tried to place the needle in the femoral vein in Lockett's right groin. That vein runs deeper than the veins in the arm, neck, or chest and so required a longer needle. No such needle had been provided, but Zellmer proceeded anyway with a shorter needle. That time he was finally

Death, Oklahoma Style

able to place the needle in the vein. The IV was taped in place and a sheet thrown over Lockett's body. At that point, Trammell opened the blinds to the chamber and ordered that the execution begin. When Trammell asked Lockett if he had any last words, he did not respond.

Nonetheless, the execution began.

First, the midazolam was released into Lockett's bloodstream only to have Lockett unexpectedly found to be still conscious when he was checked after five minutes. After another two minutes, Lockett appeared to be unconscious, and the paralytic, vecuronium bromide, was released into his body, and then the potassium chloride was injected to stop his heart. As the third and final fatal drug was entering his body, Lockett began to lift his head and raise up from the table. He made sounds and might have said something. David Autry, one of Lockett's attorneys who witnessed the execution, reported that he saw Lockett try to lift himself and heard him "moan and groan."

Zellmer lifted the sheet over Lockett's body and observed an area of swelling around the IV site larger than a golf ball but smaller than a tennis ball. That indicated that the IV had come loose, and some of the drugs had been injected into the tissue rather than into the bloodstream.

Warden Trammell then lowered the blinds so witnesses could no longer see inside the execution chamber. Zellmer frantically tried to insert a new IV into Lockett's left femoral vein but was unsuccessful. Instead, it caused prolific bleeding.

Trammell made a panicked phone call to Robert Patton, director of the Oklahoma Department of Corrections, who was in the witness room. As too often happens in a crisis, instead of making a decision, the decision was kicked up the chain of command to another bureaucrat. Patton, likewise uncertain what to do, called Steve Mullins, Governor Fallin's legal counsel in Oklahoma City.

The whole charade took ten minutes. By the time Patton—on the authority of Mullins—ordered the execution stopped, Lockett was dead, having finally absorbed a fatal dose of the lethal drugs.

The entire execution lasted forty-three minutes.

According to a 2002 study in the *Journal of Forensic Sciences*, the average length of time from the first injection to death in a lethal-injection execution is 8.4 minutes.

Given the massive mess that had been made of Lockett's execution, Charles Warner's execution was delayed by Fallin, who had been reached at an Oklahoma City Thunder basketball game. The next day, the governor ordered an investigation by the Oklahoma Department of Public Safety. The DPS interviewed witnesses, examined records, consulted with experts, and ultimately issued a written report. The report was extensive and made some limited recommendations.

News of Lockett's botched execution exploded across the country, and Oklahoma received an avalanche of unfavorable national publicity. Fallin called a press conference to assert her continued support for the death penalty and to remind the public of Lockett's heinous crimes, but no amount of posturing could restore her credibility or that of all the parties involved.

Although Lockett's execution elicited outrage from some people, it provoked a different reaction from some supporters of the death penalty. State Representative Mike Christian suggested solving the problems with lethal injection by reinstating the firing squad, death by hanging, and the electric chair. Tulsa County Assessor Ken Yazel threw his weight behind the idea of restoring public hanging, citing the suggestion of a former Los Angeles mayor.

At least Oklahoma's prison officials would get it right next time—or would they?

CHAPTER EIGHTY-THREE

The Warner Case

THE NEXT PRISONER SLATED for execution was Charles Warner. He had been convicted of a cruel and obscene crime—raping and killing eleven-month-old Adrianna Waller, the daughter of his girlfriend. Adrianna had suffered a crushing injury to her head and injury to her brain. The baby's jaw and three ribs were broken, her liver was lacerated, and her spleen and lungs were bruised. There were bruises on her chest the size of adult fingertips, and tears to her rectum indicated sexual assault. Adrianna had been left in Warner's care by her mother, Shonda Waller, while she ran an errand. When Waller returned home, she discovered the baby's injuries and immediately rushed her daughter to the emergency room.

Warner was found guilty by a jury and sentenced to death.

At the trial, Warner's five-year-old son testified that he had seen his father shaking the victim. During the penalty stage of the trial, evidence revealed that Warner had also physically abused his former wife and his daughter. The verdict against Warner, however, was reversed by the Oklahoma Court of Criminal Appeals for an error in the seating of a potentially biased juror. Warner's second trial ended in a mistrial. His third trial resulted in another guilty verdict and again a sentence of death. As with Lockett, Warner had exhausted his state and federal appeals and was scheduled for execution, but also like Lockett, he did not want to die. Lockett's botched execution was an invitation to Warner to challenge Oklahoma's execution protocol.

Along with twenty other condemned men, including Richard E. Glossip, Warner filed a case in the U.S. District Court for the Western District of Oklahoma challenging Oklahoma's execution procedures. In particular, the condemned men alleged that the drugs used violated their rights under the Eighth Amendment to the U.S. Constitution. One of the most litigated amendments to the Constitution, the Eighth Amendment prohibits "cruel and unusual punishments."

The plaintiffs also asked the court to issue a preliminary injunction against the state staying executions until the case was decided.

After Lockett's clumsy demise, the Oklahoma Department of Corrections had adopted new execution procedures. The new procedures were far more specific and were designed to avoid the kind of mess that had occurred in Lockett's case. Under the new procedures, any one of four drug protocols could be used in an execution, and the condemned person was to be given notice of which protocol was to be used. The drugs chosen for Warner's execution included five hundred milligrams of midazolam as an anesthetic, one hundred milligrams of the paralytic rocuronium bromide, and 240 milligrams of potassium chloride to stop the heart. In Lockett's case, the dosage of midazolam had been only one hundred milligrams.

A trial on the condemned inmates' constitutional challenge was conducted before U.S. District Judge Stephen P. Friot of the U.S. District Court for the Western District of Oklahoma, with both parties calling expert witnesses to support their sides of the case.

The plaintiffs focused on the Lockett case and particularly on the use of midazolam. The plaintiffs' witnesses questioned whether the drug was capable of rendering a person unconscious. On the other hand, the state's expert witness said midazolam would render a prisoner unconscious and, coupled with the paralytic, would negate any pain or suffering. Judge Friot ruled in favor of the state, approving the three-drug lethal-injection formula and denying the plaintiffs' request for an injunction. The prisoners appealed to the Tenth Circuit Court of Appeals in Denver, which affirmed the trial court's decision. The case was then appealed to the U.S. Supreme Court.

Death, Oklahoma Style

The U.S. Supreme Court subsequently both accepted certiorari and stayed Oklahoma's executions, but not in time to halt Charles Warner's execution. As a result, at 7:28 p.m. on January 15, 2015, Warner was put to death by lethal injection for the 1997 rape and killing of Adrianna Waller.

Warner was so patently guilty of heinous crimes, including crimes against society's most innocent and vulnerable, that even those who opposed the death penalty could mount little more than a token protest to his execution. One unexpected voice of opposition was Adrianna's own mother, who opposed the execution on religious grounds.

"For me, morally it's wrong," said Shonda Waller. "God has the final say-so on life and death, and after everything I have been through I wouldn't want his family to suffer the way I've suffered, or his child have to endure losing his father. I wouldn't wish that on anyone."

In spite of the new and improved Oklahoma Department of Corrections protocol, Warner's execution was not without drama. Forty-four reporters from twenty-five media organizations vied for the five open seats reserved for the press in the execution room. Prior to the 6:00 p.m. time set for the execution to begin, Warner consumed his last meal of Kentucky Fried Chicken, a Big Mac, Gummy Worms, fruit-cocktail cup, potato wedges, coleslaw, and a cola. Warner then made a lengthy statement that included his assertion, "I'm not a monster."

Abby Broyles of KFOR-TV, one of the five members of the media to witness the execution, said she heard Warner scream after the midazolam drip began at 7:10 p.m., "It feels like acid!" and "My body is on fire!" His last words before the drugs took full effect were, "I'm not afraid to die; we's all gonna die." Broyles said Warner did not appear to be in pain; he never raised his head off the gurney and did not move or convulse as Lockett had.

With no apparent complications in the process, Warner was pronounced dead eighteen minutes after the execution began. But all was not as it seemed.

The subsequent autopsy of Warner's body would not be released for nearly nine months. When it was finally made public in early October 2015, it once again raised doubts about the competence of the Oklahoma Department of Corrections to preform executions.

Charles Warner had been executed with the wrong drug. The Oklahoma medical examiner found that instead of potassium chloride, the drug required by the Department of Corrections protocol, Warner had been injected with potassium acetate. The syringes used to inject the drug were labeled "120 mEq Potassium Chloride," but the vials used to fill the syringes were labeled "20 ML single dose potassium acetate injection."

The drug cocktail had certainly done its job, but the revelation that one of the three drugs in the cocktail was used in error raised questions about whether the Oklahoma Department of Corrections could competently carry out any execution.

And the dark comedy of errors was not over.

CHAPTER EIGHTY-FOUR

State v. Glossip

NEXT IN LINE FOR EXECUTION in Oklahoma was Richard Glossip. He had been convicted by a jury that also recommended the death penalty. His original conviction had been overturned on appeal, but at his second trial, the outcome was the same. However, unlike the Lockett and Warner cases, the facts surrounding Glossip's crime remained controversial.

Glossip was convicted of the murder for hire of his boss, Barry Van Treese. Under Oklahoma statutes, murder for hire is grounds to assess the death penalty. The murder had occurred on January 7, 1997, at the Best Budget Inn in southwestern Oklahoma City. Van Treese was the owner of the sleazy motel, and Glossip was its manager. Glossip lived at the motel with his girlfriend, D Anna Wood. The night he was murdered, Van Treese, who lived in Lawton, was staying at the hotel.

The murder was committed by Justin Sneed, a maintenance man at the motel. Sneed brutally beat Van Treese to death with a baseball bat in Room 102 of his own motel.

Glossip's conviction was largely based on Sneed's testimony. According to Sneed, Glossip offered him ten thousand dollars to kill Van Treese. Sneed confessed to the murder and accepted a deal to be sentenced to life in prison without parole in exchange for a guilty plea. He became the principal witness for the state against Glossip.

The death-penalty opponents who would later protest Glossip's execution seized on Sneed's unreliability as grounds for claiming that Glossip was wrongfully convicted. Over time, Sneed gave several versions of his story; he was also a meth addict. The protestors also professed outrage at Sneed's having received only life without parole for killing Van Treese whereas Glossip got the death penalty. An odd argument for people categorically opposed to the death penalty.

What the protestors chose to ignore was the evidence corroborating Sneed's story. Before Van Treese left Lawton on January 6, the day before his murder, he told his wife he had found that more than six thousand dollars was missing from the motel's receipts. After stopping in Oklahoma City to see Glossip, Van Treese visited a hotel he owned in Tulsa and discussed the missing funds with the manager of that hotel, William Bender. Angry that receipts and registration cards were missing at the Oklahoma City motel, Van Treese told Bender he had instructed Glossip to come up with the records by his return that day. Van Treese also asked whether Bender would be interested in managing the Oklahoma City motel.

According to Sneed's testimony, Glossip participated in both the murder cover-up and stealing money from Van Treese after his death. Glossip had told Sneed after the murder to move Van Treese's car away from the motel and advised Sneed that he would find an envelope with money under the front seat. Sneed moved the car to the parking lot of a nearby credit union and found the envelope, which contained four thousand dollars. Sneed testified that he had split the money with Glossip.

When the two men were later arrested, Glossip was in possession of twelve hundred dollars and Sneed of seventeen hundred. Glossip claimed that the money came from his paycheck and other sources. Yet Glossip's salary was fifteen hundred dollars per month, divided into two payments and subject to ordinary taxes and deductions.

The murder took place at about four in the morning on January 7. Sneed let himself into Van Treese's room with a passkey and attacked him in his bed with a baseball bat. Van Treese struggled and tried to get away, but Sneed threw him to the floor and beat him to death, something that involved hitting Van Treese ten or fifteen times. Sneed also tried unsuccessfully to stab Van Treese.

During the struggle, a window was broken. Glossip told Sneed to fix it and to buy a saw and chemicals for disposal of Van Treese's body. Glossip assisted Sneed in hanging a shower curtain over the windows of the room. The next day, Glossip helped Sneed cover the broken window with Plexiglas. Glossip also directed a maid not to clean any of the first-floor rooms.

The morning after the murder, another hotel employee, Billye Hooper, noticed that Van Treese's car was gone. She asked Glossip about it, and he said Van Treese had left that morning to get supplies to remodel some of the motel rooms. He told her Van Treese had stayed in Room 108, not Room 102. Glossip told a security guard at the motel a conflicting story about where he had last seen Van Treese and later told the police yet another story.

The same afternoon as the murder, Van Treese's car was discovered, and a search begun to locate him. When the body was found, Detectives Bob Bemo and Bill Cook took Glossip to the police station for questioning. Glossip said Sneed woke him at about five in the morning to tell him two drunks had been fighting and had broken the window in Room 102.

The next day, Glossip began to sell his personal property and told the motel security guard that he was "moving on." Glossip was scheduled for another interview with the police but never showed. The police tracked him down and brought him in to be questioned again. Glossip admitted to lying about his early morning conversation with Sneed and said Sneed had told him that Sneed had killed Van Treese.

In Oklahoma, the statement of an accomplice cannot be used against another accused person unless other evidence exists that connects the accused to the crime. In Glossip's case, the judge and jury found such corroborating evidence. This was upheld on appeal. The Court of Criminal Appeals found that "Glossip's motive, along with evidence that he actively concealed Van Treese's body from discovery, as well as his plans to 'move on,' connect him with the commission of this crime." The court also stated, "The State presented an enormous amount of evidence that Glossip concealed Van Treese's body from investigators all day long and he lied about the broken window." The court then cited specific evidence supporting those conclusions.

Many media accounts, particularly during the frenzy that surrounded Richard Glossip's scheduled execution, ignored this corroborating evidence and incorrectly stated that Glossip was convicted based solely on Sneed's biased testimony. Regardless, Glossip's conviction remains highly controversial, and he has denied any guilt.

CHAPTER EIGHTY-FIVE

Glossip v. Gross

PRIOR TO CHARLES Warner's execution, the U.S. District Court and the Tenth Circuit Court of Appeals both refused to halt Oklahoma executions in the case filed by Warner, Glossip, and other death-row inmates who challenged the use of midazolam as part of the lethal-injection protocol. Shortly after Warner's execution, the U.S. Supreme Court agreed to consider the case and stayed all Oklahoma executions.

On June 29, 2015, the U.S. Supreme Court issued a decision in the case of *Glossip v. Gross*. (Kevin J. Gross, chairman of the Oklahoma Pardon and Parole Board, was one of the named defendants). The case was decided in favor of the state of Oklahoma by a five-to-four vote. The multiple opinions written by various judges not only say a lot about the status of the death penalty in the United States but also underscore how pivotal Supreme Court Justice Antonin Scalia's death in 2016 and his 2017 replacement, Neil Gorsuch, might be for law and public policy in this country.

The 2015 majority opinion was written by Justice Samuel Alito, who was joined by Chief Justice John Roberts, Scalia, and Justices Anthony Kennedy and Clarence Thomas. Scalia and Thomas wrote concurring opinions, and Justices Stephen Breyer and Sonia Sotomayor wrote dissents. Justice Ruth

Bader Ginsburg joined in the Breyer opinion, and Ginsburg, Breyer, and Justice Elena Kagan joined in Sotomayor's opinion.

Alito and the majority denied the prisoners' request for relief for two reasons. "First," Alito stated, "the prisoners failed to identify a known and available alternative method of execution that entails a lesser risk of pain, a requirement of all Eighth Amendment method-of-execution claims. Second, the district court did not commit clear error when it found that the prisoners failed to establish that Oklahoma's use of a massive dose of midazolam in its execution protocol entails a substantial risk of severe pain."

The requirement that the prisoners identify an alternative method of execution was based on Supreme Court precedent established in the previous case of *Baze v. Rees*. Alito also succinctly summed up the state of the law: "Because capital punishment is constitutional, there must be a constitutional means of carrying it out."

As to the matter of pain when it came to capital punishment, Alito stated, "Because some risk of pain is inherent in any method of execution, we have held that the Constitution does not require the avoidance of all risk of pain. After all, while most humans wish to die a painless death, many do not have that good fortune. Holding that the Eighth Amendment demands the elimination of essentially all risk of pain would effectively outlaw the death penalty altogether."

As with many cases that end up being heard by the U.S. Supreme Court, the Glossip case seemed to have been decided as much on ideology as on law. Justice Breyer in particular strayed from the issues raised in the case to advocate for the abolishment of the death penalty. Breyer concluded that the death penalty constituted "cruel and unusual" punishment no matter what means of execution was used. He cited three reasons for his decision, which led him to a fourth conclusion. "Today's administration of the death penalty involves three fundamental constitutional defects: (1) serious unreliability, (2) arbitrariness in application, and (3) unconscionably long delays that undermine the death penalty's penological purpose. Perhaps as a result, (4) most places within the United States have abandoned its use."

In support of his conclusions, Breyer offered extensive arguments based mostly on facts outside the record of Glossip's case, including articles in legal journals, newspapers, and on the Internet. Those sources had led Breyer

Death, Oklahoma Style

to conclude that innocent persons had been convicted and executed in the United States. Such a conclusion is pure speculation, but given human fallibility, is likely correct. According to *Newsweek*, between 1973 ad 2014, 144 people on death row have been exonerated, about 1.6 percent of all death sentences.

Breyer concluded that the death penalty was inherently unconstitutional. Given the inevitable imperfection of human nature, such an argument carried to its extreme would negate the entire justice system, not just the death penalty. Breyer cited what he called "evolving standards of decency" that should be applied in interpreting the Constitution. That very concept drives constitutional conservatives insane, and Breyer's opinion provoked a predictable response from Justice Scalia.

Scalia called Breyer's dissent "gobbledygook" and "full of internal contradictions." Scalia also wrote, "Capital punishment presents moral questions that philosophers, theologians, and statesmen have grappled with for millennia. The Framers of our Constitution disagreed bitterly on the matter. For that reason, they handled it the same way they handled many other controversial issues: they left it to the People to decide. By arrogating to himself the power to overturn that decision, Justice Breyer does not just reject the death penalty, he rejects the Enlightenment."

Justice Sotomayor's dissent focused more on the issues of the case. She challenged the majority opinion on both the facts and the law. She concluded that the plaintiffs had sufficiently proven that midazolam was ineffective as a lasting anesthetic and that its use would entail cruel and unusual punishment. She also disagreed that the *Baze v. Rees* case required the plaintiffs to furnish an alternate means of execution.

Whatever solace Glossip's lawyer could take from the fact that their arguments had not fallen entirely on deaf ears, Glossip had lost his appeal and had to prepare to die.

CHAPTER EIGHTY-SIX

Don't Kill Glossip

RICHARD GLOSSIP'S EXECUTION was rescheduled for September 16, 2015, but to be sure his fight to stay alive was far from over. He now had a cadre of lawyers working on his behalf, and maybe more to his benefit, he had the powerful force of an international public-relations effort behind him.

It did not hurt his cause that Oklahoma's ineptitude when it came to recent executions had also made the state a target. Glossip's case gave death-penalty opponents a cause célèbre.

Unlike Warner and Lockett, Glossip was not directly involved in a hideous, abhorrent crime. His guilt was once removed, and at least in the eyes of those who opposed execution in principle, it was based on insufficient grounds.

Some of those groups portrayed Glossip as an "innocent" man, a conclusion they clung to despite two jury convictions and numerous appellate reviews of his case. For others who were against the death penalty in all cases, it was more about doing away with the death penalty than it was about saving Glossip's life. Glossip's case was simply an opportunity to make a case against the death penalty. And make a case they did.

MoveOn.org circulated a petition on the Internet to gather support against Glossip's execution that ultimately attracted 244,000 signatures. Its efforts also generated more than seven thousand phone calls to Governor Fallin, a great expression of public sentiment but in this case an unsuccessful one. Sister Helen Prejean, made famous by her book *Dead Man Walking* and the 1995 film adaptation in which actress Susan Sarandon played the nun, came to Oklahoma and advocated for a stay of execution. A group of well-meaning citizens highlighted by former U.S. Senator Tom Coburn and former OU football coach Barry Switzer signed a letter to Governor Fallin in support of the stay.

All of those efforts, however, failed to move Fallin, who continued to deny any and all pleas made on Glossip's behalf. His execution appeared to be inevitable.

That was when Glossip's lawyers stepped forward with new evidence that they claimed would exonerate him. What they called new evidence was three affidavits. One came from Justin Sneed's drug dealer, who had sold meth to Sneed. The other two were from convicted felons who had served time with Sneed. All the affidavits attacked Sneed's truthfulness and character. One of the felon's affidavits claimed that statements by Sneed indicated he had set Glossip up for the murder in exchange for a deal to save his own life.

In another interesting twist, Sneed's daughter indicated that Sneed might be considering recanting his testimony that implicated Glossip in the crime. All this evidence was presented to the Oklahoma Court of Criminal Appeals with a request that the court stay Glossip's execution so further investigation could be conducted to help develop exonerating evidence.

By September 16, 2015, the date set for Glossip's execution, the Court of Criminal Appeals had not granted a stay, and Governor Fallin had declined to act. Glossip prepared to die, but just two hours prior to his scheduled execution, the Court of Criminal Appeals issued a two-week stay to allow review of the evidence submitted by the lawyers.

The evidence Glossip pinned his hopes on was controversial. Generally, statements by a prisoner about another prisoner have the lowest possible level of credibility. The affidavits in question were no exception. Michael Scott—one of the prisoners who claimed Sneed had mentioned sending Glossip "up the river"—had previously admitted to the Department of Corrections that

Death, Oklahoma Style

"he lies all the time." Scott, as it turned out, was also in violation of his parole and had been brought in by the Rogers County sheriff. David Prater, the Oklahoma County district attorney, whose office had prosecuted Glossip, questioned Scott. That questioning set off a barrage of accusations by Glossip's lawyers that the district attorney had intimidated Scott to get him to change his story.

Prater's response was blunt: "The day will come where it will be clear that everything the defense lawyers and their witnesses say in this case are lies." He also called Glossip's efforts to avoid execution "a bullshit PR campaign."

Perhaps so, but the campaign continued and accelerated. Archbishop Carlo Maria Viganò wrote to Governor Fallin on behalf of Pope Francis and pleaded for the governor to spare Glossip's life, stating, "Together with Pope Francis, I believe that a commutation of Mr. Glossip's sentence would give clear witness to the value and dignity of every person's life and would contribute to a society more cognizant of the mercy that God has bestowed on us all."

Meanwhile, Sister Prejean, Susan Sarandon, and the groups that opposed the death penalty maintained a barrage of rallies, press releases, and Internet campaigns to keep the case on the front page.

On September 28, two days before Glossip's rescheduled execution, the Oklahoma Court of Criminal Appeals issued its ruling, turning down the request for a stay by a three-to-two vote.

The majority of judges had not found anything "new" about the evidence presented. Judge David Lewis, citing corroborating evidence, said, "Glossip's conviction is not based solely on the testimony of a codefendant." Judge Robert Hudson said, "Glossip's proffered evidence is as dubious as that of a jailhouse informant." In dissent, however, Judge Arlene Johnson called Glossip's trial "deeply flawed." She wanted a further review of the evidence.

Judge Johnson's statements rallied those who objected to the planned execution, and they quickly organized demonstrations in Oklahoma and on the steps of the U.S. Supreme Court in Washington, D.C. where another last-ditch appeal was pending. On September 30, with no relief in sight, Sir Richard Branson, the English billionaire who had founded Virgin America airline, took out a full-page ad in the *Daily Oklahoman*. Branson declared, "Your state is about to kill a man who may well be completely innocent. . . . This is not about the rights and wrongs of the death penalty. This is about every person deserving a fair trial. . . . Your state is about to execute a man whose guilt has not been proven beyond a reasonable doubt."

Branson's last assumption no doubt came as a revelation to those jurors who, after hearing the evidence and arguments of both sides, had found Glossip guilty beyond a reasonable doubt twice.

Despite efforts such as Branson's, both the campaign for clemency and the appeal to the U.S. Supreme Court failed. What continued was the unrelenting incompetence of the Oklahoma Department of Corrections.

With no facilities in which to store the lethal drugs to be used in Glossip's execution or the legal authority to keep them at the prison, the department had opted to have the drugs delivered to the prison just hours before the scheduled execution. On the arrival of the drugs, prison authorities found that as in the Warner execution, potassium acetate had been substituted for potassium chloride. They contacted the provider and were told that the two drugs had the same effect—either one would stop a prisoner's heart—and that the scheduled drug, potassium chloride, was not available.

Substitution might have seemed an insignificant detail to the provider, but potassium acetate was not part of the department's own protocol nor was it the drug that Glossip and his lawyers had been notified would be used. As usual, the glitch flummoxed the powers that be.

As the scheduled time for the execution slipped by, prison officials consulted with the governor's office and searched for a source to provide the potassium chloride. Finally, more than an hour after the appointed time, Governor Fallin stayed the execution for thirty-seven days. Glossip was again saved, and his supporters celebrated once again.

It was the fourth time Glossip had been scheduled to die only to have the execution postponed. Some legal scholars and death-penalty opponents argued that the repeated scheduling of the executions—followed by last minute stays—amounted to torture and cruel and unusual punishment. That argument was consistent with Justice Breyer's dissent in *Glossip v. Gross* and one that no doubt will be argued when Glossip's execution is next rescheduled.

Attorney General Scott Pruitt stepped forward the next day to ask the Oklahoma Court of Criminal Appeals to stay all executions until he could

Death, Oklahoma Style

investigate the situation. The stay was granted on October 2. That investigation soon evolved into a statewide grand jury. During the grand jury investigation, Pruitt announced he would not seek to schedule any executions for at least the next five months after the Oklahoma Department of Corrections adopted new rules based on the grand jury's findings.

Pruitt subpoenaed Anita Trammell, Robert Patton, and Steve Mullins before the grand jury in October. Ten days after her grand jury appearance, Warden Trammell announced she was retiring. She had been with department more than thirty years. DOC Director of Communications Terri Watkins immediately stated, "[Trammell's] thought for a couple of years about retiring. So if anybody's trying to say she's resigning with the stuff going on, they're wrong. Or if anybody's trying to say she's been asked to resign, they're wrong."

In December, Patton resigned his job as the director of the Department of Corrections, a post he had held for about three years. Watkins was quick that time to also say Patton's resignation had nothing to do with the grand jury investigation. "It's to go spend more time with his five grandchildren in Arizona," she said.

The purely coincidental resignations continued in February 2016 when Mullins also resigned. He said it was on his doctor's advice "to control the stress in my life." Mullins also wrote in his resignation letter that he knew "the office needs to eliminate personnel costs in the upcoming budget."

CHAPTER EIGHTY-SEVEN

The Grand Jury's Report

AFTER HEARING THE TESTIMONY OF A LONG parade of witnesses over eight months' time, the grand jury issued its report on May 19, 2016. The report ended up being a scathing condemnation of the Oklahoma Department of Corrections and the governor's office. The grand jury found blame and cast the blame where it belonged.

Because Clayton Lockett's execution had previously been investigated by the Oklahoma Department of Public Safety, the attorney general's office had focused the investigation on the Warner execution and the planned Glossip execution. The report was thorough, covered the facts, and made clear the incompetence of those involved in the process: "The Multicounty Grand Jury finds that Department of Corrections staff, and others participating in the execution process, failed to perform their duties with the precision and attention to detail to exercise of state authority in such cases demands, to wit:

- the Director of the Department of Corrections ("Director") orally modified the execution protocol without authority;

- the Pharmacist ordered the wrong execution drugs;

- the Department's General Counsel failed to inventory the execution drugs as mandated by state purchasing requirements;

- an agent with the Department's Office of Inspector General ("OIG Agent 1") failed to inspect the execution drugs while transporting them into the Oklahoma State Penitentiary;

- Warden A failed to notify anyone in the Department that the potassium acetate had been received;

- the H Unit Section Chief failed to observe the Department had received the wrong execution drugs;

- the IV Team failed to observe the Department had received the wrong execution drugs; the Department's Execution Protocol failed to define important terms, and lacked controls to ensure the proper execution drugs were obtained and administered;

- and the Governor's General Counsel advocated the Department proceed with the Glossip execution using potassium acetate."

As a result of those findings, the grand jury concluded, "Based on these failures, justice has been delayed for the victims' families and the citizens of Oklahoma, and confidence further shaken in the ability of this state to carry out the death penalty."

No one was indicted for any crime, but some of the testimony revealed a high level of inattention, careless behavior, indecision, indifference, and bad judgment. In Charles Warner's case, the warden examined the vials containing potassium acetate, rather than the scheduled drug potassium chloride, but exhibited no concerns about the switch and did not alert anyone else to it. The IV team members who prepared the syringes to be used in Warner's execution did not notice the discrepancy, and thus the execution proceeded with the wrong drug.

In Richard Glossip's case, the warden did not even know who had supplied the drugs. The warden testified that such knowledge was above his level

Death, Oklahoma Style

and that "there are just some things you ask questions about and there's some things you don't. I never asked questions about the process."

Probably the most inflammatory testimony involved conversations held with the governor's lawyer, Steve Mullins, related to the delay in Glossip's execution. After it was found that the wrong drug had been delivered and the correct drug was not available, Mullins still wanted to press on with the execution. Assistant Attorney General Jennifer Miller was prepared to file a motion for a stay of execution if the governor did not grant a stay. Mullins argued that the execution should proceed, stating that potassium chloride and potassium acetate were the same, suggesting that Miller "google it."

A conference call was convened that included the attorney general, his chief of staff Melissa Houston, and Deputy Attorney Generals Kindanne Jones and Miller, as well as Governor Fallin and Mullins. At the insistence of Pruitt and over the objections of Mullins, the governor agreed to stay Glossip's execution. The call was followed by a series of back-and-forth e-mails between the attorney general's office and the governor's office. Mullins wanted to spin the facts and avoid admitting any kind of error. He was particularly opposed to calling potassium acetate "the wrong drug." Finally, Governor Fallin issued the stay, including the following language: "This stay will give the Department of Corrections and its attorneys the opportunity to determine whether potassium acetate is compliant with the Execution Protocol and/or to obtain potassium chloride."

Regardless of the wording of the stay, the aborted execution further hurt the already damaged credibility of the Oklahoma Department of Corrections.

After reporting its criticism of the execution process and meticulously documenting its findings, the grand jury made a series of recommendations that called for straightforward and commonsense changes in the protocol and procedures for executions. According to the grand jury, the protocol should be revised to include the following changes:

"i. This time, key terms should be defined and duties clearly assigned; ii. The Protocol should require verification of execution drugs at every step; iii. Administrators should not serve in dual roles; iv. The Department should follow laws requiring the documentation of purchases and inventories while still safeguarding the privacy of those participating in execution of the death penalty; and, v. The Quality Assurance Review called for in the

Protocol should be performed by an independent third party bound by confidentiality."

The grand jury also recommended that individuals involved in the execution be thoroughly trained. Training those involved might seem obvious, but it had not been done in the executions of Lockett and Warner and the planned execution of Glossip.

Reactions to the report were political and predictable. Fallin avoided commenting on the substance of the report but went on record to say, "It is imperative that Oklahoma be able to manage the execution process properly."

The new interim director of the Oklahoma Department of Corrections, Joe Allbaugh, "reserve(d) comments until a full vetting process had been undertaken by the department."

Attorney General Scott Pruitt, whose office had held a steady hand through the turmoil, said the treatment of the protocol by the Department of Corrections and the governor's office was "callous, cavalier, and in some circumstances dismissive."

Most opponents of the death penalty seized on the report to call for the abolition of all executions. Don Heath, vice chair of the Oklahoma Coalition to Abolish the Death Penalty, after voicing opposition to the death penalty, also suggested a moratorium on executions while the state researched executions by means of nitrogen hypoxia.

CHAPTER EIGHTY-EIGHT

Recent Developments

IN 2015, REACTING TO Richard Glossip's challenge of Oklahoma's drug protocol, the state legislature passed a statute authorizing nitrogen-induced hypoxia as an alternate method of execution if lethal injection was ruled illegal by the courts or if the appropriate drugs were unavailable.

Oklahoma became the first state to authorize nitrogen hypoxia as a means of execution.

Although execution by nitrogen hypoxia seems to be a painless way to die, it should be noted that it has not been tested in an execution setting.

In reaction to the *Glossip v. Gross* case and in light of the continued incompetence of the Oklahoma Department of Corrections, the legislature passed a resolution placing a change in the Oklahoma Constitution on the 2016 election ballot (State Question 776).

The measure was designed to short-circuit future challenges to the manner of execution or the death penalty itself. The proposed constitutional amendment read as follows:

> All statutes of this state requiring, authorizing, imposing or relating to the death penalty are in full force and effect,

subject to legislative amendment or repeal by statute, initiative or referendum. Any method of execution shall be allowed, unless prohibited by the United States Constitution. Methods of execution may be designated by the Legislature. A sentence of death shall not be reduced on the basis that a method of execution is invalid. In any case in which an execution method is declared invalid, the death sentence shall remain in force until the sentence can be lawfully executed by any valid method. The death penalty provided for under such statutes shall not be deemed to be, or to constitute, the infliction of cruel or unusual punishments, nor shall such punishment be deemed to contravene any other provision of this Constitution.

The last sentence, declaring that the death penalty is not "cruel and unusual punishments" smacked of window dressing and posed dubious legal effect because of the wording of the Eighth Amendment to the U.S. Constitution.

Regardless of the necessity or efficacy of the constitutional amendment, Oklahomans expressed their support for the death penalty by adopting the amendment in November 2016. Support was strong, with 66.37 percent of voters backing passage.

In 2014, the Estate of Clayton Lockett filed a civil suit for damages against Governor Fallin, Robert Patton, Anita Trammel, Dr. Johnny Zellmer, and unknown executioners, drug manufacturers, and compounding pharmacies. The suit, filed in U.S. District Court for the Western District of Oklahoma, alleged violations of Lockett's rights under the Sixth, Eighth, and Fourteenth amendments to the U.S. Constitution. U.S. District Judge Joe Heaton dismissed the suit based on the qualified immunity of the defendants.

The plaintiffs appealed to the Tenth Circuit Court of Appeals, which affirmed the trial court's ruling in November 2016. There was no question that Lockett had suffered during his execution, but the court ruled that this kind of isolated mishap could occur during an execution and did not, according to U.S. Supreme Court precedent, constitute cruel and unusual punishment or otherwise violate Lockett's constitutional rights.

Death, Oklahoma Style

In March 2016, motivated by the state's problems with administering the death penalty, a group of prominent Oklahoma citizens formed the Oklahoma Death Penalty Review Commission. The group was headed by former Governor Brad Henry, retired Oklahoma Court of Criminal Appeals Judge Reta Strubhar, and former U.S. Magistrate Judge Andy Lester. This volunteer commission, which included law professors, lawyers, and representatives of different ethnic groups, undertook a comprehensive review of the death-penalty process in Oklahoma from initial arrest and interrogation through execution.

In April 2017, the commission published its report. The 271-page report is thorough and voluminous, reflecting a tremendous amount of work by the eleven commission members. The principal recommendation of the commission is that Oklahoma extend its current moratorium on the death penalty until the serious flaws in the system can be reformed.

The report makes forty-five specific recommendations, each supported by extensive information, research, and comment. The sense of the report is to provide a death-penalty system that is as modern and as scientifically correct as possible. There are also recommendations that all persons involved in the system, including police, prosecutors, defense lawyers, expert witnesses, judges, and executioners, be properly trained and properly compensated.

Specifically, the commission recommended the Oklahoma Department of Corrections "adopt the most humane and effective method of execution possible, which currently appears to be the one-drug (barbiturate) lethal injection protocol." Given the difficulty of obtaining a lethal barbiturate, that recommendation might not be practically possible.

The report as a whole is a useful source of information for the courts, the Department of Corrections, and the Oklahoma Pardon and Parole Board. On the other hand, the proposals in the report might constitute a panacea that is, practically speaking, unattainable because of the public's attitude about the death penalty and state's current financial problems. Taken as a whole, the report could easily be translated by opponents of the death penalty into a manifesto to abolish the death penalty entirely because of the inability of the judicial system to guarantee a perfect result in every case. Human nature will always render that an impossible goal.

The Oklahoma Board of Corrections has met several times since the issuance of the grand jury's report, but at the time of the writing of this book, has yet to finalize new rules for executions. Thus the moratorium on the death penalty in Oklahoma remains in effect.

As for Richard Glossip, at least for now, he remains on death row.

Acknowledgments

I want to thank all the defense lawyers, prosecutors, judges, and law enforcement professionals who took the time to talk to me about the cases in this book. Their input and information were invaluable and helped me to give an accurate account of the cases. Without their help, this book would simply not have been the same.

I particularly want to thank Debra Osborne Spindle, Judge Thomas Walker, and Larry Floyd for helping me with research on the Clara Hamon story. They provided me with information and documents that made my task much easier, including some facts that have never been published before.

Thanks also to Nancy Samuelson for reading the Bill Tilghman story and correcting some of the facts.

Thanks to Don Davis for introducing me to Granville Long and to Granville Long for sharing his experience with me. His insights were important for telling the Geronimo Bank story.

I also appreciate Dr. John Hamilton for corresponding with me and telling me his side of the story. He still maintains his innocence in the death of his wife.

BIBLIOGRAPHY

Valentine's Day Murder

Newspaper
The Oklahoman.

Television
Channel KFOR-TV.
Channel KOCO-TV.
Channel KWTV.
Dateline, NBC, March 26, 2010.
Forensic Files, "Deadly Valentine," HLN, July 6, 2010.

Interviews
Horton, Richard. Interview by Kent Frates, October 19, 2015.
Lane, Wes. Interview by Kent Frates, October 13, 2015.
Martin, Mack. Interview by Kent Frates, September 28, 2015.
Smothermon, Connie Pope. Telephone interview by Kent Frates, September 22, 2015.
Sterling, Teresa. Interview by Kent Frates, September 15, 2015.

Correspondence
Hamilton, Dr. John, correspondence with Kent Frates, 2016.

Court Cases
Documents of record, including motions, pleadings, briefs, decisions, and orders in the following cases:
John Baxter Hamilton v. Randall G. Workman, No. 06-6212, U. S. Court of Appeals, Tenth Circuit.
John Baxter Hamilton v. State of Oklahoma, Court of Criminal Appeals of the State of Oklahoma F-2002-35.
John Baxter Hamilton v. Warden Randall G. Workman, No. 04-6V-01392-T, U.S. District Court for the Western District of Oklahoma.
State of Oklahoma v. John Baxter Hamilton, District Court of Oklahoma County, Oklahoma CF-2001-1147.

Transcripts of Legal Proceedings
Deposition of Connie Pope, August 7, 2002.
Deposition of Tom Bevel, July 2, 2002.
Deposition of Wesley Lane II, August 7, 2002.
Depositions in the case of Richard R. Horton as the personal representative of the *Estate of*

Susan Hamilton, deceased, et al. v. John Baxter Hamilton, District Court of Oklahoma County, Oklahoma CJ-2002-1103.
Preliminary hearing of John Baxter Hamilton, May 25, June 15, and June 25, 2001.
Jury trial of John Baxter Hamilton, December 3–19, 2001.
State of Oklahoma vs. John Baxter Hamilton, District Court of Oklahoma County, Oklahoma CF-2001-1147.

Clara Hamon, a Woman Scorned

Books
Lewis, Jon, and Eric Smoodin, eds. *Looking Past the Screen: Case Studies in American Film History and Method.* Durham: Duke University Press, 2007.
McCartney, Laton. *The Teapot Dome Scandal: How Big Oil Bought the White House and Tried To Steal the Country.* New York: Random House, 2009.

Journals, Newspapers, and Wire Service
Chicago Herald-Examiner.
Daily Ardmoreite.
Dallas Morning News.
El Paso Daily Herald.
Floyd, Larry C. "Jake Hamon: 'The Man Who Made Harding President.'" *Chronicles of Oklahoma* 87, no. 3, Fall 2009.
Kansas City Post.
Lawton Constitution.
Los Angeles Times.
New York Times.
Robinson, Gilbert L., "Transportation in Carter County 1913–1917." *Chronicles of Oklahoma* 19, no. 4, December 1941.
Tulsa Daily World.
Universal Services.

Electronic Sources
Goodman, Bonnie K., "Presidential Campaigns & Elections, Overviews & Chronology 1920," *http://www.presidentialcampaignselectionsreference.wordpress.com/*.
Shafer, Stephanie, "Hamon, Jacob Louis" (1873–1920), Oklahoma Historical Society, *http://www.okhistory.org/*.

Interview
Walker, Thomas W. Telephone interview by Kent Frates, August 26, 2016.

Court Case
State of Oklahoma v. Clara Smith Hamon, No. 1925, District Court, Carter County, Oklahoma.

Roger Wheeler's Bad Investment

Books
Carr, Howie. *Hitman: The Untold Story of Johnny Martorano*. New York: Forge Books, 2011.
Cullen, Kevin, and Shelley Murphy. *Whitey Bulger: America's Most Wanted Gangster and the Manhunt that Brought him to Justice*. New York: W. W. Norton & Company, 2013.
Foley, Thomas J., and John Sedgwick. *Most Wanted: Pursuing Whitey Bulger, the Murderous Mob Chief the FBI Protected*. New York: Simon & Schuster, 2012.
Lehr, Dick, and Gerard O'Neill. *Black Mass: The True Story of an Unholy Alliance between the FBI and the Irish Mob*. New York: BBS Public Affairs, 2000.
Lehr, Dick, and Gerard O'Neill. *Whitey: The Life of America's Most Notorious Mob Boss*. New York: Crown, 2013.
Yadon, Lawrence J., and Robert Barr Smith. *One Murder Too Many: Whitey Bulger and the Computer Tycoon*. Gretna, Louisiana: Pelican Publishing Company Inc., 2014.

Newspapers
Boston Globe.
Boston Herald.
New York Times.
The Oklahoman.
The Tulsa Tribune.
Tulsa World.

Film
Whitey: United States of America v. James J. Bulger, Magnolia Pictures, documentary film, 2014.

Interviews
Green, Robert G. Telephone interview by Kent Frates, August 4, 2016.
Huff, Michael. Online interview by *Voices of Oklahoma*, Oklahoma Center for the Humanities, University of Tulsa, September 23, 2013.
Huff, Michael. Telephone interview by Kent Frates, August 23, 2016.

Court Cases
Telex Corp. v. International Business Machines Corp., 367 F. Supp. 258 (N. D. Okla. 1973).
Telex Corp. v. International Business Machines Corp., 510 F.2d 894 (10th Cir. 1975).
United States v. Francis P. Salemme, James J. Bulger, et al., U. S. District Court, District of Massachusetts, Crime No. 94-10287.
United States v. James J. Bulger, 928 F Supp. 2d 294 (D. Mass 2013).
United States v. James J. Bulger, No. 13-2447 (1st Cir. 2016).
Walker v. Telex Computer Products, Inc., et al., 583 P.2d 482 (Okla. 1978).
Wheeler v. United States, No. 02-10464-RCL (D. Mass 2003).

Author's note: The definitive work on the Roger Wheeler case is *One Murder Too Many* by Lawrence Yadon and Robert Barr Smith. Those authors have extensively explored the connection between Whitey Bulger and Roger Wheeler. For further reading on the Wheeler case, Yadon and Smith's book is recommended.

The Geronimo Bank Case

Newspapers
Lawton Morning Press-Constitution.
The Oklahoman.

Electronic Document
Howarth, Joan W. *The Geronimo Bank Murders: A Gay Tragedy.* 17 Law & Sexuality, Rev. Lesbian Gay Bisexual & Transgender legal issues 39 (2008).

Interviews
Henricksen, Mark. Interview by Kent Frates, March 7, 2016.
Long, Granville. Interview by Kent Frates, January 12, 2016.

Correspondence
Johnson, Robert Grady, and Jay Wesley Neill, correspondence to the *Lawton Constitution*, Dr. Paul Dunn, and Granville Long.

Court Cases
Johnson v. Mullin ,505 F.3d 1128 (10th Cir. 2007).
Johnson v. State, CaseNo. F-2002-918 (Ok. Cr. 2003), unpublished opinion.
Neill v. Gibson, 263 F.3d 1184 (10th Cir. 2001).
Neill v. Gibson, 278 F.3d 1044 (10th Cir. 2001).
Neill v. State, 827 P.2d 884 (Ok. Cr. 1992).
Neill v. State, 896 P.2d 537 (Ok. Cr. 1994).

Government Documents
Federal Bureau of Investigation records, reports, and photographs.
Comanche County (Oklahoma) district attorney's office investigative reports.
Lawton (Oklahoma) Police Department statements and reports.

The Death of Bill Tilghman

Books
Boggs, Johnny D. *Great Murder Trials of the Old West.* Plano, Texas: Republic of Texas Press, 2003.
Butler, Ken. *Oklahoma Renegades: Their Deeds and Misdeeds.* Gretna, Louisiana: Pelican Publishing Company, 1997.
Dorman, Robert L. *It Happened in Oklahoma.* "It Happened In" series. Guilford, Connecticut: TwoDot, 2006.

Owens, Ron. *Oklahoma Justice: The Oklahoma City Police: A Century of Gunfighters, Gangsters and Terrorists*. Paducah, Kentucky: Turner Publishing Co., 1995.

Samuelson, Nancy B. *Shoot from the Lip: The Lives, Legends, and Lies of the Three Guardsmen of Oklahoma and U. S. Marshal Nix*. Dexter: Shooting Star Press, 1998.

Shirley, Glenn D. *Guardian of the Law: The Life and Times of William Matthew Tilghman, 1854–1924*. Austin, Texas: Eakin Press, 1988.

Tilghman, Zoe Agnes Stratton. *Marshal of the Last Frontier: Life and Services of William Matthew (Bill) Tilghman, for Fifty Years One of the Greatest Peace Officers of the West*. Glendale, California: Arthur H. Clark Company, 1949.

Newspapers
Cromwell News.
Guthrie Leader.
Holdenville Democrat.
Oklahoma City Times.
Oklahoma State Capitol (Guthrie, Oklahoma).
The Oklahoman.
The Tulsa Tribune.
Tulsa World.
Wewoka Capital Democrat.

Author's note: The most definitive work on the life of Bill Tilghman is Nancy B. Samuelson's book, *Shoot from the Lip*. This book is thoroughly and independently researched, in many cases from primary sources. *Marshal of the Last Frontier*, by Tilghman's wife, Zoe Agnes Stratton Tilghman, is based as much on legend as on fact yet should not be completely discounted because she was privy to so much personal oral history. Glenn Shirley's book, *Guardian of the Law*, relies heavily on Mrs. Tilghman's book and adds very little information regarding her husband's death. No transcript of the evidence in the Wiley Lynn murder trial is known to exist. It is probable that no transcription was ever made by the court reporter. A jury verdict of "not guilty" is final and not subject to an appeal by the state. Because there was no appeal, there was no reason to pay for a transcript of the proceedings. It would be extremely rare to have a transcript made when there was no appeal of a case.

The Case of the Talking Pharmacist

Newspapers
The Oklahoman.
The Norman Transcript.

Television
Channel KFOR-TV.
Channel KOCO-TV.
Channel KWTV.
Fox News.

Interviews
Box, Irven. Interview by Kent Frates, July 7, 2015.
Chance, Jennifer. Telephone interview by Kent Frates, October 12, 2015.
Friesen, Doug. Interview by Kent Frates, July 6, 2015.

Court Cases
Documents of record, including motions, pleadings, briefs, decisions, and orders in the following cases:
Emanuel Dewayne Mitchell v. State of Oklahoma, Court of Criminal Appeals of the State of Oklahoma, 2016 OK CR 21.
Jerome Jay Ersland v. State of Oklahoma, Court of Criminal Appeals of the State of Oklahoma F. 2011-638.
State of Oklahoma v. Emmanuel Dewayne Mitchell, Anthony Devale Morrison, and Javontai Ingram, District Court of Oklahoma County CF 2009-3297.
State of Oklahoma v. Javontai Cartez Ingram, District Court of Oklahoma County CF 2014-4851.
State of Oklahoma v. Jerome Jay Ersland, District Court of Oklahoma County CF 2009-3199.

Transcripts of Legal Proceedings
Hearing on removal of trial judge, December 6–7, 2010.
State of Oklahoma vs. Jerome Jay Ersland, District Court of Oklahoma County CF 2009-3199.
Jury trial of Jerome Jay Ersland, May 16–26, 2011.
Preliminary hearing of Jerome Jay Ersland, November 4, 2009.

Death, Oklahoma Style

Book
McGuigan, Pat, Chris Querry, and Byron J. Will, *Bob Macy: The Man behind the String Tie*. Mustang, Oklahoma: Tate Publishing, LLC, 2011.

Journal, Periodical, and Newspapers
Astle, Doris J. "Dorie." "The Death Penalty: Baze, Glossip and Beyond." Oklahoma Bar Journal 87, no. 8, March 12, 2016.
New York Times.
Stern, Jeffrey E. "The Cruel and Unusual Execution of Clayton Lockett." *The Atlantic*, June 2015.
The City Sentinel.
The Oklahoman.
Tulsa World.

Electronic Documents and Source
Canon, Gabrielle. "Richard Glossip Awaits Execution or Life on Death Row." Upvoted.com, November 11, 2015.

Creel, Von Russell. "Capital Punishment." The Encyclopedia of Oklahoma History and Culture, *www.okhistory.org*, accessed September 26, 2017.
Death Penalty Information Center, *www.deathpenaltyinfo.org*.
Gajanan, Mahita. "Oklahoma Used Wrong Drug in Charles Warner's Execution, Autopsy Report Says." *The Guardian*, theguardian.com, October 8, 2015.
Hellerstein, Erica. "Oklahoma Death Row Inmate's Lawyer Speaks Out Hours before His Execution." *ThinkProgress.org*, September 30, 2015.
Segura, Liliana, and Jordan Smith. "What Happened in Room 102: Oklahoma Prepares To Execute Richard Glossip." *theintercept.com*, July 9, 2015.

Television
Berlinger, Joe, director. "Killing Richard Glossip." Investigative Discovery Channel, April 2017.
Channel KFOR-TV.
Channel KOCO-TV.
Channel KWTV.

Interviews
Autry, David B. Interview by Kent Frates, May 4, 2016.
Day, Seth. Interview by Kent Frates, May 6, 2016.
Knight, Don. Telephone interview by Kent Frates, June 15, 2016.

Report
Constitution Project, The. The Report of the Oklahoma Death Penalty Review Commission, March 2017.

Court Cases
Estate of Clayton Lockett v. Fallin, et al., 15-6134 (10th Cir. 2016).
Glossip v. Gross, 135 S. Ct. 2726 (U.S.S.C. 2015).
Glossip v. State, 157 P.3d 143 (Ok. Cr. 2007).
Glossip v. State, 29 P.3d 597 (Ok. Cr. 2001).
Lockett v. State, 53 P.3d 418 (Ok. Cr. 2002).
Warner v. State, 144 P.3d 838 (Ok. Cr. 2006).
Warner v. State, 29 P.3d 569 (Ok. Cr. 2001).
Warner, et al. v. Gross, 776 F.3d 721 (10th Cir. 2015).

Government Documents
Interim Report Number 14, In the Matter of the Multicounty Grand Jury, State of Oklahoma, Case Number SCAD-2014-70 D. C., Case Number GJ-2014-1, in the Supreme Court of the State of Oklahoma, in the District Court of Oklahoma County.
Oklahoma City Police interview of Justin Sneed, January 14, 1997.
Oklahoma Department of Public Safety investigation report. The Execution of Clayton D. Lockett, Case Number 14-018951.
The State of Oklahoma's Response to Charles Frederick Warner's Request for Executive Clemency.

Author's Note: In 1976, I was a member of the Oklahoma House of Representatives. I voted in favor of the death penalty. At that time, I reasoned that if the death penalty deterred the killing of one innocent person, it was worth it. In the forty years that have passed since my vote, I have developed more doubt about the death penalty, particularly in its administration. My strongest reservation comes because of the excessive delays associated with carrying out an execution that can undermine the public's faith in our judicial system. However, I still favor the death penalty; to me, there are some crimes that are so horrible, depraved, or subhuman that the perpetrator has to be permanently removed from society.

About the Author

Kent Frates is a historian and attorney who has practiced law in Oklahoma since the 1960s. He is the author of *Oklahoma Hiking Trails*, *Oklahoma Courthouse Legends*, and the nationally acclaimed *Oklahoma's Most Notorious Cases*, which won the Benjamin Franklin Award for nonfiction. A graduate of Stanford University, he served in the Oklahoma house of representatives from 1970 to 1978 and as minority leader for the house from 1976 to 1978. He makes his home in Oklahoma.